Many a coach has noted that the most important distance in any sport is the few centimetres between the player's ears. We have other ways of putting it – words like commitment, confidence, teamspirit, and morale among them. They all add up to much the same thing: attitude. How many times has an athlete of superior ability been beaten by one of lesser skill but with a more determined frame of mind?

– Ken Hodge, editorial for the *Otago Daily Times*

From my experience physiology defines a good athlete, but psychology defines a great one … Take another step and imagine if all our top athletes had this psyche, it would be incredible what they could achieve. I haven't seen a live endurance performance so outstanding that in the end it didn't come down to the top six inches to decide the race.

– Jon Ackland (NZ sport scientist – trainer; author of *The Complete Guide to Endurance Training*).

That's why I won. Physically, I wouldn't have a chance against her but it's funny, in tennis sometimes the mind is more important than the rest.

– Martina Hingis (Swiss tennis player) explaining how she claimed her third Australian Open title in beating Amelie Mauresmo.

I believe very firmly that in the power of the mind lies the key to winning, as opposed to performing well and losing… After the Montreal Olympics, I became a keen and serious student of sport psychology, so as soon as I was appointed skipper of *Australia II*, I began to look for the right man to deal with the mental attitudes of my crew.

– John Bertrand (Skipper, *Australia II*: In 1983 his boat was the first team to win the America's Cup from the USA in its 132 year history)

Other titles in **THE COMPLETE GUIDE** series

The Complete Guide to
Circuit Training
by Debbie Lawrence, Bob Hope

The Complete Guide to
Postnatal Fitness
by Judy DiFiore

The Complete Guide to
Endurance Training
by Jon Ackland

The Complete Guide to
Strength Training
by Anita Bean

The Complete Guide to
Exercise in Water
by Debbie Lawrence

The Complete Guide to
Stretching
by Christopher Norris

The Complete Guide to
Core Stability
by Matt Lawrence

The Complete Guide to
Sports Massage
by Tim Paine

The Complete Guide to
Studio Cycling
by Rick Kiddle

The Complete Guide to
Sports Nutrition
by Anita Bean

The Complete Guide to
Exercise to Music
by Debbie Lawrence

The Complete Guide to
Exercising Away Stress
by Debbie Lawrence

THE **COMPLETE GUIDE TO**

Ken Hodge

SPORT MOTIVATION

A & C Black • London

For my 'Home Team' –
Nicky, Kayla and Jack.

Published in 2005 by A&C Black Publishers Ltd
37 Soho Square, London W1D 3QZ
www.acblack.com

First published in New Zealand in 2004 by
Reed Books, a division of Reed Publishing (NZ) Ltd,
39 Rawene Rd, Birkenhead, Auckland.
Associated companies, branches and representatives throughout the world.

Copyright © 2004 Ken Hodge

ISBN-10: 0 7136 7465 2
ISBN-13: 978 0 7136 7465 1

A CIP catalogue number for this book is available from the British Library.

A&C Black uses paper produced with elemental chlorine-free pulp, harvested from managed sustainable forests.

Cover image © Zefa/digitalvision/Digital Vision Ltd.

Typeset in 10½ on 12pt Baskerville BE Regular by Palimpsest Book Production Limited, Polmont, Stirlingshire

Printed and bound in Great Britain by
Biddles Ltd, Kings Lynn.

CONTENTS

PREFACE AND ACKNOWLEDGEMENTS

In my opinion sport is all about passion. Sport is an inherently emotional experience; you can experience all the human emotions from excitement to worry, contentment to depression, pride to shame, boredom to anxiety, and frustration to fun! The thrill of victory, the agony of defeat, the frustration of failure, and the satisfaction of success are ingrained in sport.

Of course sport is not alone in providing a venue for these experiences; they are to be found equally in other activities such as art, music, dance and theatre. But in sport the emotions are perhaps more pronounced and more volatile, since sport has direct competition and opponents. In general, sport has no utilitarian value in the sense that work or an occupation has, but success in sport matters to a great many people. That is what makes sport both challenging and threatening, and makes the psychological aspect of sport so interesting and important for those involved.

In short, sport is a passionately human undertaking; we care about sport and we care about being good at it!

> 'Sport is a glorious nonsense.'
>
> Cliff Morgan (Former Welsh and Lions rugby player)

Once you choose to be involved in competitive sport you are stating your desire to set and achieve goals, to develop new skills and competencies, to test your physical and mental limits, and to pursue some level of excellence. For most sportspeople this is a voluntary decision, motivated by intrinsic reasons such as facing a challenge, feeling competent, having fun, and feeling good about yourself. However, like all areas of human endeavour, sport has the potential for negative as well as positive experiences.

Sport psychology is all about helping sportspeople to have consistently positive experiences. My motivation for writing this book is to share with you my ideas and insights about how to make sport more positive and enjoyable by enhancing your performance through Psychological Skills Training (PST).

As in any aspect of life, experience is one of the best coaches or teachers available in sport psychology. My experience has been enriched by a number of people, and I would like to take this opportunity to express my gratitude to these 'coaches'. First, I owe a huge debt to my greatest coach, my father Richard. He provided me with the best psychological principle I have ever found – 'There is no such word as can't; if it's not possible this way there is always another way; never give in and never give up.' Richard taught me ways to develop my mental toughness based on this principle. Second, I am eternally indebted to my PhD advisor Dr Dan Gould. Dan was a mentor, teacher, coach, role model and good friend – I learnt a lot about the humanity of sportpsych from Dan. Thanks. I have also learnt a great deal from a number of colleagues over the years, in particular my mates Alex McKenzie, Linda Petlichkoff, Tom Hanson, Bob Eklund and Sue Jackson. Finally, a special word of thanks to all the players, athletes and coaches with whom I have been privileged to work over the years – I learned a great deal from these people, for they were using psych skills on a day-to-day basis. Their experiences pervade the ideas in this book.

With respect to the book itself I wish to thank Peter Janssen, Peter Dowling and Sam Hill at Reed Publishing NZ for proposing the idea of a second edition, and for once again knocking my writing into shape. Many, many thanks.

INTRODUCTION: Psychological Skills Training (PST)

Coaches often refer to 'mental strength' and 'mental toughness' when attempting to describe that elusive quality that distinguishes the great players from the good ones in any sport. But what do we mean by mental toughness, and what can you as an athlete do to develop your mental toughness?

Sport psychology focuses on teaching practical psychological skills and methods such as goal setting and mental preparation to athletes/players so they can develop their psychological abilities (i.e. mental toughness) to the same high level as their physical abilities.[1] The key difference between winning and losing, or between a good performance and a poor performance, may be the psychological skill level rather than the physical skill level. Like physical skills, these 'psych' skills need to be taught correctly, fine-tuned by the player/athlete and coach, and then practised regularly.

The real contest is in the mind.

I prefer the label 'Psych Skills Training' (PST), but I also call it Mental Toughness Training, and some players and coaches like to label it Mental Skills Training. It doesn't matter too much what you call it, as long as you understand the principles of 'psych' training and feel motivated to put the effort into improving your own mental toughness.

Some athletes/players and coaches are sceptical of psych training, dismissing it as unnecessary for tough sportspeople, or asserting that such skills can't be trained – 'you've either got them or you haven't!' In contrast, I argue that psych skills are a lot like physical skills; some people do have natural abilities (but still need to fine-tune them), while most of us need to work hard at improving our psych skills through planned practice and consistent training. There is considerable evidence from coach and player endorsements[2] and scientific research[3] demonstrating that psych skills can be trained and improved.

Some athletes/players and coaches reckon that 'psych' training has a place for junior/age-group players and development squads, but they dismiss it as unnecessary for senior and elite athletes, believing that by that stage of an athlete's career they must have a high level of mental toughness.[4] While such a belief has some superficial logic to it, top-level athletes still need a coach, and most now have specialised 'fitness trainers' as well. So if you have identified the need for specialised coaching and fitness advice, why wouldn't you also use a 'mental coach'? The old saying that you need to use the 'top six inches' in competition suggests that mental toughness is a vital component of success. I believe all athletes/players need to train their 'thinking' skills along with their physical, technical and tactical skills. If you want to be the best athlete/player you can be, you should train *all* aspects of your sport skill needs.

> 'The mental approach is one of the most important things in running. The man who can drive himself further once the effort gets painful is the man who will win. Most people train by racing. I tried to make each race an event in my life.'
>
> Roger Bannister (British runner; first athlete to run the mile in under four minutes)

The primary purpose of Psychological Skills Training (PST) is to focus on positive aspects of psychological performance, thus avoiding the stigma of being labelled a 'headcase' or having an 'abnormal problem'[5]. The philosophy is that 'you don't have to be sick to get better'; i.e., you don't have to be suffering from a mental problem or be abnormal to use psychological skills. PST assumes that the dedicated athlete is already an above 'normal' performer – he or she just wants to increase his or her psychological skills to a level that matches his/her above-normal physical skills.

'Champion athletes/players are not extraordinary people, they are ordinary people who do extraordinary things.'

It is important to realise, however, that this focus on PST is not just for Olympic athletes or elite players. These skills are equally appropriate and important for players/athletes of all ages and levels of physical performance. Anyone who wants to consistently perform to the level they know they are physically capable of can use PST to help them play to the best of their abilities and to thoroughly enjoy their participation in sport.

'The key to handling pressure is to enjoy it when you're confronted with it rather than worry about it too much … I'm not overwhelmed by it. I probably was when I was younger.'

Steve Waugh (former Australian cricket captain)

To be able to fully learn psych skills it is helpful to understand the fundamental principles behind the applied PST programme. Given this requirement, I will briefly cover some basic sport psychology principles before I outline the practical PST programme in detail. Using PST effectively is a bit like driving a car – most people can drive a car or can learn to drive, but if the car breaks down they do not know how to fix it, because they do not know 'how' or 'why' the car actually works. Because they do not understand the 'principles' behind what makes the car work, most people have to call in an expert to fix the car when it breaks down.

PST works on the same principle: if you as an athlete or coach do not know why PST works (i.e., the principles), then you will have to call in an expert (a sportpsych consultant) when it breaks down or doesn't work properly! The major goal I have for this book is for you to learn PST so well, both at a principles level and at a practical level, that you will be able to be your own 'expert' and troubleshoot any problems that arise with your PST programme.

This book is written for the average athlete, although elite athletes and coaches at all levels will also find it very useful. Indeed, many of the examples and quotes I use are from elite athletes, since it is easier for most of us to identify with someone whose performance we have witnessed live or on TV.

This use of elite athletes as examples is not meant to suggest that PST is only for elite performers – PST is just as useful for the 60-year-old lawn bowler, the 10-year-old netball player and the average club hockey player as it is for an Olympic athlete. PST is about performance enhancement in general, not just elite performance!

The myth of the natural athlete/player

The best players do have natural ability, but they believe that what sets them apart is their psych skills.

Most athletes know they should relax, be positive, stay focused and so on, but they don't always know how to do it. When PST skills and methods are explained to experienced sportspeople they often respond by saying, 'I wish I'd had this information when I first started competing; I do most of this stuff now but it took me years of trial and error to figure it out!'

> 'I think my mental ability has improved drastically, and maybe my physical ability has diminished a little bit. But I think, in the overall picture, I am a better basketball player.'
>
> Michael Jordan (US basketball player, after being named MVP when the Chicago Bulls won the NBA champs in 1996)

Indeed, many athletes/players already use these skills in some form or another, but it is the haphazard and often lengthy learning process they had to endure that PST is designed to eliminate. The PST programme seeks to teach players basic psych skills and psych methods that have both an intuitive appeal and a sound scientific basis.[3] PST will reinforce a number of things that you already do based on commonsense wisdom, but have probably never structured or practised in the way the PST programme recommends. Just because it's 'commonsense' doesn't mean that PST is commonly used! PST will also provide you with answers to psych skill needs you have not been able to work on before, and you will learn PST methods that you would probably not have discovered through trial and error. To quote the old saying, we are 'trying to put an old head on young shoulders'. PST is designed to ensure that the old head is a 'smart' one!

> 'The psychology of golf goes a step further than course management. It entails mental toughness, self-confidence, intimidation, gamesmanship, conquering inner demons, instant recall of past successes and being able to quickly purge failures. It is the game within the game.'
>
> Tiger Woods (US golfer).

Why train psych skills?

Ask yourself the following questions.

First, in competition, what percentage of your performance is dependent on the psychological aspect? Elite players (for example Steve Waugh, Tiger Woods, Pete Sampras) say about 90 per cent, other players say about 50 per cent.[3]

Second, how many hours a week (or minutes a day) do you as an athlete spend on physical training? Many elite-level athletes report that they devote as much as 20 hours a week (two to three hours a day) to physical training.

> '[Sport is] a self-inflicted stressful situation . . .'
>
> Graham Mourie (former All Black captain)

Third, how many hours a week (or minutes a day) do you as an athlete spend on psych training? Most athletes report devoting only a few minutes a day to psych 'training', and that is typically only 'daydreaming' about their sport (hardly a planned PST programme!). Although most players agree that psych skills account for at least 50 per cent of performance, much less than 50 per cent of training time is spent on developing specific psych skills – usually between 0 and 5 per cent.[5]

Why is so little time spent on psych skills?

First, coaches and players often don't know how to develop psych skills. PST is still a relatively new addition to sports science and coaching education. Second, psych skills are often viewed as unchangeable, based on the mistaken belief that 'either you have it or you don't'. We seldom make such assumptions about our physical skills or fitness, yet we often assume that we cannot change our psychological abilities, or our lack of them. Third, players sometimes feel there must be something wrong with them (you must be a 'headcase' to need sport psychology) if they try to work on psych skills.

It is important to understand that PST is not for players with abnormal problems. As noted above, PST focuses on conveying knowledge about practical sport psychology to 'normal' individuals involved in sport. This involves normal athletes who have to deal with the abnormal stress of competitive sport.

PST is for 'normal' people who are required to perform at an 'above-normal' level in the 'abnormal situation' of competitive sport (e.g. in front of spectators, meeting the expectations of the coach). Clearly, this 'abnormal' situation requires 'above-normal' psych skills! Rather than focusing on 'what is wrong and how to treat it', PST focuses on 'what is right and how to use it'. We are concerned not with problems, but with answers and solutions. Consequently, PST is not about being a 'shrink', it is about being a 'stretch'. Rather than shrinking problems, PST is designed to stretch capabilities!

Objectives of PST

The PST programme outlined in this book has three major objectives:

- To help you perform consistently to the best of your ability – performance enhancement;
- To help you enjoy sports participation more by reducing stress and improving performance;
- To help you develop psych skills for use in other life situations (e.g. anxiety/stress management).

Overall, the PST programme is designed to help you reach your Ideal Performance State on a regular basis. The Ideal Performance State is that mood, feeling or state in which an athlete feels totally focused, mentally and physically, on the performance and is confident they will perform to their best; like being on 'automatic

pilot'[6] (see chapter 1, 'The Ideal Performance State', for more on this). Unfortunately, for most athletes the Ideal Performance State usually proves to be quite elusive – it doesn't happen often enough!

So, the PST programme is directed at identifying your particular Ideal Performance State, then at fine-tuning your psychological skills to help you reach that Ideal Performance State more often: to move from conscious control (e.g. 'paralysis by analysis') to 'automatic pilot', and to get into automatic pilot regularly!

Remember: performance enhancement and the Ideal Performance State are not just for elite athletes (see chapter 1). Any athlete, at any level of performance, who wishes to enhance her or his performance and perform to his or her personal potential more often can use PST.

Performance enhancement doesn't just mean elite performance.

Realistic expectations of PST

Psych skills are only one of the building blocks of outstanding performance – successful sport performance is a combination of psych skills, physical skills and physical fitness. The goal of PST is to have the brain and the body working together as a team. Psych skills are not quick and easy gimmicks or a magic formula for success. They must be learned correctly and practised, practised, practised.

'I've always said that to be good at this [game], you need three things. You need to have the game, you need to have the heart, and you need to have the mind.'

Pete Sampras (US tennis player; World No. 1 for six consecutive years; winner of 14 Grand Slam titles)

Outstanding performance = willpower + horsepower

Psych skills will not turn a 'draught horse into a thoroughbred' – you must have the necessary 'horsepower' for your chosen sport. However, psych skills will help you to consistently perform to the best of your ability, whether that be at thoroughbred or draught horse level!

PST takes time and effort

Psych skills greatly influence performance. At the elite level the difference between a successful and an unsuccessful athlete/player may only be five to ten per cent – and mental toughness may account for that five to ten per cent! In addition, few athletes/players develop their psych skills to the full. Consequently, there is considerable potential for improvement in psych skills when physical and technical skills are already at their peak. Players/athletes must be as determined and disciplined about their PST as they are about their technical skill and fitness training. Psych skills are like physical skills in that they are developed by learning basic skills, then fine-tuning, and then continuing to practise, practise, practise.

Individualised PST

PST programmes must be separately designed for each *individual* athlete or player: 'One size does not fit all!' In order to individualise your psych skills training you first need to identify your mental strengths and mental weaknesses (i.e., your psych skill needs). Consequently, you will need to do a psych skills assessment by completing one or more of the following: (i) a 'peak performance profile' (filled out by you and, if possible, your coach; see chapter 6); (ii) an interview/discussion with your coach or a sportpsych consultant; or (iii) game/race/event/match or video observation by you, your coach or a sportpsych consultant.

Once you have completed some form of psych skills assessment you then need to identify your key psych skill strengths and weaknesses, which should then be categorised into three types of skill. These categories are important in planning your PST programme (see chapter 5). The three categories are: (i) foundation skills (e.g. commitment, self-confidence); (ii) performance skills (e.g. controlling activation/psych-up); and (iii) facilitative skills (e.g. team building, communication). In order to individualise your psych skills training you need to identify your PST skill needs and then 'match' the PST methods to those skills to form your own PST 'game plan' (this is dealt with in chapter 19).

> 'Mental toughness is my big plus as a cricketer. Technique's important, ball skills… but sheer talent isn't the answer. There's a lot of people with talent to burn but they don't use it properly. It's your attitude more than anything. You use your skills as much as possible, recognise your limitations, and mentally you're tougher than the guy next to you.'
>
> — Allan Border (former Australian cricket captain)

Once you have identified your psych skill needs and categorised them you will be in a position to select appropriate psych methods to practise/train for enhancing specific psych skills; i.e. you need to 'match' methods with skills. Methods are the 'means', not the 'end'. The key distinction between psych skills and psych methods, and the matching of methods with skills, is explained in detail in chapter 5. It is vital to individualise your PST so you can practise the psych skills and methods required for you to reach your personal Ideal Performance State.

What this book will do for you

PST is not intended to 'over-complicate' your sport performance. Not all the skills and methods in this book will be necessary for you – it will depend on your psychological strengths and weaknesses. There is an old saying that is very appropriate in this regard: 'If it ain't broke, don't try to fix it!' In other words, only work on those PST skill areas that need it. However, having said that, all athletes have the potential to improve some aspect of their PST abilities. Humans are not perfect machines; we all make mistakes and we all have weaknesses. Athletes who are committed to performing to their best do not accept these weaknesses, they actively work to turn them into strengths. The challenge is for you to identify your particular PST needs then design a PST programme for yourself using the instructions in this book (see the peak performance profile exercise in chapter 6).

Different players have different psych skill abilities. However, all players can develop psych skills with practice. The development of psych skills does not replace physical ability and physical fitness, nor does it guarantee success. But, at the level of 'ideal performance' physical ability and fitness is not enough; the player seeking consistent best performances needs psych skills as well.

'We all have dreams. But in order to make dreams into reality, it takes an awful lot of determination, dedication, self-discipline, and effort.'

Jesse Owens (US athlete; winner of four gold medals at the 1936 Olympics)

The aim is to have the brain and the body working together as a team; that is, 'brains + brawn'. From the neck down we may be relatively equal, but from the neck up the potential is endless!

How to use this book

The Complete Guide to Sport Motivation is a practical resource book. It is designed to take you step-by-step through the process of developing a Psychological Skills Training (PST) programme for yourself – one that is specific to your needs. This programme incorporates the development of appropriate PST skills, and includes many practical PST methods and evaluation techniques. It provides you with the basic sportpsych information that you will require for designing a new PST programme or evaluating your current programme. In each of the PST skill chapters (see chapters 7–9) worksheets and examples will help you take the necessary steps in designing your own PST programme.

After completing your 'peak performance profile' (chapter 6) and identifying your psych skill needs, you may wish to go directly to the relevant PST skill chapters in Part Three and complete the specific PST skill worksheets before you choose the PST methods you will use to 'train' each specific PST skill. On the other hand, you may choose to read/skim through all the PST skill/method information in Parts Three and Four before you begin to put together your PST programme. The choice is yours. In chapter 19 I provide a five-step process for designing your own PST 'game plan'.

As stated earlier, the PST programme is not designed to overcomplicate your sport or your training; not all of the information in this book will be necessary for your PST needs. The PST programme is designed so you can develop your own individual programme, tailored to fit your needs, and address your weaknesses and strengths.

The gain from pain is mainly in the BRAIN!

ROGER BANNISTER

'It was a psychological barrier, rather than a physical barrier'

British runner: First person to run a sub-4 minute mile

In 1953, the fervour to break four minutes for running the mile was rekindled. A number of runners (including Roger Bannister, with 4 min 2 sec) had gone under 4 min 3 sec. It became evident that breaking the four-minute barrier, like climbing Mt Everest, was just a question of time.[1] Roger Bannister stepped up his plans and chose the Amateur Athletic Association Championships, on the Iffley Road track at Oxford on 6 May 1954, for his attempt. 'In my mind,' he wrote, 'I had settled this as the day when, with every ounce of strength I possessed, I would attempt to run the four-minute mile… I had reached my peak physically and psychologically. There would never be another day like it.'[2]

Brasher led the first lap in 57.5 sec, with Bannister behind urging him to go faster. But Brasher kept his head and stayed at the pace he knew would bring success. Any faster and Bannister might falter on the last lap.[2] Brasher took them to the half-mile in 1 min 58 sec, then Chataway took over, bringing up the three-quarter mile time in 3 min 0.7 sec. Bannister then had to run the last lap in 59 seconds.

Bannister wrote of the mix of joy and anguish on that last lap: 'There was no pain, only a great unity of movement and aim.' He crossed the line and fell, exhausted, into the arms of a friend. The time was 3 min 59.4 sec, taking almost two seconds off the old record.[3] 'I always expected people would break the four-minute mile much more easily. It was a psychological barrier, rather than a physical barrier.'[4] At the time, Bannister also stated that 'records are made to be broken. The human spirit is indomitable.'[3]

Bannister opened the gates and within weeks of his epic performance, John Landy (Australia) had run even faster – just 46 days (26 June 1954) after Bannister's breakthrough Landy ran a mile in 3 min 57.9 sec to clip 1.5 sec off the record.[3]

The 4-minute mile stands as a salutary example of a psychological barrier in sport – once Bannister proved that it could be done, dozens of other runners broke the 4-minute barrier. Indeed, in the two years following Bannister's triumph at least 11 athletes broke four minutes, and by the end of 1959 some 21 runners had gone under four minutes for the mile. In 1975, the 3:50 minute barrier was finally broken by John Walker (New Zealand) who ran a time of 3 min 49.4 sec[5,6] – 1.6 seconds faster than the previous record. While that run seemed just as remarkable as Bannister's, by 1985 the record had been reduced to 3 min 46.3 sec, and in 2003 the World Record for the mile stood at an incredible 3 min 43.1 sec – a full 16 seconds faster than Bannister's epic run 49 years earlier![7]

'If you can believe it, you can achieve it!'

PRINCIPLES OF PSYCHOLOGICAL SKILLS TRAINING

PART **ONE**

THE IDEAL PERFORMANCE STATE 1

> 'Guys know when they're going to go out there and get runs. You just feel in that sort of mood. For me, I've got to be relaxed, I've got to be not thinking about what I'm doing. I'd rather be sitting there joking around with someone and have my mind completely off batting beforehand, so when I get out there the subconscious takes over and I know how to play … I was just in a state of mind where I was positive, I wasn't nervous, I was relaxed, my feet were moving, I was playing straight – everything was happening perfectly for me. My subconscious was taking over; I wasn't thinking about anything. That's the best way you can be.'
>
> Nathan Astle (New Zealand cricketer) describing his World Record double-century innings in 2002; he reached 200 runs in just 153 balls and 217 minutes!

The Ideal Performance State is that mood, feeling or state in which an athlete/player feels totally focused, both mentally and physically, on their sport performance and is confident they will perform to their best. It's like being on auto-pilot. Unfortunately, for most athletes the Ideal Performance State can prove quite elusive.

Considerable research in sport psychology has identified the elite athlete's psychological profile as consisting of the following 'skills'[1]:

- mental preparation, mental readiness (control activation)
- complete concentration on the task at hand (concentration)
- a high degree of self-confidence (confidence)
- high motivation and determination to do well in their sport (commitment)

- ability to control activation and anxiety (control activation)
- ability to cope with pressure and anxiety (cope with pressure).

Collectively these psych 'skills or abilities' represent the Ideal Performance State. However, the Ideal Performance State is not just for elite athletes; any athlete performing to his or her full physical ability is performing in an Ideal Performance State.

> 'It was a type of euphoria; I felt I could run all day without tiring, that I could dribble through any of their team or all of them, that I could almost pass through them physically. I felt like I could not be hurt. It was a very strange feeling and one I had not felt before. Perhaps it was merely confidence, but I have felt confident many times without that strange feeling of invincibility.'
>
> Pele (Brazilian soccer player; three-time World Cup winner: 1958, 1962, 1970)

The PST programme is designed to help you reach your Ideal Performance State on a regular basis. So, the programme is directed first at identifying your particular Ideal Performance State, then helping you to reach it more often (see Chapter 5, 'The PST programme').

Peak performance

One of the most positive performance feelings you can experience as an athlete is the perception of peak performance.[2] This is a state of superior functioning that creates optimal sports performances, resulting in personal bests and outstanding achievements. Peak performance describes the upper limits of functioning; that is, the Ideal Performance State.[2]

The 'flow' experience is almost identical to peak performance. Flow is an emotionally enjoyable feeling that occurs when there is a perceived balance between your competencies and the demands of the task. Compare this with the definition of stress that will be discussed in Chapter 4; stress is defined as a perceived 'imbalance' between skills and demands. A critical aspect of the flow situation is that flow does not depend on the objective nature of the challenges present or on the actual skills of the individual. In fact, whether an athlete is in flow or not depends entirely on her or his *perception* of the challenges and skills.

Peak performance occurs when there is a balance between the perceived challenges of the situation and the athlete's perceived abilities to meet the challenges. The perception of a challenging situation thus becomes critical. If the athlete believes that he or she has the ability to achieve the goal, then action and effort will be sustained until the goal is achieved or until the perception of ability changes, making the goal seem either unattainable or not as highly valued. Perception of your own ability and the subjective meaning of the task are therefore critical to flow, and to peak performance and the Ideal Performance State.[2] Figure 1.1 illustrates how important it is to get a match or balance between the perceived challenges of the situation and your perceived abilities to meet the challenge.

For example, you have no doubt played with or against players who have all the ability required to play the sport at the level you are currently at, but who are not able to perform up to their potential consistently. They are able to perform the required skills perfectly at practice or in minor competitions, but in 'big' games they

Figure 1.1 Peak Performance

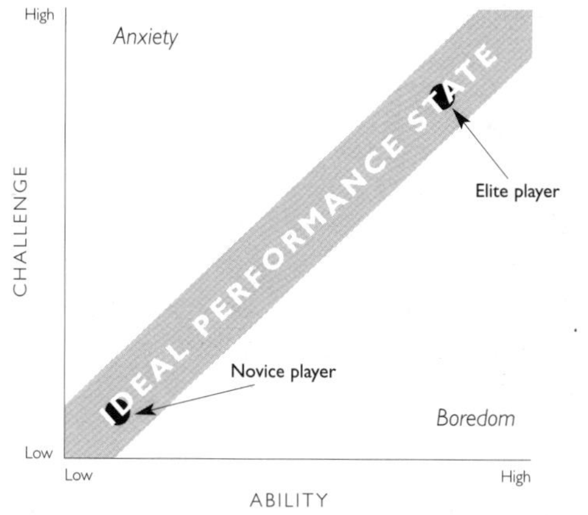

seldom play as well as they are capable. These players usually perceive the 'big' game to be beyond their capabilities. This perception is usually not accurate, but if they believe they don't have the ability then that is how they will play! They are not able to switch on their Ideal Performance State because they perceive the 'big game' situation inaccurately. PST is designed to help these players develop a more accurate perception of the situation and of their capability to meet the challenge of that situation.

Perceived ability is also a central idea in achievement motivation (see Chapter 3). Research on peak performance in sport suggests that the Ideal Performance State is related to the adoption of a task/performance goal.[3] Complete task involvement has also been identified as a key aspect of flow.[2] While a task goal helps an athlete achieve peak performance, an outcome goal (e.g. win/loss, score) sometimes hinders them from achieving peak performance.

Athletes who primarily focus on 'outcome' goals may be distracted by how well they are performing compared to others, and may focus on the anticipated outcome of their performance rather than on the immediate tasks that need to be mastered for successful performance. That is, they will be focused solely on 'winning' instead of on *how* to win as well.

Research has found that athletes tend to perceive the challenge of the task as high in both best and worst performances, but it is the perception of the necessary skills to cope with the challenge that differs markedly.[4] Skills are perceived to match the challenge in the best performance, but to be much lower than the challenge when performance is poor. The individual has to believe that he or she has the required skills to meet the challenge.

To be an achiever, you have to be a believer (in yourself).

In one research study nearly 88 per cent of athletes reported an 'outcome' focus during their worst performance.[4] By examining worst performances it becomes clear that an over-emphasis on outcome goals prevents athletes from performing well. The focus during best performances should be primarily on skill mastery and be process-centred. This focus of attention is also discussed later when we look at the PST skill of 'concentration and attention' (see Chapter 8, 'Performance PST skills'). However, the bottom line is that if an athlete adopts a task-focused, personal-best approach she or he is more likely to achieve peak performance.

Practical implications

It is important for athletes to understand the distinction between task (process-focus) goals and outcome (win-focus) goals, and the enormous impact that their 'goals' have on their performance. Athletes must work hard to develop a task-goal orientation, since these goals are related to the skills in which the athlete must be competent in order to perform well, and are goals that she/he has control over (see Chapter 3, 'Motivation for peak performance', and Chapter 10, 'Goal setting').

During actual performance it is vital that the athlete primarily adopts a task goal; however, that does not mean she/he should never be focused on the outcome. Winning is not a dirty word! We all want to win in competitive sport, but during the actual performance we should primarily focus on *how* to win. Since competitive sport is designed to decide which athlete is the best, it is natural that athletes will want to compare their competitive ability with others (an outcome focus). Such a focus is not necessarily bad. An outcome goal can provide motivation and incentive for training just as much as a task goal can. However, during performance the athlete must be primarily task-focused to get into the Ideal Performance State and achieve peak performance.

> 'That's when I come alive: on the basketball court. As the game unfolds, time slows down and I experience the blissful feeling of being totally engaged in the action. My mind is completely focused on the goal, but with a sense of openness and joy… That's when you realise that basketball is a game, a journey, a dance – not a fight to the death… It's life just as it is.'
>
> Phil Jackson (Chicago Bulls and LA Lakers basketball coach, nine-time winner of the NBA Championship)

Since it is the *perception* of ability that affects the Ideal Performance State, the athlete needs to develop a high, stable level of self-confidence in her/his sporting ability (see 'Self-confidence' in Chapter 7, and the section on positive self-esteem in Chapter 2).

> 'I was in such a zone today, working on every shot, working so hard on every shot. At the end I walked over to the side and I just started thinking, you know, I don't have any more shots to play. I'm done. I won the Masters.'
>
> Tiger Woods (US golfer); commenting on his Ideal Performance State when he won the 2001 US Masters.

Peak performance and the Ideal Performance State require a perceived balance between challenges and skills. Therefore a balance should be sought, either by matching opponents or by matching the athlete with an achievable personal 'performance' or 'task' goal. That is, if it is not possible to change the actual situation for a challenge/skill balance, then athletes should redefine the challenges of the situation so that they approach the performance with confidence (e.g. set task/performance goals, be assertive).

Summary: the Ideal Performance State

Remember, the Ideal Performance State contributes to both success and enjoyment in sport. However, it doesn't occur by chance very often – you need to plan your PST programme to help you get into the Ideal Performance State more often. That is, you need to learn how to 'switch on' your automatic pilot, so the Ideal Performance State becomes second nature.

PST is designed to help you deliberately switch on your auto-pilot, but it is *not* intended to overcomplicate your performance. You should only plan a PST programme to work on the psych skill areas that you need to kick-start your auto-pilot and your Ideal Performance State. Working on your 'thinking skills' like this does not necessarily mean you will increase your amount of thinking and run the risk of overcomplicating your sport. On the contrary, PST is all about limiting your 'thinking' to the bare minimum required to help you get into your Ideal Performance State, to get into that wonderful mental rhythm and flow where you barely need to 'think' – instead, you 'just do it'!

The eight C's of peak performance: 'tough stuff'

(Self-) Concept (see Chapter 2)
(Self-) Confidence (see Chapter 7)
    Commitment (see Chapter 7)
    Control of activation (psych-up) (see Chapter 8)
    Cope with pressure and anxiety (see Chapter 8)
    Concentration (see Chapter 8)
    Communication (especially for team sports) (see Chapter 9)
    Cohesion (for team sports) (see Chapter 9)

A peak performance creed

If you think you are beaten you are;
If you think you dare not, you don't;
If you'd like to win, but think you can't,
it's almost a cinch you won't.

If you think you'll lose, you're lost;
For out in the world we find success begins
with a person's will;
It's all in a state of mind.

Life's battles don't always go to the stronger
or faster hand;
But sooner or later the person who wins
is the one who thinks 'I can'.

Author unknown

'TOUGH STUFF': THE BUILDING BLOCKS OF MENTAL TOUGHNESS

2

Mentally tough players make things happen. This chapter focuses on the psychological 'tough stuff' that is the foundation of a player's mental toughness in sport. The mental qualities of positive self-esteem, assertiveness and commitment are vital to peak performance in sport. Without the required 'tough stuff' a player is unlikely to be a consistent peak performer. He or she may achieve peak performance occasionally, but the hallmark of a peak performer is consistency. If you can achieve consistent peak performance you are likely to be more successful and enjoy your sport more.

> 'There are three types of people in the world: those who make things happen; those who watch things happen; and those who ask 'what the hell happened?'. Successful people, people who reach their goals, make things happen.'
>
> Anon

Succeeding vs surviving

Ask yourself this key question: 'When you play competitive sport are you "playing not to lose" or are you "playing to win"?' There is an essential difference between these two mindsets – people who succeed on a regular basis are 'playing to win', to be the best they can possibly be, whereas those who only succeed on occasion (despite having the physical ability) are typically more focused on 'survival' and a 'playing not to lose' attitude.[1] Athletes/players who don't want to risk losing typically set their sights low, they avoid taking any risks, they focus on defence at

the expense of attack, they seldom challenge the status quo regarding their race/game plan or their training programmes, and they drift along happy with modest success. These athletes/players are what we might call 'survivors'; they hang in there, always close to real success, always threatening to score the big win or smash a personal best, but never quite cracking the barrier to peak performance. What is holding these athletes back?

Success is not easy. It is challenging, frightening, demanding and costly. It's risky and often it is lonely.[1] But most of all it is 'personal'. Deciding to be successful and committing to being a winner is a personal decision – you can't expect help from others on this one. *You* must make the bold decision to set your standards high, to always strive to win and be the best, to expect and want to succeed every time you compete. You must be brave enough to want to win/succeed even though you know such an approach may lead to failure when you match up against tough opponents and difficult personal best standards, and even though you know that failure is a very real outcome against such tough standards. You need to be made of 'tough stuff' to accept this challenge!

'If it's to be, it's up to me!'

Self-esteem and peak performance

Self-esteem is a vital building block of peak performance, because peak performance requires you to have a realistic perception of your ability and a complete faith in your ability to match the challenges and demands of the situation.

What is self-esteem?

Self-esteem is made up of the descriptive and evaluative perceptions we have of ourselves in different areas of our experience, as well as the perception of our overall worth.[2] For example, you might describe yourself as good sports-person, an average academic student, and an awful musician, but a great 'social' person with lots of friends. These descriptions represent your self-concept. Self-esteem is the evaluative perception of 'worth' you attach to these descriptive perceptions (i.e. description = self-concept); that is, do you like the description, does it matter to you? For example, you may not like describing yourself as a good sportsperson (you want to be an outstanding sportsperson), but not mind describing yourself as an average academic. Self-concept descriptions are only important to your mental toughness if they matter to you, if they are important to you.

> 'No one can make you feel inferior without your permission.'
>
> Eleanor Roosevelt

Key points

Self-esteem is both a descriptive (i.e. an 'objective' self-assessment) and an evaluative (i.e. a 'subjective' assessment) perception. You have multiple perceptions of various aspects of your life. For example, you make self-assessments of your skills in social relationships, your physical ability, physical appearance and academic ability, and an overall assessment of yourself as a person. These multiple assessments are organised and structured depending on your individual preferences. Some

of these assessments 'matter' to you while others may not.

For many, or most, dedicated sportspeople, their self-concept of physical ability is their major source of self-esteem. Someone who is not a sportsperson will probably have another aspect of self-concept (e.g. an academic self-concept) as their major source of self-esteem. Therefore the relative importance of each area of self-concept is very important for an individual to fully understand her/himself. Too many sportspeople allow the self-concept of physical ability to be their only source of self-esteem, and develop a sports-only 'identity' as a result.[3] This narrow focus has major implications for retirement from sport (see Chapter 18), but is also very important for current levels of self-confidence and commitment (see Chapter 7, 'Foundation PST skills'). That is, it has an important impact on your level of mental toughness.

'Self-esteem: look in the mirror, what you see is what you get.'

Why concern yourself with self-esteem?

First, self-esteem has a profound effect on your psychological well-being (i.e. your moods, happiness and life satisfaction) and your consequent ability to achieve peak performance. Second, self-esteem affects what sports and skills you learn (i.e. choice), and whether you learn (effort). Third, self-esteem affects behaviour; that is, the selection of behaviours, motivation to achieve behaviours, persistence and selection (or not) of appropriate options to achieve goals.

How is self-esteem formed/affected?

Self-esteem is a product of learning, especially through social interactions with others, and a culmination of personal experiences (i.e. successes and failures). One way of explaining the development of self-esteem is the 'looking-glass' theory, which suggests that an individual looks in the 'mirror' of other people's evaluations of him/herself. Self-esteem is therefore dependent upon the individual's perception of other people's evaluations of her/him. In addition, socially individuals compare themselves directly with others.

Self-esteem is influenced by success and failure in terms of skills, control over actions, and social acceptance by others. It is also influenced by emotions; for example, pride, shame, anxiety and stress. It is vital for psychological well-being and peak performance that you do not have a sports-only source of self-esteem, or a sports-only identity.[3] Your self-esteem must have a 'balance' of different sources. Positive self-esteem is a 'tough stuff' building block, and it is developed by using more than sport as the basis of your overall self-esteem.

Developing a positive level of self-esteem

Emotional self: 'Everyone hates me!'

Analytical self: 'Don't be ridiculous, not everyone knows you.'

Positive self-esteem helps you to be more analytical, rational and logical, and less emotional in your self-assessment. To maintain a positive level of self-esteem you need to be analytical rather than emotional. However, this does not mean that the emotions of pride and passion should be totally discounted. What it does mean is that a strong dose of realism through some analytical thinking helps with the maintenance of a positive level of self-esteem.

Consistently successful sportspeople have this general attribute called 'positive self-esteem'.

Often a positive level of self-esteem develops as a person ages and gains experience. However, positive self-esteem does not always equal experience. There are many older players who have the same low or average level of self-esteem they had ten years earlier. Conversely, there are young athletes who display a positive level of self-esteem beyond their years.

'You are what you believe yourself to be.'

As your physical and psychological skills develop you should aim to develop your level of self-esteem as well. Although self-esteem will develop with age and successful experiences in sport, it may take a little longer than you want. There are a number of ways you can speed up the development of your self-esteem. The first step is to understand what is meant by self-esteem. What are the characteristics of an athlete with a positive level of self-esteem? The following characteristics are most commonly found among successful people, whether they be athletes or businesspeople.

Self-awareness and acceptance

If you wish to accept your sporting strengths and weaknesses you should first learn to accept yourself, to be self-aware. Players with a positive level of self-esteem appear relaxed and confident under pressure, some say arrogant, because they have a belief in their ability to cope with any situation. They understand themselves. That is part of self-esteem development. Become aware of your own perceptions, accept them as yours and accept the fact that others' are different.

'Athletes with a positive level of self-esteem do not try to be like others or waste time comparing themselves to others.'

They accept themselves for the person they are and strive to develop their skills to the very best of their own ability. They take up the challenge to bring out the best of themselves. Athletes with high self-esteem place more emphasis on self-comparison (e.g. with personal bests, performance goals) than social comparison (i.e. with other athletes). You need to develop skills in self-awareness and self-monitoring. The more you understand yourself the more effectively you can plan and take action to eliminate weaknesses and maintain strengths (see the 'peak performance profile' in Chapter 6).

'To be an achiever you have to be a believer (in yourself).'

Realistic and rational

To accept yourself you must be realistic. People with a positive level of self-esteem have the ability to be honest about themselves and the world around them. They have the skill to step out of themselves and view the world a little more objectively. This is very difficult to achieve when emotions are high. It is particularly difficult to be objective after a disappointing performance or an injury. Often our emotions can get the better of us and we temporarily lose our sense of objectivity. You can become more realistic by setting short-term realistic goals and having a solid set of standards against which to compare your performance. It helps to list the factors that make-up your Ideal Performance State (see Chapter 1, and also Chapter 6, 'Peak Performance Profile'). Regard failures and setbacks as positive opportunities for learning.

A further sign of positive self-esteem is rational beliefs. We carry around in our heads two kinds of beliefs – rational and irrational. Rational beliefs help us think realistically and positively. They help us to move towards our goals, and to keep a balance on the pressures that build up in sport. A common rational belief is 'I will strive in this game/event to play to the very best of my ability.'

Irrational beliefs, on the other hand, tend to make us think unrealistically and negatively. They interfere with our ability to 'switch on' our Ideal Performance State. For example, common irrational beliefs held by athletes/players are 'I must always win', and 'I must be perfect'. It is important to strive for the highest standard possible, but to always win (what about the standard of your opponents?) or to be perfect? Athletes who hold such beliefs set themselves up for failure. They must fail, because try as they might they cannot always win or ever achieve perfection.[4] Athletes who hold irrational beliefs are those who suffer from over-activation, anxiety and stress (see Chapter 4, 'Anxiety, activation and peak performance').

Athletes with positive self-esteem are careful to be rational in their beliefs. For example, instead of perfection they believe in their commitment to strive to achieve the highest standard possible; that is, they are 'process' focused. They identify irrational thoughts and effectively change them so they are more rational and productive. They regularly check and adjust their beliefs and thoughts (see also Chapter 13, 'Self-talk').

'Both require total belief in yourself and the ability to live with the outcome, whether good or bad. The road to failure is paved with negativity. If you think you can't do something, chances are you won't be able to. Conversely, the power of positive thinking can turn an adverse situation into a prime opportunity for heroism.'

Tiger Woods (US golfer).

Self-responsibility/self-discipline

When we make a decision we choose from a number of options. Rarely is there only one option. Players with a positive level of self-esteem recognise that they have options and that they have the right to make a choice. Unfortunately many people fail to recognise these things. They allow others to make decisions for them, rely on others for reinforcement, or believe that their old habits are ingrained and incapable of being changed. When something goes wrong they are quick to attribute blame to external factors such as other people, bad luck, or the situation.

Athletes/players with a positive level of self-esteem accept responsibility by allowing internal factors to dominate. They make their own decisions, they set their own goals, they reinforce themselves when they achieve their goals – they take control of their own lives. They are assertive without being arrogant. Successful athletes like Stacey Jones (New Zealand Warriors, New Zealand Kiwis rugby league player) and Barbara Kendall (Olympic boardsailor) do not rely on others for motivation, reinforcement or direction. They are self-reliant and think for themselves. Both these athletes are willing to learn from others, both have specialist coaches and advisers, but in the end they make their own decisions. The first step in accepting responsibility is to accept that you have a choice, and that you and only you make the final decision.

Another characteristic of athletes with a positive level of self-esteem is a willingness to accept responsibility for their strengths and weaknesses. They do not try to hide their limitations or exaggerate their strengths. They can distinguish between limitations that can be overcome with persistent effort and those that cannot be altered. Part of accepting responsibility is accepting your sporting strengths and weaknesses at a particular moment in time. You should strive to overcome your weaknesses and develop your strengths, but not get hung up on your limitations. You should adopt an action attitude, not a passive one. Do not depend on others to do your thinking or your work. Take responsibility and do it yourself. Be assertive!

Self-management

High achievers find they do not have enough hours in the day to achieve all they want. With training, family lives, and work or study they often find themselves pulled in many conflicting directions. Those athletes who handle the conflict are good at allocating their time and energy. They have plans and priorities, they have the discipline to stick to their plans and to achieve their goals, and at the end of the day they evaluate their progress (see Chapter 10, 'Goal setting'). Use your training diary/logbook, and create and use a 'daily planner' in which you allocate your time on a daily basis. Your decisions on time allocation should be based on your long-term and short-term goals and your training cycle. Be organised, and be assertive!

Persistence and commitment

The road to success is long, hard, and a battle to overcome obstacles. In sport these obstacles include injury, financial problems, slow improvement, lack of competition and numerous other hassles. It seems that the top performers have learned that obstacles can be overcome, either through personal effort or with assistance from coaches, sport scientists and administrators. Do not expect steady, constant improvement. There will be ups and downs and setbacks. Successful athletes handle the setbacks effectively. Patience is a common characteristic. A useful exercise to complete is to make a list of obstacles that you have faced and dealt with in your life (inside and outside of sport). This reminds you that you have the ability to handle setbacks, and highlights ways to improve in this area. Do not avoid important tasks just because they are associated with discomfort and hassle. Reject the irrational idea that change should be painless and easy. If change and success were painless and easy then anybody could be a top athlete; but top athletes are not just anybody!

> 'The training is hard in any sport at high level. There are just a few people who are mentally and physically prepared to take the hard work, and these people are going to make it... If it was easy, everybody would be an Olympic champion.'
>
> Nadia Comaneci (Romanian gymnast; winner of three gold medals, and three perfect '10s' in artistic gymnastics at the 1976 Olympics)

Summary: positive self-esteem

- Take a long-term approach to developing a positive level of self-esteem. It will not happen in a day, but you can take a short step each day if you know where you are going.
- Adopt an active attitude, not a passive one. Be assertive. Do not depend on others to do your thinking or work. Take responsibility and do it yourself.
- Accept yourself for the person you are at a particular point in time. Challenge yourself to develop and improve.
- Develop skills in self-awareness and self-monitoring. The more you understand yourself the more effectively you can plan and take action to improve.
- Regard failures and setbacks as positive opportunities for learning.
- Develop the skill to manage your time and energy by setting priorities and goals and disciplining yourself to achieve them.

- Do not avoid important tasks because they are associated with discomfort. Reject the irrational idea that change should be painless and easy.
- Do not expect steady, constant improvement. There will be ups and downs and setbacks. Successful athletes, those with positive self-esteem, handle the setbacks effectively.

Assertiveness and peak performance

Closely associated with positive self-esteem is the development of assertiveness as a building block for mental toughness. Coaches often describe assertive players as those who make things happen, those who are keen and confident, who never give up, and who consistently challenge themselves, their teammates and their opponents.[5] Assertive athletes do not let opponents take advantage of them, nor are they easily dominated tactically or physically by others, yet they are respectful of their opponents – assertive doesn't mean aggressive!

Non-assertive players, on the other hand, tend to be hesitant and cautious. They allow others to set the pace and dominate the situation (e.g. tactically), and are often afraid of failing or making a mistake. Rather than being focused on and committed to their goals, they tend to allow the ideas, goals and needs of others to dominate. Non-assertive players tend to have low self-esteem, and to worry and keep their feelings to themselves rather than freely expressing their thoughts and feelings. The non-assertive athlete commonly experiences frustration, stress, low self-confidence, low self-esteem, poor concentration, and a lack of initiative.

Rarely do players conform to one extreme of an assertiveness continuum; they are seldom totally assertive or totally non-assertive. Most athletes show a combination of assertive and non-assertive behaviours depending on the situation. Successful players are able to control their assertive behaviour and decide themselves when it is appropriate to be assertive or non-assertive.

Assertiveness training

The aim of assertiveness training is to help you develop the self-esteem, skills and attitudes necessary to control your assertiveness so that you can consistently tailor it to suit the situation. Here are some important points about assertiveness that reflect the skills noted above regarding positive self-esteem.[5]

First, assertiveness is not arrogance. Assertive behaviour is forceful and active, yet acceptable to others. It is an outward expression of your self-esteem and self-confidence, but not at the expense of the respect or rights of others (also see 'Self-confidence', Chapter 7).

Second, assertiveness is not aggression. Many players and coaches talk about the need to be more 'aggressive', when in fact what they mean is more assertive. Aggression is defined as a deliberate act intended to physically or psychologically harm another person. Assertive behaviour is forceful and active, but it is not meant to harm an opponent or show him/her a lack of respect. Assertive players avoid the extremes of either aggressive or non-assertive behaviour.

Learning and maintaining assertive behaviours

- As part of the peak performance profile process outlined in Chapter 6, you should spend some time defining for yourself what precisely you mean by assertive behaviour in your sport. Write down specific examples. Write out a list of the actions and qualities of a particularly assertive elite athlete/player in your sport. Identify the actions and behaviours that you need to improve upon. Make sure you clearly understand the difference between non-assertive, assertive, and aggressive behaviour in your sport. You should also discuss this with your teammates and your coach.

- Rate yourself against the actions and behaviours of non-assertive, assertive and aggressive players in your sport (see the peak performance profile in Chapter 6).

- Set goals to improve the assertive behaviours you are poor on (see Chapter 10, 'Goal setting'). Assertive players have a 'process' goal focus, as these goals are within their control and are the basis of successful performance (see Chapter 1 and Chapter 3). Assertive players focus on what they can control.

- Consistently 'visualise' or imagine yourself being assertive in important situations (see Chapter 12, 'Imagery').

- Develop appropriate 'self-talk' to remind and instruct yourself about being assertive (see Chapter 13, 'Self-talk').

- As part of your pre-game or pre-race mental preparation you should identify key situations in the race or game when it will be particularly important to be assertive (e.g. after an error, immediately after a time-out or injury break). Plan, as part of your performance focus plan, what you will do to make sure you react assertively (see Chapter 14, 'Mental preparation').

- Identify an appropriate role model in your sport who consistently demonstrates appropriate assertive behaviour: model yourself, to a degree, on her/his behaviour.

- As part of your peak performance profile try to identify some of the common reasons or causes of inappropriate non-assertive or aggressive behaviour (see Chapter 6). Some of the common causes are: (i) having an outcome goal orientation (see Chapter 3, 'Motivation for peak performance'); the outcome focus takes your attention away from yourself to a focus on your opponent(s) and the score, creating a fear of failure. The situation then controls you, rather than you controlling the situation; (ii) being overly concerned about the judgements and evaluations others make about you. If you worry about what others think then you will end up 'mind reading' too much, instead of focusing on putting your tactics into operation (see also 'Concentration and attention' in Chapter 8).

> 'It just comes down to your attitude. You've got to be committed, you've got to be dedicated and have a will to win. You don't have to be born tough, it can be learned.'
>
> Rod Dixon (NZ runner – bronze medal, 1972 Olympics; winner New York Marathon)

Maintaining assertiveness

Assertive players 'make things happen', they don't watch things happen. Assertive players control the situation, they don't let the situation control them. They take the initiative and they decisively choose options rather than being tentative, cautious or overly conservative. Like any psychological skill, assertiveness takes practice to develop and more practice to maintain.

Summary: 'tough stuff'

This chapter has dealt with the vital building blocks of mental toughness. As discussed previously, mental toughness is the hallmark of consistent peak performance and the Ideal Performance State. Clearly it is impossible to be a consistent peak performer without a positive level of self-esteem, an assertive attitude, and complete commitment to peak performance. The challenge you now face is to accept the task of developing the necessary 'tough stuff' to become a peak performer – you need to make the decision to be 'winner', rather than a 'survivor'. The first PST skill area you will need to develop to achieve mental toughness is motivation, which we look at in Chapter 3.

MOTIVATION FOR PEAK PERFORMANCE

**'Success is getting what you want.
Happiness is wanting what you get.'**

My job in this chapter is not to 'motivate' you – the only person who can motivate you is you! Motivation must come from within – intrinsic motivation – to be effective and meaningful. Extrinsic motivation provided by someone else like your coach and captain, or the opposition, is unlikely always to be meaningful for you or have a lasting effect. Too often captains and coaches label themselves as 'motivators' and portray themselves as being able to motivate others; in reality it just isn't possible to motivate someone unless that person wants to achieve the dreams and goals the coach or captain is providing for them. More accurately, these 'motivators' are only providing an inspirational sparkplug for people. While inspiration is useful, it is little more than a spark that can't start a real fire unless the right 'fuel' is available. That fuel must come from within – the dreams, goals and aspirations that matter to you. Motivation is your own internal combustion engine!

Consequently, I often refer to the 'motivator/ inspirational' approach to motivation as petrol station psychology – someone fills up your fuel tank and blows up your tyres, but the benefit is short-lived as the fuel tank will soon be empty again, and the tyres will go flat. You must be able to supply your own 'fuel' for effective motivation in the long run. As noted earlier, mental toughness is all about self-reliance and personal responsibility, so you need to be responsible for your own motivation. You must take some time to identify a dream (long-term goal) and a set of goals that excite you, have meaning for you, and

will be satisfying and provide you with a sense of purpose.

Motivation is both 'wanting to' and 'having to' do something. You must identify sporting goals that you 'want to' achieve – this is the long-lasting fuel for goal accomplishment – but also be realistic enough to realise that there will be times when you need to motivate yourself to do something because you 'have to' do it (e.g. training motivation). When you reach the stage of having to do something, rather than wanting to do it, you will need strong self-discipline and mental toughness to tough it out. So motivation covers both wanting to and having to do something. Commitment, on the other hand, is a decision to commit to something you really want to do – intrinsic motivation. We will get to commitment in Chapter 7, but first let's talk about motivation.

Motivation is all-important for success in sport. You need motivation for the season (dreams, vision, goals), for your fitness training, for your skill training/practice, and for your pre-game/race/event 'psych-up'. Motivation is a Foundation PST skill for developing mental toughness (see Chapter 5). Consequently, motivation is a skill that you need to have well and truly mastered before you can expect to have consistent success at developing Performance PST skills like peak activation, peak concentration, or coping with pressure.

What is motivation?

What is your definition of motivation? Does it mean 'psych-up', 'be committed', 'desire to win'? Motivation is a necessary, but not sufficient, condition for mental toughness and peak performance. It energises, selects, and directs performance. Without sufficient motivation you will not perform well in competition or train effectively. Motivation is primarily made up of the direction and intensity of effort.

- Direction – the tendency to approach or avoid a particular situation (e.g. competition). This represents the goals you are trying to achieve, your reasons for playing.
- Intensity – the activation of a person, on a continuum from low intensity (asleep) to high intensity (all-out effort). This is the 'psych-up' aspect of motivation related to effort, activation and intensity (more on this in Chapter 4).

> 'There's no such thing as coulda, shoulda, and woulda. If you shoulda and coulda, you woulda done it.'
>
> Pat Riley (coach of the LA Lakers 1981–89, four-time NBA champions)

There are many different types of motivation. We can look at motivation for a number of aspects of sport. For example, long-term motivation – such as commitment to training and practice; short-term motivation – for example, motivation for an upcoming game/race/event; intrinsic motivation – for example, playing for fun, enjoyment, and mastering the skills of your sport or playing position; extrinsic motivation – such as rewards, trophies, money, recognition, and trips away with teams; and pre-game motivation – such as the 'psych-up' before your game/race/event (also see Chapter 14, 'Mental preparation').

Explanations of motivation

There exist a number of differing explanations of motivation in sport.[1] Unfortunately many of these 'explanations' are based more on guesswork than on successful experience or research. However, we need to be aware of them in order to understand motivation fully. The first of these explanations is common among players/athletes, while the second explanation is common among coaches – both are partially correct!

Person-centred models (intrinsic motivation)

Here player/athlete or personal factors determine motivation. People have underlying dispositions (i.e. traits) that account for their level of motivation. The behaviours of players are viewed as signs of their underlying traits. This model suggests that you have either got motivation or you haven't, and that motivation isn't something that can be developed.

Situation-centred models (extrinsic motivation)

In this model situational factors determine motivation (e.g. the coach, captain, opponents, spectators). Something in the situation causes a response in the athlete/player. This model suggests that the athlete/player has no drives or other motivational forces or traits that affect behaviour; it's all up to the coach or captain to provide motivation.

Interaction model (person × situation)

Motivation is a function of the person, the situation, and the interaction between these two factors. There is mutual interaction between the person and the situation – people actively change situations and situations change people. This is the most accurate and useful explanation of motivation in sport as it accounts for both the athlete/player's goals and the situation. While this model includes the effects of the goals and motives that the athlete/player brings to the situation, it also takes into account the effect that situational factors such as the coach, captain, opponents and the crowd have on his/her motivation.

> 'You don't have to be a fantastic hero to do certain things – to compete. You can be just an ordinary chap, sufficiently motivated to reach challenging goals.'
>
> Sir Edmund Hillary (New Zealand mountain climber; with Tenzing Norgay, the first climber to reach the top of Mt Everest)

Implications of the interaction model

This model assumes that athletes/players are motivated by both the situation and the goals and motives they bring with them. For example:

Player/athlete motives

1. To beat my opponent/win
2. To master the tasks/skills
3. To get approval/praise
4. To get rewards (trophies/money)
5. ...

Situational motivators

1. Crowd, spectators
2. Opponent(s)
3. Coach
4. Captain/teammates
5. ...

There has been considerable research into common participation motives for athletes/players in different sports in New Zealand.[2] The interesting aspect of these studies, from junior through to senior and elite players, was the consistent focus on 'fun', 'friendship' and 'achieving goals'. As you would expect, at the senior/elite level 'winning' was a more important motive, but not at the expense of these others. Perhaps the other motives indicate more of a focus on 'how to win', rather than just winning itself.

To understand your particular motivation, you must know why you participate in your sport. What are your reasons for being involved? What is your definition of success in sport? You must consider your motives, reasons or goals, and the situation that you participate in. The coach is a critical part of the sports situation, and directly and indirectly influences motivation. Consequently the coach should structure the sport situation to meet players' needs (e.g. adjust their coaching style) and/or change athletes'/players' motives if they are inappropriate. Try to ensure successful participation.

> 'It's my motivation to always improve. I'm sort of fuelled by that. Overall I do feel stronger... It's not easy to come down here [to the Australian Open] very prepared, but it sure beats the alternative!'
>
> Andre Agassi (US tennis player) commenting on his career goals at the 'mature' age of 33 years!

To help sort out your own definition of success you need to understand the basic principles of a motivational factor called 'goal orientations'. Getting a handle on your profile of goal orientations will help you enhance your levels of motivation and strengthen your commitment.

Goal orientations

You need to define success in specific terms. People have different personal definitions of success, which are referred to as 'achievement goal orientations'[1]. Your goal orientations affect your perception of a situation (e.g. confidence, perceived ability) and systematically affect your overall motivation in sport. Goal orientations are based on the principle that people are intentional, goal-directed individuals who operate in a rational manner.[1] Thus, your motivation is the result of intentional and rational thought. The behaviour you choose has some meaning to you, therefore it is necessary to understand the meaning of success for you – that is, your individual perceptions of success and failure.

Individuals typically have multiple goals; your own combination of multiple goals forms your goal orientation for sport.[1] There are two major goal orientations that most athletes/ players develop in sport (task and outcome), plus a third goal orientation that is less common (social approval) but which can be important for some athletes/players.

Task orientation (or mastery)

The focus is on succeeding at a task or mastering a skill; people with a task orientation are interested in the process – how competently they actually complete a particular task. These athletes/players are ability-oriented, but they focus on personal performance in relation to their previous level of ability or skill. Other ways to describe this goal orientation are mastery-focused, or intrinsically motivated. These players assess performance on the task and the process of mastering the task. They also assess the effort needed to complete or master the task. Perceived ability is judged on task performance.

Outcome orientation (or ego)

The focus of success here is social comparison. The athlete/ player compares their ability with others or with a recognised standard; they are interested in the product – how performance is related to the final outcome or result (e.g. winning/losing), and how that relates to being better than someone else.

With this goal orientation the aim is to be able to claim high ability for yourself, so it is very ego-driven. The primary concern is your own ability in relation to others; that is, social comparison with others' abilities, especially winning! Outcome-oriented athletes/players make three assessments in order to demonstrate high ability. The outcome of these assessments significantly affects their motivation:

- Assess opponents' abilities in relation to all other opponents; usually win/loss record.
- Assess own ability in relation to opponent; social comparison. This assessment is usually based on the outcome of the game/race/event (i.e. win or lose).
- Assess effort applied by yourself and your opponent; effort is emphasised and rewarded in sport. A minimal effort required to beat an opponent will enhance your perceived ability.

Social approval orientation

The focus here is on demonstrating ability and effort to others and trying hard; these people want to gain approval, recognition and praise from other people who matter to them (e.g. coaches, teammates, selectors, spectators, family).

Players with a dominant social approval goal orientation aim to demonstrate ability or try hard in order to gain approval from other people who matter to them, especially the coach, teammates and family. This goal orientation is especially relevant to athletes/players under the age of 12. Athletes/players at this age tend to equate effort with ability.[3]

Every athlete/player has acquired a little bit of each of these three major goal orientations. There may be other goal orientations as well, but these are the most common. It is your unique combination of these goal orientations that determine your level and type of 'motivation'.

Multiple goal orientations

Each athlete/player has multiple motives or goals – a combination of goal orientations for being in a particular sports situation.[1] Your combination of goals will likely include the three major goals discussed above, plus other goals as well.

For example, an athlete/player who competes at a senior club level may have a combination of goals that is predominantly outcome-oriented, and to a lesser degree task-oriented. An individual who plays occasional social sport with friends may have a combination that is predominantly oriented to social approval, with task as a secondary goal, and some desire to demonstrate competitive ability (i.e. outcome/ego). Goal orientations are dynamic, and the combination may change from situation to situation and over time.[1] The competitive athlete/player mentioned above may change to a task and social approval orientation when he or she plays social touch football with friends. Your combination of goal orientations, and the emphasis you place on particular goals, represents your definition of success.

'At the end of the day you play rugby because you enjoy it, for what it gives you in satisfaction, physical and mental, and for what playing it well does for your country.'

Grant Fox (All Black 1985–93)

In the quote from Grant Fox, he talks about some of his multiple goals for being involved in rugby; it would appear that he mainly played for task (i.e. enjoyment, satisfaction) as well as social approval (i.e. doing something for your country)

reasons. To begin to understand his motivation he needs to know his multiple goals for playing. Similarly, you need to identify your own goals when playing your sport if you want to maintain existing levels of motivation and create extra motivation.

Research into the goal orientations of New Zealand rugby players shows that most elite players (i.e. Provincial/Super 12 level) have a goal profile of high task orientation (i.e. 4 on a scale of 1 to 5) and a medium outcome orientation (3 on a scale of 1 to 5).[4] So it would seem that the major goal orientation focus of elite rugby players is one that is high in task (mastery of skills/improvement), but also has a significant focus on the outcome (winning, beating an opponent). Both these goal orientations are useful for motivation in sport and both contribute to mental toughness.

'I play to have fun, to get better, and to win.'

Jeff Wilson (All Black 1993–2001)

You need to consider your own goal orientations in order to understand your motivation for sport. Goal orientations are also important in developing a number of other PST skills (e.g. self-confidence, peak activation), and are especially useful in learning the PST method of 'goal setting' (see Chapter 10). Finally, an understanding of goal orientations is vital in achieving peak performance; you need to focus primarily on a task-mastery orientation in order to switch on the Ideal Performance State.

Example: Nicky's pre-game motivation

Nicky is a senior-level hockey player. Her pre-game motivation had been a real problem for her for a number of seasons, until she decided to take the bull by the horns and take charge of it herself. Typically she had left her pre-game motivation and mental preparation to her captain and coach, assuming it was their job to get her and the rest of the team motivated and 'psyched-up' for each game. However, before some games the captain and coach failed to do much to psych-up Nicky, so finally she decided to do it herself. Most of her coaches had emphasised 'winning' and 'beating the opposition' in their pre-game motivation, but Nicky reckoned she felt better prepared when they focused on the team's game plan and a 'how to win' approach. So she set herself goals before every game that were related to her 'jobs' as a centre forward, and how these jobs fitted into the team's game plan. Her goals were based on match stats such as tackle counts, forced turnovers, ball retention, effective attacking moves, and penalty corner completions.[5] She kept track of these stats and goals by recording them in her training logbook. She used a task orientation approach, and it really paid off as she felt much more confident, motivated and psyched-up before each game without being over-psyched or too nervous. She started playing much better, and her improved play led to her selection in the provincial rep team.

Summary

Clearly, motivation is a key Foundation PST skill for developing mental toughness. However, the committed athlete/player in pursuit of their goals will necessarily be putting themselves under considerable pressure to achieve success. This pressure to achieve can lead to anxiety and stress if the player hasn't carefully thought through their commitment to their goals. It is therefore vital that you understand the role that commitment, as well as motivation, plays in peak performance (see Chapter 7, pages 59–67).

Strategies for enhancing motivation

1. Structure practice to improve skill learning:
    *   learning is not automatic
    *   learn from/with everyone, not just the 'stars'
    *   use a 'positive approach' to mistakes.

2. Keep practices and games fun:
    *   maximum participation and activity.

3. Provide time to be with friends:
    *   work on team spirit (social cohesion)
    *   organise parties, social events
    *   have a 'fun period' in practice.

4. Keep practice activities/drills exciting:
    *   be organised
    *   change pace, change drills
    *   create mini-games, add a challenge; for example four consecutive passes in a netball drill equals 1 goal; keep a score.

5. Explicitly define success for yourself (success does not equal winning):
    *   performance goals, personal bests (PB's)
    *   effort and skill, not just outcome/result.

SIR EDMUND HILLARY

'Motivation – 'I rather like to succeed''

New Zealand mountain climber: First person, along with Tenzing Norgay, to climb Mt Everest; the world's highest mountain (8,848 m/29,028 ft)

It was the desire and passion to go where no-one had never gone before – to succeed – that spurred on Edmund Hillary (New Zealand) and Tenzing Norgay (Nepalese Sherpa), to leave their footprints in history by reaching the summit of Mt Everest first.[1]

On the night of 28 May 1953, Hillary and Tenzing camped precariously on a two-level rock ledge at 27,900 ft (8450 m) in brutal temperatures of minus 27 degrees C – it was so steep that Hillary had to sleep sitting upright! At 6.30 am on the 29th, they began their historic day's work, laboriously cutting one step in the snow after another.[3] They reached a rock step about 12 m high and Hillary knew it might spell the difference between success and failure.[4] He found the solution in a crack between the rock and a pillar of ice. He jammed himself into the crack and slowly levered his way up. The obstacle was

surmounted and it has become famous in mountaineering circles as the Hillary Step.

The ridge ahead, instead of curving ever upward, suddenly dropped sharply away. 'It was 11:30 am and we were on top of Everest! … it was a great moment.'[3] They were there for perhaps 15 minutes, alone on the roof of the world.

The descent was as dangerous as the ascent, survival rather than challenge now the motivation.[2] As they approached the camp on the South Col they were met by the other New Zealander in the team, George Lowe. As they met, Hillary told Lowe in his earthy New Zealand fashion: 'Well, we knocked the bastard off.' Lowe, nodding with pleasure, replied: 'Thought you must have.'[3]

Years later, when asked about his achievement, Hillary laconically observed that: 'You don't have to be a fantastic hero to do certain things – to compete. You can be just an ordinary chap, sufficiently motivated to reach challenging goals[6] … Fearful of heart in moments of danger, I found it difficult to produce the calm

courage of the heroic mould … [However] I discovered that even the mediocre can have adventures and even the fearful can achieve. In a sense fear became my friend – I hated it at the time but it added spice to the challenge and satisfaction to the conquest[3] … I have moderate abilities, but a good deal of determination … I rather like to succeed.'[6]

Given Hillary's commitment to success, it is not surprising that in his autobiography he lamented the defeatist attitudes of many young people: '"There is nothing left to do!" is a common cry you hear from all sorts of young people and it's sad in a way because you know the speaker must be closing his [or her] eyes to the adventurous opportunities that still abound. The world is full of interesting projects – if you have the imagination and the resourcefulness to seek them out. Finding new adventures has never been a problem in my life – the big difficulty is finding time to do them.'[3]

'Real success is a continuing process – one's objectives may well change but one always has an eye for something new and exciting … In later years I became deeply involved in a new inspirational dream – the welfare of the people of the Himalayas, building schools and medical clinics, mountain airfields and fresh water pipelines. Fund raising around the world is a major effort.'[7]

Indeed, Hillary's inspirational dream was the Himalayan Trust which he formed to deliver on-going assistance to the Sherpa people of Nepal. By the mid-1990s, Hillary and the Trust had built more than 30 schools and many hospitals, bridges, and freshwater pipelines.[4] Currently the Himalayan Trust spends around $500,000 a year on projects in Nepal; with most of the money being raised solely by Hillary.[4]

In his autobiography, Hillary concluded by stating his philosophy of success in life: 'Each of us has to discover his [or her] own path – of that I am sure. Some paths will be spectacular and others peaceful and quiet – who is to say which is the most important? For me the most rewarding moments have not always been the great moments – for what can surpass a tear on your departure, joy on your return, or a trusting hand in yours? Most of all I am thankful for the tasks still left to do – for the adventures still lying ahead. I can see a mighty river to challenge; a hospital to build; a peaceful mountain valley with an unknown pass to cross; an untouched Himalayan summit and a shattered Southern glacier – yes, there is plenty left to do.'[3]

ANXIETY, ACTIVATION AND PEER PERFORMANCE

4

'While the game itself at times appears to move in slow motion, some things occur in a millisecond that can have a dramatic effect on the execution of a shot or outcome of a tournament. Knowing how and when to jack yourself up and calm yourself down are two of those things. For example, if I need to hit a big drive and I've been a little lethargic, I can get the adrenaline going immediately. On the other hand, I can throttle back on a shot simply by composing myself and inducing calm. No one can do it for you. You have to do it yourself. It's a matter of being in touch with yourself mentally, physically and emotionally.'

Tiger Woods (US golfer).

In the previous chapter we focused on the importance of having a realistic sense of motivation in order to perform to your potential. Hand in hand with the need for motivation is the need to learn how to control your levels of activation. For many athletes/players, this means controlling their nerves and learning how to reduce their level of physical and mental activation in order to maintain a peak level of pre-game motivation/intensity.

For most athletes/players, being nervous is a normal and expected part of the build-up to a game or event.[1] However, the additional 'psych-up' routines that coaches and other athletes/players sometimes use can make a player's nervousness even worse, so that by the time the event begins they are 'over-psyched' or too fired-up for it. This often means they don't perform well because they are too busy trying to

calm themselves down! How often do you hear coaches, commentators and spectators commenting that a player or team took a while to settle down and play to their game plan? The reason for this can often be put down to their being over-psyched, or over-activated, for the event. However, for some athletes/players the problem is not that they get too nervous or over-activated for competition, but just the opposite – they can't seem to get themselves psyched up enough. They feel they just can't get into it![1]

'I know what makes me play well, and passion is not part of it. If I get passionate, I don't seem to play the way I like. The games when I get really fired up are the ones where I don't go any good. I've got to go and do the little things right and do my job.'

Gorden Tallis (Australian rugby league player) – belying his nickname of 'Raging Bull'.

So what can athletes/players and coaches do to ensure their level of activation ('psych-up') is just right for them, and that they don't take 20 minutes to settle into a game or event? How can you psych-up or calm down enough so that your level of activation is optimal for you? What exactly is activation, what causes it, how can it affect your performance, and how can you control it?

Activation and motivation

As discussed in Chapter 3, motivation can be described in terms of multiple goal orientations. However, motivation is also affected by activation and competitive anxiety.[1] Many common sayings with regard to motivation indicate the use and/or control of activation and anxiety; for example, 'psych-up', 'fire-up', 'get psyched', 'psyched-out', 'put them under pressure', 'attack of the nerves' and 'choke'. Have you ever seen a player 'choke' in an important game or event because of the pressure? Have you ever 'choked' yourself? Situations that are potentially stressful or anxiety-producing might include playing in a competition final, playing against a traditional rival, or performing in selection trials. Do players get 'psyched-up' or 'psyched-out' in these potentially stressful situations? Is it possible for athletes/players to prevent themselves being 'psyched-out' in such situations? Can players control their activation levels enough to remain 'psyched-up' rather than 'psyched out'? As an athlete/player, what do you do?

> 'Nerves can give you the edge, the tension makes you more focused and the pressure makes you perform. When two players are physically equal it's the one who prepares best that wins the battle.'
>
> Jeff Wilson (All Black 1993–2001)

What is activation?

Activation is the level of physiological and psychological activity that an athlete/player experiences in a particular situation.[1] It is represented in the continuum in fig. 4.1.

Activation is not the same as anxiety.[1] Anxiety represents a high activation level that produces feelings of discomfort and concern, and is a response to a specific situation. Stress, which is the basis of this excessive concern, results from the athlete/player thinking they cannot perform a particular task successfully when it is important for them to be able to do so. In more scientific terms, it is a perceived imbalance between situational demands and the person's abilities, under conditions where failure to meet the demand has important consequences.

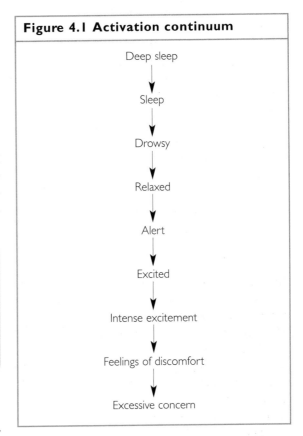

Figure 4.1 Activation continuum

Deep sleep
↓
Sleep
↓
Drowsy
↓
Relaxed
↓
Alert
↓
Excited
↓
Intense excitement
↓
Feelings of discomfort
↓
Excessive concern

For example, Jack, an elite golfer, is down by one stroke on the last hole of a tournament; he needs a birdie to win. His drive on the par-4 18th hole lands in a fairway bunker, about 160 metres from the green. Jack knows the green is surrounded by four deep bunkers and that it slopes away sharply at the front and back. He knows that to birdie the hole and win the tournament he has to make the green with this shot to give himself the chance for a birdie putt. Given the fact that Jack has already missed the 18th green 'short' twice before in this tournament, and has only ever played a long iron out of a fairway bunker once before in competition, he doesn't believe he can do it, but he has to make the attempt because there is no other way to win the tournament. As he calculates his yardage and thinks about club selection, Jack is aware that his heart is racing, his stomach is churning, and his palms have suddenly become very sweaty. He is anxious, and definitely under stress. He starts to worry about how the provincial selectors will respond if he misses the green, and wonders if anybody else can hear his thumping heart. He thinks to himself, 'I can't do this – it won't have the distance out of this fairway bunker and I'm gonna lose!' He selects his club without talking to his caddy and steps behind the ball to start his pre-shot routine – he tries to clear his head, but can't. He moves in to address the ball, settles into his stance, tries unsuccessfully to calm his twitching leg muscles, and to shake his negative thoughts about his club selection and his worries about missing short of the green. He makes his swing and tries to put something 'extra' on the shot, but at the point of contact with the ball he lifts his head slightly and miscues the strike, sending it short and hooking to the left, thus sinking his chances of taking the championship and making the provincial team.

Jack's situation illustrates clearly how a perceived imbalance between task demands and a player's abilities can affect concentration and self-confidence, which in turn affects performance. Compare this with the Ideal Performance State described in Chapter 1. The Ideal Performance State results from a perception of a balance between the situational demands and the player's abilities. This perceived balance or imbalance is also related to the 'perceived ability' discussed in Chapter 3 ('Motivation for peak performance'). Before we discuss some practical ways to deal with

activation levels, we need to understand how 'activation' can affect performance.[2]

The relationship between activation ('psych-up') and performance

There are two types of activation ('psych-up'). Mental psych-up represents excitation, apprehension and nervousness, whereas physical psych-up represents bodily responses such as increased heart rate, increased breathing, muscle tension, sweating and 'butterflies'.[2] There are a number of theories that attempt to explain the relationship between activation and performance. The first of these, drive theory, states that there is a direct relationship between performance and activation. It says that the more highly psyched-up or activated the athlete/player is the better will be their performance, provided the game/race plan and their skills and moves are either simple or well-learned.[2] This approach to motivation suggests that more is better. The reasoning behind this is that if a certain level of psych-up is followed by a good performance, then a greater degree of psych-up will increase performance even more!

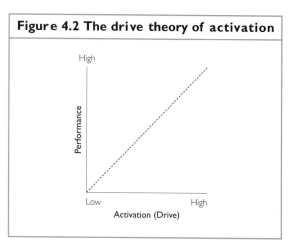

Figure 4.2 The drive theory of activation

Traditionally many coaches and captains have adopted the drive theory approach in preparing for a game or event, using such strategies as emotional pre-game speeches, pre-game yells and team chants to 'psych up' the players. Unfortunately, this theory doesn't explain why athletes/players often perform poorly when they are super-'psyched-up'. In such cases, it is clear that more is definitely not better.

As a consequence of the failure of drive theory to adequately explain the activation–performance relationship, the catastrophe theory was developed.[2] This theory states that there is an inverted-U relationship between activation and performance, in that performance will increase in proportion to increases in activation up to a certain optimal or peak point, beyond which performance will dramatically decrease (see fig. 4.3).[2] Such dramatic performance decreases as a result of over-activation are called 'performance catastrophes', and in such cases peak activation levels can only be regained once the athlete/player has reduced their activation levels to a very low level and has built up to peak levels once more.[2]

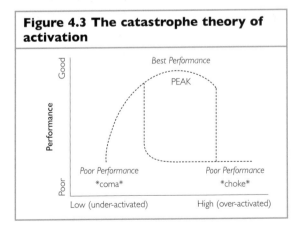

Figure 4.3 The catastrophe theory of activation

Under-activation can lead to boredom and poor performance, whereas over-activation can lead to 'choking' (i.e. anxiety). In fact, there is a fine line between getting psyched-up to peak activation levels and being uptight (over-activated), and the relationship between activation and performance can perhaps be more easily understood in terms of the activation 'thermometer' shown opposite. If you imagine your activation level in terms of 'temperature', you can imagine that you will have a healthy/optimal temperature at which you operate best, just as your body has an optimal/healthy temperature (i.e. 37.4°C; 98.6°F). If you are under-activated (i.e. cold) you will perform poorly; if you reach your optimal/peak 'temperature' or activation level then you will perform to your best, and if you are over-activated (i.e. choke) you will perform very poorly.

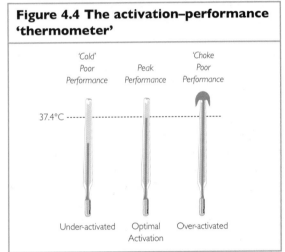

Figure 4.4 The activation–performance 'thermometer'

Key points

- Peak performance results from peak activation levels.
- Peak levels of activation are task-specific (e.g. driving vs putting in golf).
- Each of us has a different peak level of activation that will produce peak performance. You need to recognise when you are at peak activation, over-activated and/or under-activated.

Different skills or tasks within your sport may require different peak levels of activation (i.e. both mental and physical activation).[2]

For example, the tasks of goal-kicking and tackling in rugby require very different physical skills to be successful. Goal-kicking demands a very high level of precise control over physical movement, force, strength and timing. Tackling requires a high level of strength, and players often have to use large amounts of force and effort to successfully execute a tackle. Both skills require high levels of concentration and motivation, however the type of motivation is necessarily different. For example, if you were Andrew Mehrtens (All Black goal-kicker 1995–2002) standing over a 45-metre penalty kick, with the score at 15-all and time up on the clock, you would not want to be as psyched-up (i.e. activated) as Anton Oliver (All Black hooker 1995–2002) would be when preparing to pack down in an attacking five-metre scrum in the last seconds of the same test match with the scores still tied!

These two situations, and the skills required for them, are very different, therefore they require different levels of motivation and activation. Both players are no doubt equally determined to succeed, but the level of 'activation' needed for each skill is vastly different.

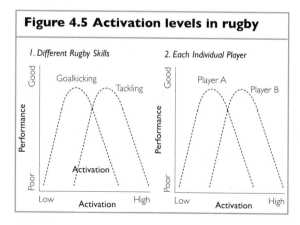

Figure 4.5 Activation levels in rugby

In addition, each athlete/player has his or her own slightly different peak level of activation for each of the skills required for their sport or activity.[2] For example, in the demanding professional sport of tennis the activation levels of Andre Agassi and Leighton Hewitt could not be more different. Leighton Hewitt plays tennis with a very high level of psych-up/activation, often shouting at himself, his opponents, the umpires and the crowd to keep himself activated. Andre Agassi, on the other hand, plays with a seemingly very low level of mental activation. He seldom seems upset or excited by the situation, and plays in a very controlled fashion. Clearly, these two players have played the same sport at the same level of competition, and both have been phenomenally successful despite using very different levels of activation or psych-up. Thus, peak levels of activation are individually specific; each athlete/player has his/her own peak level. Indeed, as Jeff Wilson points out, each player needs to identify his or her own personal level of activation and a pre-game routine to match that peak level.

Signs of over-activation

In order to control activation and over-activation, and in order to consistently achieve your individual peak level of activation, you have to learn to recognise the signs of peak activation and over-activation for yourself. Some of the immediately obvious physical signs of over-activation are 'butterflies' in the stomach, racing heart rate, increased breathing or hyperventilation, uncontrolled and increased muscle tension, feeling tired, a dry mouth, clammy hands, frequent desire to urinate, trembling or twitching muscles, flushed face, voice distortion, yawning and nausea or vomiting.

Some of the obvious mental signs include being abnormally irritable and/or confused, forgetting details, an inability to concentrate and make decisions, self-doubts, fear, worry and changes in communication levels. Obviously if you demonstrated all these signs at once you would be a complete wreck! Typically, most athletes/players have an individual pattern or combination of physical and mental signs that indicate when they are over-activated. In addition, they differ in how much their performance is affected by over-activation. Consequently it is vital that you learn to identify your own personal signals associated with over-activation.[2]

What happens when players become over-activated?

In addition to being able to identify the signs of over-activation, you should also be aware of the effects of over-activation on your mental and physical performance. That way you can more fully appreciate the need for regaining your peak activation level.

Mental effects of over-activation

Negative thoughts such as self-doubt, loss of self-confidence, worry and fear usually accompany over-activation, and often lead to anxiety, which is very detrimental to performance.[2] Over-activation is also commonly associated with a shift in concentration, where your focus of attention becomes too narrow and important cues or pieces of information (such as an unmarked player outside you shouting for the ball) can be missed (i.e. tunnel vision). The idea here is that as activation increases, the amount of information that you can 'scan' reduces.[2] Different tasks entail different concentration demands (e.g. a penalty corner shot in hockey vs 'reading' the opposition's defence pattern), and you must voluntarily control your activation levels to match the concentration demands of

the skills you are trying to execute. Over-activation can interfere with your control of your concentration levels (see 'Concentration and attention' in Chapter 8).

Over-activation can also cause a concentration shift from task-related concerns to other factors such as the score, the crowd and/or the expectations of others. Further increases in activation can then shift your concentration to internal factors such as worry and self-doubt, which in turn leads to stress and anxiety and further decreases in performance.[2]

Physical effects (muscle tension)

Over-activation commonly results in decreased co-ordination and timing, and tight jerky movements as a result of uncontrolled increases in muscle tension.[2] If you can recognise when you are in this state you will know when you need to relax both the mind and the body, and bring unwanted muscle tension under conscious control in order to achieve success.

In summary, over-activation leads to problems with concentration and muscle tension. These problems can inhibit performance, and destroy the enjoyment and satisfaction that come with achieving peak performance and the Ideal Performance State. But why? Why would an athlete/player perceive a situation as stressful? What factors cause stress and high activation?

What causes players to be over-activated or over-psyched?

Sources of stress

Stress results from a perceived imbalance between situational demands and your ability to meet those demands. Competitive sport is designed to socially evaluate your performance against known standards,[1] which means that other people (e.g. coaches, other athletes/players, spectators, selectors) can make comparisons between your abilities and those of others, or with your previous performances. This 'threat' of social comparison can cause stress before, during and after the game or event. Consequently, competitive sport can be a stressful experience for some participants under some conditions.[1]

Stress occurs if you perceive that you are not capable of successfully meeting the demands of the game or event, and feel that it is important to be successful because of the perceived threat to self-esteem and self-confidence that comes with failure. This is linked to the perceptions of ability that you make in the process of deciding if you have achieved your goal (see 'Goal orientations' in Chapter 3, and Chapter 1, 'The Ideal Performance State'). There are a number of sources that affect your perception of your ability to meet the demands of a situation.

Personal/player factors

These include high levels of anxiety, low self-esteem, low personal performance expectancies (uncertainty), low team performance expectancies (uncertainty), fear of failure (win/loss), and lack of fun.[2]

Situational factors

Factors such as the criticality of a game, race or event, the presence of significant others (e.g. coaches, selectors, family, teachers) and the actual outcome (win/loss) can cause uncertainty in your mind about your perceived ability to meet the demands of the situation.[2]

Significant other factors

There are other factors that are often a major source of stress, including parental and family pressure (e.g. to compete, to win), unrealistic expectations from coaches, teammates, administrators or selectors, worry about negative social evaluation by others (this is a particular source of post-game/race stress), and the importance placed on winning by other people.[2]

Summary: sources of competitive stress

The critical feature of these sources of stress is that it is your perception or interpretation of the personal, situational and significant other factors that determines whether or not they cause stress and 'choking'.[2]

Of all the factors mentioned above, there are two that most often cause athletes/players to become stressed. The first of these is the importance that is often placed on the outcome of a game or event, in that the more important the outcome is perceived to be, the more activated you often become. The second major factor is the uncertainty you experience with regard to the outcome of the event, your ability, and your relationship with the other people involved in the game or event.

Activation and performance: practical implications

- Know yourself as an individual. Recognise your individual level of optimal activation and individualise your motivation techniques. Remember, not everyone needs to 'psych-up' for competition. In fact, many athletes/ players would benefit more from learning to relax before competition (see Chapter 11, 'Relaxation and centring', and Chapter 14, 'Mental preparation').
- Reduce the importance of the outcome of the game, race or event. Accept that winning is

the aim for most athletes/players when they enter a competition, but place your emphasis on the process of performing to achieve that aim (i.e. task orientation; see Chapter 3, 'Motivation for peak performance'). In doing so, emphasise effort and doing your best, and set technique or performance goals (see Chapter 10, 'Goal setting'). Trust in the fact that if you achieve these goals, then you will have done all you could towards winning.

- Reduce uncertainty. Do as much as you can to create a supportive atmosphere within the squad/team. Make sure your individual and squad or team goals are clear and specific. Ensure your coach knows what pre-game/race coaching you would like so that you get consistent coach support leading up to competition. If everybody is clear about their goals, their role in the squad or team, and the way they like to interact with other athletes/players and the coaches leading up to a event, then a great deal of uncertainty can be eliminated and stress reduced.

- Emphasise and develop positive mental attitudes. Focus on what you can do in a game or event, rather than what you can't do. This will help you to set more realistic and appropriate goals. Identify positive mistakes – what can be learned from a loss or poor performance – analyse mistakes, learn the lesson, then forget them.

- Develop your 'coping skills' for dealing with pressure. Chapter 8 outlines a number of methods for coping with pressure and developing the ability to control your activation levels (see also Chapter 15, 'Critical Action Response Strategies (CARS) plan').

PRACTICE OF PSYCHOLOGICAL SKILLS TRAINING (PST)

PART TWO

2

THE PST PROGRAMME

As discussed in Chapter 1, there exists considerable research in sport psychology that has identified the psychological profile of the Ideal Performance State as consisting of the following 'skills'[1] (see also the 'Eight Cs of Peak Performance' on page 5):

- mental preparation, mental readiness (control activation)
- complete concentration on the task at hand (concentration)
- high degree of self-confidence (confidence)
- highly motivated and determined to do well in their sport (commitment)
- able to control activation and anxiety (control activation)
- able to cope with pressure and anxiety (cope with pressure).

Collectively these psychological skills/abilities represent an Ideal Performance State for a mentally tough player/athlete.

The PST programme outlined in this chapter is not intended to overcomplicate your sporting performance. Indeed, you will not need all of the skills and methods to enhance your performance and enjoyment of your sport. It is your task to identify the PST skills that you believe are needed to improve your performance, then to choose the PST methods you believe are the most appropriate for your PST needs. Don't try to do too much too soon (i.e. don't work on all the PST methods at once!), otherwise you will struggle with the time and commitment necessary for effective PST practice.

The PST programme: skills vs methods[2]

The distinction between PST Skills and PST Methods is vitally important, but it is usually overlooked by athletes/players and coaches. This distinction has profound implications for the success of your PST programme.[2]

PST skills

A skill is something that needs to be developed, and this happens via the use of a number of different methods and techniques. A 'skill' in this situation means competency, capability or ability level (e.g. concentration/attention). These PST skills may be divided into foundation, performance and facilitative skills.[2]

Foundation skills, as the name suggests, are skills that must be developed as the 'PST foundation' before other skill areas can be consistently developed. Unfortunately, athletes and coaches often overlook these skills and focus solely on performance skills.

Performance skills are those that are necessary during the actual game or event for successful performance.

Facilitative skills such as communication skills are vital for the performance skills to be utilised effectively. Like foundation skills, facilitative skills are often overlooked by athletes/players and coaches as they focus on performance skills.

PST skills may be subdivided as follows:

- **Foundation skills**
  Motivation
  Commitment

Self-esteem
Self-confidence
* **Performance skills**
  Controlling activation
  Coping with pressure
  Concentration/attention
* **Facilitative skills**
  Communication (interpersonal skills)
  Team building: teamwork, team spirit
  Training motivation
  Psychological rehabilitation from injury
  Retirement and lifestyle management

One way to make sense of these skill categories is to think of them as the structure for a PST building or house (i.e. your own PST programme). In fig 5.1 below you can see that like all well-constructed buildings your PST house requires a firm foundation (i.e. foundation PST skills) for the main part of the house (i.e. performance PST skills) to be built upon. In addition, like all homes you need a roof to protect yourself against environmental conditions (i.e. facilitative PST skills – to keep the lid on things!). As the name suggests, this last category of PST skills 'facilitates' the successful execution of the other skills – these facilitative skills may be less obvious, but they are no less important for successful performance.

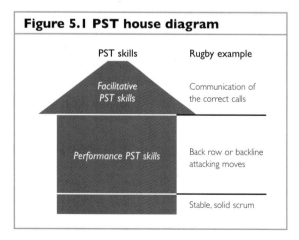

Figure 5.1 PST house diagram

PST skills	Rugby example
Facilitative PST skills	Communication of the correct calls
Performance PST skills	Back row or backline attacking moves
	Stable, solid scrum

Another way of thinking about these three categories of PST skills is to use a sport analogy; in this case the sport of rugby (see fig. 5.1). Designing a PST programme is just like putting together an attacking move in rugby from first-phase scrum ball. The foundation for such an attacking move is a stable scrum that goes forward; the actual performance of the move involves the accurate running of the back row or backline attacking move. Finally, the facilitative skills required for the attacking move involve the calling and communication of the move that has been chosen – all players need to hear and understand the call or they will miss their assigned role during the attacking move (e.g. an 8–9 back row blindside move). As you can see in the diagram, the successful performance of the attacking move from first-phase scrum ball is dependent on a solid foundation of a stable, strong scrum (not flashy, but basic and fundamental), and a sound level of communication that facilitates the co-ordination of everyone involved in the attacking move.

PST methods

A method is a technique that is used to help a player develop a particular skill; just as a physical drill is used to develop a particular physical skill.[2] Method in this sense means a procedure, technique or drill (e.g. imagery).

The PST methods are subdivided as follows:

* **Foundation methods**
  Physical practice
  Education/self-analysis
* **Specific PST methods**
  Goal setting
  Relaxation
  Imagery
  Self-talk
  Mental preparation
  CARS plan

'THE' PST programme?

Ideally, the PST programme is an individually designed combination of PST methods that are selected to attain your PST skill needs. There is no set or 'packaged' PST programme for any one sport or any one type of athlete. It needs to tailored to *your* needs!

The need for the distinction between PST skills and PST methods is especially evident when one realises that there is no set PST programme. To be able to effectively develop a PST programme for yourself it is vital that your existing PST skill levels be assessed, then the skill weaknesses can be attacked via a well-planned programme of specific PST methods. Too often players/athletes and coaches focus totally on the teaching and learning of particular methods (e.g. imagery) and lose sight of the specific PST skill the method is designed to improve (e.g. attentional control). It is easy to be seduced into thinking of the method as the end in itself, rather than as a means to an end (i.e. PST skill development). The methods chosen must have a planned purpose or the desired skill development is unlikely to occur.

You should pick and choose, and only select those PST methods that are necessary to meet your PST skill requirements, with the goal of creating your Ideal Performance State. Fig. 5.2 below illustrates how PST methods are matched with PST skills and then integrated with other types of skills (e.g. technical skills) for enhanced performance, enjoyment and life skills (also see Chapter 19 for suggestions on designing your own PST 'game plan').

Psychological skill needs analysis

The sport itself is the first area that needs to be assessed for effective planning of a PST programme. Various aspects of your sport and/ or playing position need to be considered in assessing your performance requirements – aspects such as physical intensity, type of fitness required, basic physical skills, duration of basic skills, and different critical actions or moments within the game/race/event.

The team (or squad) is also a vital area of assessment in determining the PST programme. This assessment should take account of the coach, manager, administrators, leaders, captains and the size of the team or squad.

The individual is the final and most important assessment that needs to be completed in the development of an effective personalised PST programme. There are a number of ways to assess your individual strengths, weaknesses and needs (such as coaching observations, match/ performance statistics, video analysis); however, the easiest way to complete a basic assessment of your overall PST training needs is to complete a Peak Performance Profile (see Chapter 6).

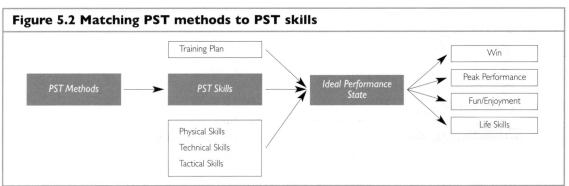

Figure 5.2 Matching PST methods to PST skills

Planning your PST programme for mental toughness

PST programme for the team (squad)

The team will have some general or common needs, such as cohesion (teamwork, team spirit), awareness of teammates' needs, leadership and communication skills. You may need to take these into account before you finalise plans for your own PST programme.

PST programme for each individual

The key aspect of any effective PST programme is that it needs to be personally designed and individually tailored to your PST skill needs (see the peak performance profile exercise in Chapter 6). This personalised programme should take into account the need for foundation skills, performance skills and facilitative skills – see the examples for Jack (an elite golfer) and Kayla (a netball centre) in Chapter 6.

Like physical skills and methods, psychological skills and methods need to be learned properly, adapted/modified to fit your strengths and weaknesses, fine-tuned with initial use, and then practised, practised, practised. See Chapter 19 for suggestions on designing your own PST 'game plan'.

Psychological skill needs: common areas

Listed below are some of the common areas of PST skills that athletes/players find they need to work on after completing a peak performance profile. I have also included some suggested PST methods that I have found useful in developing these particular skills. Do not feel you have to

use all, or even any, of the suggested PST methods for a particular PST skill. You should make your own choice of methods based on your needs and preferences.

Self-confidence (a foundation PST skill)

This involves the feelings and images you have about what you can and can't do. You need to develop and maintain a stable, realistic level of self-confidence (see Chapter 7).

PST methods:
- Goal setting
- Positive self-talk
- Mental preparation
- Imagery.

Motivation (a foundation PST skill)

Motivation is both 'wanting to' and 'having to' do something. You must identify sporting goals that you want to achieve – this is the long-lasting fuel for goal accomplishment – but also be realistic enough to realise there will be times when you will need to motivate yourself to do something because you have to do it (e.g. training motivation). When you reach the stage of having to do something, rather than wanting to do it, you will need strong self-discipline and mental toughness to tough it out.

PST methods:
- Goal setting
- Positive self-talk.

Controlling activation (a performance PST skill)

This deals with psych-up or activation regulation through the management of motivation and activation (see Chapter 8).

PST methods:
- Centring
- Relaxation
- Mental preparation
- CARS plan.

Coping with pressure (a performance PST skill)

This skill involves being able to cope with the stress and anxiety that comes with being committed to achieving challenging goals (see Chapter 8).

PST methods:
- Centring
- Relaxation
- Mental preparation
- Self-talk, parking
- CARS plan.

Concentration control (a performance PST skill)

This deals with the ability to 'tune in' what is important to performance, and 'tune out' what is not. It includes being able to maintain concentration as well as the ability to shift focus when needed (see Chapter 8).

PST methods:
- Imagery
- Centring or relaxation
- Self-talk, parking
- CARS plan.

Communication and team building (facilitative PST skills)

These are the tools that allow you to interact and communicate effectively with other players, teammates, coaches and managers (see Chapter 9).

PST methods:
- Leadership self-talk and 'key words' for team communication
- Teamwork (task cohesion), team spirit (social cohesion).

Steps in learning psychological skills

Education

Learning PST skills should initially focus on increasing your awareness of PST, increasing your understanding of PST principles, developing realistic expectations of PST, and understanding the need for PST for yourself. The 'peak performance profile' (Chapter 6) is vital in this self-education process. You have already taken an important step in this process by reading this book, and in the 'Recommended reading' section on page 179 you will find a number of other practical books about PST – these may be of interest if you are keen to learn more about the principles of PST.

Skill acquisition

Once you understand the PST programme fully you should focus on learning the specific PST methods you have selected to increase PST skill levels.

Practice

Once you have identified the best PST methods you need to systematically practise those methods.

Implementing a PST programme: practical considerations

Organisational considerations

There are a number of important organisational considerations to take into account when you are planning your PST programme.[3] First, who should conduct the programme (a sportpsych consultant, coach, you)? Second, when should you implement the programme (pre-season, early season)? Third, where and when should you practise the methods (at home, before practice, after practice, during practice)? Fourth, how much time should be spent on mental training (possible clash with physical practice time)? Fifth, assessing your psychological skill needs (when, who, how much assessment?). And sixth, determining what PST skills to include, what methods to learn, and what sequence to learn them in.

There are no 'set' answers to any of these questions. You have to be assertive and confident enough to make these decisions yourself. After learning the basics of the PST programme you should be in a position to make informed decisions on these matters – trust your own knowledge of yourself, your sport, your abilities, your strengths and weaknesses, your playing position, and now your knowledge of PST.

However, given my experience of teaching PST, I suggest the following organisational recommendations. I believe that to learn PST properly you need to work initially with a sportpsych consultant. There are currently few coaches who have enough knowledge or experience of PST to teach it effectively. Nevertheless, it is vital that your coach gains a basic understanding of your PST programme so that they can reinforce what you are doing and lend advice and support. The ideal situation would be to have a coach who is qualified in sportpsych as well as in coaching, but that is unlikely in view of the time commitment that most coaches already put into their sport. See Chapter 19 (pages 174–8) for advice to coaches teaching PST to their players.

In addition, it is important to approach your PST programme with the same commitment to planning that you would put into planning your physical training. This requires a simple periodisation plan, taking into account all periods of the season (see Hodge, Sleivert & McKenzie [1996] for details of periodised plans).[4] Ideally, PST should begin in the off-season and develop through the pre-season and early season, with the goal of peaking with your PST skills for the important games or events in the season. Experience has taught me that PST methods are best learned and practised during normal physical training or practice time. The PST skills and methods must be integrated into physical training in order to simulate their use during competition. Often you will need to do additional PST practice by yourself at home, just as extra physical practice is usually needed for fine-tuning physical skills.

PST practice considerations

In learning PST methods you should provide the what, why, when and how of mental training for yourself as an athlete/player – you need to understand the reasoning behind the PST programme. You must structure your team and individual situation for PST practice, and in doing so it is vital to stress personal responsibility and commitment as a player/athlete; you must do the hard work and practice yourself. You must also be flexible and individualise your programme and learning procedures to take account of the team or squad and your particular situation.

Evaluating the PST programme

As with the development of any new skill, your initial PST programme will probably not be perfectly matched to your individual needs. Consequently there is a need for frequent evaluation during the learning and practice of PST methods (e.g. repeated use of 'peak performance profiles'; see Chapter 6). There must also be a post-season evaluation of the PST programme to enable future recommendations, improvements and modifications to be made.

Summary

Remember, PST is not intended to over-complicate your sporting performance. Indeed, you will not need all of the skills and methods to enhance your sporting performance and enjoyment. Your task is to identify the PST skills you believe are needed to improve your performance, and then choose the PST methods that you believe are the most appropriate for your PST needs. Don't try to do too much too soon, otherwise you will struggle with the time and commitment necessary for effective PST practice.

As stated previously, PST is designed to help you with:

- performance enhancement (Ideal Performance State)
- enjoyment and satisfaction in participation
- the development of life skills.

Finally, keep in mind that PST is not just for elite players, and that it is only one part of sporting performance. You must have realistic expectations of PST – psychological skills will not make up for a lack of physical skills or fitness. Nor is PST a 'quick fix' – it takes time and effort! See Chapter 19 for ideas and advice on how you can design your own PST 'game plan'.

PEAK PERFORMANCE PROFILE: SELF-ASSESSMENT

As discussed in Chapter 5, the assessment of your individual skills is the most important factor in the development of an effective personalised training programme. The Peak Performance Profile will give you needed direction in planning your individualised PST programme.

Sense of direction

If you don't know what is important, then everything is important.

When everything is important, then you have to do everything.

When you have to do everything, you don't have time to think about what is really important.

Author unknown

Your Peak Performance Profile will give you direction by helping you identify the various physical, technical, tactical and psychological requirements for achieving peak performance.[1] Examples of qualities that might be included in each of these areas are listed below:

Physical:

- Physiological requirements (e.g. strength, speed, endurance, power, flexibility)
- Medical requirements (e.g. general health, injury prevention)
- Nutritional requirements (e.g. training diet, pre-game/race meal, fluid intake).

Technical:

- Biomechanical requirements (e.g. techniques for successful performance of individual skills for your sport or playing position).

Tactical:

- Strategies for each area of performance in the game (e.g. options/tactics/game plans for various situations).

Psychological:

- Mental skills (e.g. commitment, motivation, confidence, concentration, coping with pressure).

In identifying your PST training needs, you have to discover (or rediscover) the essential skills, qualities or themes that contribute to a successful performance in your sport (i.e., a peak performance profile). Your individuality is emphasised in this profile process, in that you decide what is important for you, and you evaluate your capabilities in a very personal and individual manner.

The Peak Performance Profile invites you to view yourself as an athlete/player involved in the process of developing a general 'jigsaw picture' of yourself and your particular technical, tactical, physical and psychological needs (see fig. 6.1 overleaf). Your jigsaw picture will enable you to design an effective PST programme to improve your performance, to achieve your goals, and to get your brain and body working together as a team. The jigsaw picture that you create will be one that readily makes sense to you, as opposed to one that has been created for you by your coach or a sportpsych consultant[1] (see 'peak performance profile' forms on pages 44–7). Once you have developed your peak performance profile you should share it with your coach(es) or a sportpsych consultant so they can help you to refine the profile and design a PST programme based upon it.

Figure 6.1 Example Peak Performance jigsaw puzzle

Peak performance profiling phases[1]

Phase 1. Understanding the idea

You need to be very clear that the profile will be used to help you understand how you currently feel about your ability to achieve your peak performance. There are *no right or wrong profiles* – you need to build the profile that you think is best for you to achieve your peak performance. When you have developed your profile you should share it with your coach or a sportpsych consultant, and possibly with teammates you respect, so they can help direct your PST programme toward the PST methods needed to enhance your ability to achieve peak performance. Many athletes/ players also use the peak performance profile assessment on a regular basis (e.g. weekly, or every four to five games/races) as a detailed form of 'performance review' so they can fine-tune their training by monitoring their skill levels.

Phase 2. Identifying themes/qualities

You need to decide on the important themes, qualities or 'performance skills' that you require to perform well. You should discuss this with your coach or a sportpsych consultant, and/or with your teammates. Qualities or skills can typically be categorised as either technical, tactical, physical or psychological, although you need to use labels that make sense to you. Technical qualities refer to the specific skills required for your sport and/or playing position (such as passing and tackling in hockey, or batting and bowling in cricket). Tactical qualities are the strategies, tactics and game plans used in your sport and/or playing position, and you will need to discuss these with your coach. Physical qualities are the endurance, strength, power, speed, flexibility, nutritional and medical requirements of your sport and/or playing position, while psychological qualities refer to mental requirements such as motivation, self-confidence and concentration. These qualities or skills collectively represent the jigsaw pieces of a peak performance in your sport.[1]

Each athlete/player will have a slightly different set of performance skills/qualities, and a slightly different combination of psychological, technical, tactical and physical skills. You must decide for yourself how important each skill area or 'performance quality' is to your peak performance jigsaw picture.

You may wish to identify these performance skills/qualities through brainstorming in small groups of four or five people within the team/squad.[1] If you choose to use the 'team brainstorming' approach, you will need to select those skills/qualities that you think are appropriate for the team, but also take into account your individual needs. You or your group should consider questions like 'What are the essential skills/qualities of a good player/ athlete in our sport?' It can also be useful to talk to a former elite player, or invite one to participate in the group discussion.

Use the peak performance skill worksheet on page 42 to write out an exhaustive list of all the performance skills/qualities they can identify (see an example of a completed list on page 43). When you have completed the peak performance skill worksheet you should select the top three or four skills in each category of performance (e.g. pick out the top three technical skills/qualities), and transfer these to either of the peak performance profile forms on pages 44 and 45.

I have included two versions of the peak performance profile for you to choose from. The first, labelled 'Peak Performance Profile (I)', is a simplified version that only includes two of the four rating assessments (i.e. 'Current' and 'Best Ever' ratings; see below). The second, labelled 'Peak Performance Profile (II)', is the full version that includes all four rating assessments (i.e. 'Current', 'Best Ever', 'Improvement' and 'Stability' ratings; see below).

Phase 3. Assessment of the skills/qualities/themes

You now need to rate yourself on each of the skills/qualities you have identified, using the four scales described below.[1] See examples of completed peak performance profiles on pages 46 and 47.

Current performance

Using a scale of 0–10 (where 0 = poor, 5 = average, and 10 = excellent) rate yourself on each of the skills/qualities of peak performance according to how you feel currently (i.e. right now). You may also want to ask your coach to rate you on these same skills/qualities. Their assessment may or may not agree with yours, and this can become a basis for greater discussion and understanding between you and your coach.

Best-ever performance

Another assessment that you (and your coach) should complete is to rate your best-ever performance in relation to these skills/qualities. Most athletes can recall their best-ever performance, and although that performance might not have been ideal, it represents your best so far. Your best-ever profile will not necessarily have ratings of '10' for each skill/quality, because some skills that are important for performance may not be absolutely vital for peak performance. Completing a best-ever rating profile helps you decide which skills/qualities require and deserve the most work to improve your ability to reach peak performance consistently.[1]

Improvement

You should also complete ratings on the skills/qualities that need improvement, and determine how much improvement is needed (i.e. 0 = huge improvement needed, 5 = moderate improvement, and 10 = no improvement possible). These ratings are a bit deceptive as the scoring works the opposite way to the others; that is, lower scores (e.g. 2 or 3) mean the player/athlete rates him/herself as having considerable room for improvement, while high scores like 8 or 9 mean virtually no room for improvement. Consequently, elite players/athletes with well-developed skills often have high scores on 'improvement', indicating there is little room for improvement. The 'improvement' ratings will help you to decide which skill areas have the most room for improvement, which areas you should work on immediately, and which you should leave till later. Clearly, the areas that have significant room for improvement and are important for your peak performance are the qualities that you should be designing a PST programme to improve!

Stability/consistency

The final rating is of the stability or consistency of your performance skills/qualities (e.g. 0 = very unstable, needs control, 5 = moderate stability, and 10 = very stable, maintain). It is likely to be most important to improve the skills/qualities that are unstable or inconsistent, because their instability works against your ability to consistently produce peak performance. For example, as a netball centre you may rate yourself as currently having good technical skills for long passing into the goal circle (rating = 8), and in your best-ever performance you may have rated yourself highly (rating = 9), but unfortunately your long passing into the goal circle is inconsistent from game to game and sometimes in the same game (rating = 4). At this stage your skill at passing into the goal circle is inconsistent and unstable, possibly due to low levels of psych skills like concentration and coping with pressure.

Phase 4. Planning

Use your profile ratings to set goals for improving your peak performance profile. For example, you may set a goal to increase a technical skill like tackling in hockey from a 'current' rating of 6 to 8, or set a goal to improve your concentration from 5 to 7. It is important to identify both strengths and weaknesses – then plan your training to maintain your strengths and to improve on your weaknesses. You should not regard weaknesses as a sign of failure or incompetence – everyone has weaknesses and the key issue is admitting them and working hard to improve them. For example, some people say that Michael Jordan was the greatest basketball player ever. Despite his successful basketball career there were many things that he couldn't do – he had a number of 'weaknesses':

> 'I can't skate. I can't swim. If you threw me in the water I'd be able to survive. But I never learned how. I grew up near the beach, but I was never taught to swim as a child. I won't go out on a boat unless it's a big boat. If I'm at a party, I'll make sure to stay away from the edge of the pool. I don't think I ever will learn how. But I do want my children to learn. Any four-year-old boy or girl who's just learning to swim can do something that I can't.'
>
> Michael Jordan (US basketball player, member of the

You can also use your profile ratings to gain a greater understanding and agreement between yourself and your coach. To work in harmony you and your coach must eliminate any major differences in assessments. The profile will not only allow your coach to understand you better, but you will gain a greater appreciation of their assessment of your performance profile. As noted above, many players also use the peak performance profile assessment regularly as a detailed form of 'performance review' so they can fine-tune their training and monitor their skill levels. On the other hand, you may wish to use the profiling procedure during the 'business end' of the season (e.g. during play-offs, semi-finals, national tournaments), as repeated profiling can help you assess your progress and degree of readiness for a peak performance.

Once you have identified your PST needs you can begin to design your PST programme. You need to choose the appropriate PST methods to develop or improve the performance qualities identified in your peak performance profile. On pages 46 and 47 you will see the peak performance profiles completed by Jack (an elite golfer) and Kayla (an elite netball player). Based on these assessments we will be able to follow the logic of Jack's PST programme and then help design a PST programme for Kayla to work on.

PEAK PERFORMANCE SKILLS WORKSHEET

Write an exhaustive list of all the performance skills/themes/qualities/characteristics of your **sport** and/or **playing position**.

TECHNICAL	TACTICAL	PHYSICAL	PSYCHOLOGICAL

PEAK PERFORMANCE SKILLS WORKSHEET

Write an exhaustive list of all the performance skills/themes/qualities/characteristics of your **sport** and/or **playing position**.

TECHNICAL	TACTICAL	PHYSICAL	PSYCHOLOGICAL
Playing long irons.	'Reading' putts/green.	Aerobic/endurance fitness.	Pre-game psych-up — psych-up without psyching-out (activation levels).
Playing short irons.	'Clubbing' (club selection).	Upper body strength.	
Playing fairway woods.	Yardages.	Leg strength.	Pre-shot routine for every golf shot.
Driver & tee shots.	'Game plan' for the round.	Flexibility — shoulders, torso, hips.	Coping with pressure during the game/round.
Chipping.	Course management.	Recovery from injuries.	
Pitching.	Shot selection.		Confidence for each game/round.
Putting — long.	'Hole' plan for each of the 18 holes.		Concentration for every shot over 18 holes.
Putting — short.	Communication with caddy — yardages, club/shot selection.		Ability to shift concentration — focus on the right info at the right time.
Bunker shots.			
Fairway bunker shots.			Communication with caddy — yardages, club/shot selection.
Deliberate 'fade'.			Commitment to my goals and objectives.
Deliberate 'draw'.			Motivation for skill training.

PEAK PERFORMANCE PROFILE (1)

List and rate the performance skills/themes/qualities/characteristics of your peak sport performance. Rate yourself on each of the skills/qualities using the following scale:

	0	1	2	3	4	5	6	7	8	9	10
Current + Best:	Poor					Average					Excellent

	Current (right now)	Best Ever

Technical:

.... |..........| |..........|

.... |..........| |..........|

.... |..........| |..........|

Tactical:

.... |..........| |..........|

.... |..........| |..........|

.... |..........| |..........|

Physical:

.... |..........| |..........|

.... |..........| |..........|

.... |..........| |..........|

.... |..........| |..........|

Psychological:

.... |..........| |..........|

.... |..........| |..........|

.... |..........| |..........|

.... |..........| |..........|

PEAK PERFORMANCE PROFILE (II)

List and rate the performance skills/themes/qualities/characteristics of your peak sport performance. Rate yourself on each of the skills/qualities using the following scale:

	0	1	2	3	4	5	6	7	8	9	10

Current + Best:	Poor	Average	Excellent
Improvement:	Huge improvement needed		No improvement possible
Stable:	Unstable, needs control		Very stable

	Current	Best	Improvement	Stability
Technical:				
....	|.........|	|.........|	|.........|	|.........|
....	|.........|	|.........|	|.........|	|.........|
....	|.........|	|.........|	|.........|	|.........|
Tactical:				
....	|.........|	|.........|	|.........|	|.........|
....	|.........|	|.........|	|.........|	|.........|
....	|.........|	|.........|	|.........|	|.........|
Physical:				
....	|.........|	|.........|	|.........|	|.........|
....	|.........|	|.........|	|.........|	|.........|
....	|.........|	|.........|	|.........|	|.........|
....	|.........|	|.........|	|.........|	|.........|
Psychological:				
....	|.........|	|.........|	|.........|	|.........|
....	|.........|	|.........|	|.........|	|.........|
....	|.........|	|.........|	|.........|	|.........|
....	|.........|	|.........|	|.........|	|.........|
....	|.........|	|.........|	|.........|	|.........|

PEAK PERFORMANCE PROFILE (II)

List and rate the performance skills/themes/qualities/characteristics of your peak sport performance. Rate yourself on each of the skills/qualities using the following scale:

	0	1	2	3	4	5	6	7	8	9	10

Current + Best:	Poor	Average	Excellent
Improvement:	Huge improvement needed		No improvement possible
Stable:	Unstable, needs control		Very stable

	Current	Best	Improvement	Stability
Technical:				
Putting – long	5	8	5	7
Pitching	6	9	8	9
Short irons	4	8	5	7
Tactical:				
Reading greens	4	6	3	8
'Hole' plan for each hole	6	8	6	9
'Clubbing' – yardages, club choice	6	9	7	9
Physical:				
Greater shoulder flexibility	4	6	4	9
Upper body strength	8	9	9	9
Aerobic fitness/endurance	4	7	3	8
Leg strength & hip rotation	8	9	7	8
Psychological:				
Cope with pressure	5	9	3	2
Pre-shot routine	5	9	5	7
Concentration	7	8	3	5
Commitment	5	9	3	8
Communication with caddy	8	9	7	8

PEAK PERFORMANCE PROFILE (II)

List and rate the performance skills/themes/qualities/characteristics of your peak sport performance. Rate yourself on each of the skills/qualities using the following scale:

	0	1	2	3	4	5	6	7	8	9	10
Current + Best:	Poor					Average					Excellent
Improvement:	Huge improvement needed									No improvement possible	
Stable:	Unstable, needs control									Very stable	

	Current	Best	Improvement	Stability
Technical:				
Long passing – chest & overhead	6	8	5	7
Dodging & avoiding 'contact'	8	9	8	9
Passing into the circle	5	7	5	7
Tactical:				
Making space & shaking defender	7	9	7	8
Awareness of teammates' court positions	5	8	5	8
Defensive pattern – options	4	7	2	5
Physical:				
Acceleration & power	8	9	9	8
Upper body strength	4	8	4	9
Aerobic fitness/endurance	5	7	5	8
Leg strength & leaping	8	9	7	8
Psychological:				
Self-confidence	5	9	3	2
Teamwork – coordination	5	9	5	7
Concentration & decision-making	4	8	3	5
Communication with teammates	6	9	5	7
Coping with pressure	8	9	9	9

Jack's profile indicates that he has a number of technical, tactical, physical and psychological skills that need improvement and/or stability. Jack's coach and fitness trainer will help him with his technical, tactical and physical skills needs; our focus here is on his psychological skill needs.

As you can see from the psych skills section of Jack's profile, at the start of the season he needed to commit himself fully to his golf and his training, take control of his own pre-shot psych-up (i.e. calm down!), sharpen up his concentration, and learn to cope with pressure. On the other hand, you can see from the psych skills section of Kayla's profile that she currently needs to gain some self-confidence, get back her concentration, improve her decision-making, be a better team player, and pick up her on-court communication.

Jack was able to follow a PST programme that allowed him to improve his skill weaknesses. The first step he took was to sort his skill needs into different types of training. He labelled his training as follows: fitness/strength training; technical skills practice; and psych skills training. Among his different skill needs he decided that it was his psych skills that were most in need of improvement. So his next step was to categorise his psych skill needs into foundation, performance and facilitative needs; these were: (i) commitment (foundation skill); (ii) pre-shot psych-up = peak activation (performance skill); (iii) concentration (performance skill), and (iv) coping with pressure (performance skill). Then, based on this skill categorisation, he concluded that he first needed to identify some psych methods that would help him improve his foundation skill need for greater commitment – he chose to use the methods of goal setting and self-talk to improve his commitment.

Once Jack saw some gains in commitment he was in a position to work on some PST methods to enhance his performance skills of pre-shot psych-up and concentration. He chose to combine the use of mental preparation, imagery and self-talk to work on both these performance skills together. Finally, he decided to use self-talk and a Critical Action Response Strategies (CARS) plan to help him cope with pressure and be smarter in his on-course decision-making.

At the moment Kayla needs some help to design her PST programme based on the peak performance profile information presented on page 47. To help her out we will follow the same procedure that Jack used for sorting out his training needs. Our first step is to separate Kayla's skill needs.

It would appear that Kayla has some serious limitations in fitness and upper body strength (physical skills) that need to be addressed if her general play and especially her long passing (a technical skill) are to improve. She also has some significant problems with her passing into the circle (a technical skill) that will need some specialist coaching, and she needs improvement in her awareness of teammate positioning on court (a tactical skill). In addition, she sometimes struggles with the correct options for the defensive pattern (a tactical skill). These last two tactical skills are also connected to her psych skill needs for improved teamwork and improved communication. She also has some other areas of psych skills that need strengthening (i.e. confidence and concentration).

Before making any definitive decisions it will be important for Kayla to discuss her assessments with her coach, and compare her assessments with the profile her coach has completed. Once Kayla and her coach are in agreement, the next step for us and Kayla is to categorise her psych skill needs: (i) self-confidence (foundation skill); (ii) concentration and decision-making (performance skill); (iii) teamwork (facilitative skill), and (iv) communication (facilitative skill).

Now, based on this classification of Kayla's psych skill needs, we will help her pick some likely PST methods to match with each psych skill. Following the logic of the PST programme (see Chapter 5) we should sort out her foundation needs first. We would suggest to Kayla that a blend of goal setting, imagery and self-talk could be a useful way to enhance her self-confidence (a foundation skill). This decision would need to be discussed with Kayla and her coach, then fine-tuned with her input.

Once Kayla was happy that her self-confidence was starting to improve we would make some suggestions regarding PST methods to improve her concentration and decision-making. Likely methods here are mental preparation, self-talk and possibly a modified version of a CARS plan. At the same time as she is working on her concentration skills she should also work on her need for improved teamwork and communication – likely methods here are self-talk, modified imagery, and possibly a modified version of a 'Team Destruction Worksheet' focused on individual sabotage (see pages 98–99).

As you read through Chapters 7 to 15 you will see the detail of the various psych skills and psych methods that Jack used, and the ones we have suggested for Kayla. Finally, in Chapter 19 there is a five-step process for designing your own PST 'game plan'.

DAME SUSAN DEVOY

'Mental toughness'

Squash player: 4-time World Champion, 8-time British Open Champion

Susan Devoy, who first became World Squash Champion at twenty-one, wasn't content with pushing the boundaries in her sport – she fought for and won equal prize money for women, and an equal share of the sponsorship dollar. She was also a fine example of an athlete who succeeded because she not only trained hard, but she 'trained smart and she was Mentally Tough'.[1]

'I always wanted to be the best at something. It just happened to be squash. I've done nothing else in my life but play squash. I had to be the best or I'd be a failure. I put all my time into the game – even gave up school. My pride wouldn't let me fail. The hard part now is trying to be normal.'[2]

'If you want to be good at a sport you've got to decide really young and stick with it. You've got to do it for yourself, not your family, and enjoy it. If you're happy being second or third there's no shame, but if you want to be the best you've got to apply yourself and be responsible to yourself, not blame anyone else. The ones who want to be the best will succeed.'[2]

'I was a maniac for training. I believed you could never train hard enough, so I couldn't possibly comprehend the possibility that I might 'overtrain'. Early on, the only rest days I had were days that I was so rundown and so sick I couldn't drag myself out of bed. But you live and learn, and after a few years I began to take people's advice, to listen to my body and appreciate more of the science of training'.[3]

'I become single-minded on the court. You have to rely on yourself. You're not part of a team; there's no one else there. I don't give in. I keep coming back. Though it's a hard grind. Ten months of the year it's squash every week and weekend, playing about thirty tournaments. There's always pressure; I'd like to live without that pressure but I can't. I love competing. Ultimately I love winning more than anything. You have to be tough, and strong-willed to succeed.'[2]

PST SKILLS

PART THREE

FOUNDATION PST SKILLS

> 'When you doubt yourself, it's like joining your enemy's army and bearing arms against yourself. You make failure certain by being the first person to be convinced of it.'
>
> Adapted from Alexandre Dumas

PST skill: self-confidence

Ask any coaches or top-level athletes/players about the key ingredients of successful performance in sport and one of the first things they will mention is belief in one's own ability. What they are talking about is the skill of self-confidence, and they will be quick to tell you that athletes/players who are self-confident think and act differently to those who lack confidence. Think of some international athletes who could be described as confident (even arrogant), and ask yourself, 'What causes us to describe them as being confident?' If we think of some of the great performances by athletes such as Tiger Woods (golf), Andre Agassi (tennis), Michael Jordan (basketball), David Beckham (soccer), Michael Schumacher (Formula 1 car racing), Andrew Mehrtens (rugby) and Chris Cairns (cricket) we can probably come up with some common characteristics of their performances that would lead us to label them as confident athletes/players. All are (or were) willing to take risks in order to display their skills, and words like 'composure', 'timing' and 'effortless rhythm' can be used to describe their great performances.[1] They are never hesitant, rarely make unforced errors, and if they do, they are still willing to try a particular move again, even if it may not have worked the first time. They are *confident* athletes/players. In the following quote Michael Jordan outlines a key characteristic of his famous self-confidence – he isn't the least bit scared of failure!

> 'I've missed more than 9000 shots in my career. I've lost almost 300 games. Twenty-six times I've been trusted to take the game-winning shot and missed. I've failed over, and over, and over again in my life – and that is why I succeed.'
>
> Michael Jordan (US and Chicago Bulls basketball star), explaining why you have to be prepared to fail in order to be able to succeed – fear of failure is not a healthy focus for self-confidence

Self-confidence greatly influences your performance in situations where you are physically capable of performing the task but are uncertain about your capabilities. The feelings and images you have about what you can or can't do strongly determine performance. The athlete who perceives that she/he is capable of meeting the demands of a task typically feels less anxiety and stress about her/his performance (see Chapter 4, 'Anxiety, activation and peak performance'). Self-confidence is especially important when you face adverse consequences or failure, and it has consistently been found to be related to peak performance; it is essentially the same as positive self-esteem. The mentally tough player has a strong level of self-confidence without being over-confident. Self-confidence is one of the 'tough stuff' building blocks for mental toughness.[1]

'Confidence is easier to define than it is to measure. It is an assuredness in one's ability to accomplish a task even under the most stressful circumstances. Success breeds confidence. It's similar to when you're on a roll with the putter. Seems like the hole is a big as a basketball hoop.'

Tiger Woods (US golfer).

What is self-confidence?

So what exactly is self-confidence? Why is it so important? How can we learn to develop this skill for ourselves as athletes/players and coaches, and how is it possible to instil confidence in others?

Self-confidence has been described in numerous ways by various people over the years, but in relation to performance in sport we can define it as an athlete or player's belief in their ability to execute the various skills required for playing their sport or playing position. Essentially it is whether or not you expect to be successful when you attempt a particular skill.[1] If you expect to succeed, then you are confident. In addition, there is a difference between being confident in your ability to perform certain specific skills (e.g. goal-shooting in netball), which could be described as 'specific self-confidence', and a general belief in your ability to be successful overall in sport. This could be described as 'general self-confidence'.

**'If you think you can,
or if you think you can't
– you're probably right!'**

This saying tells us that belief in one's own ability is often a self-fulfilling prophecy; if we expect something to happen, then that expectation helps to make it happen.[2] For example, if you expect to be able to tackle an opposing rugby player who is running straight at you, you are more likely to make the tackle successfully than if you expect him/her to break through your tackle attempt. In other words, if your confidence in your ability to tackle is high, you are more likely to be successful than if your confidence is low. In fact, the positive relationship between self-confidence and success is one of the most consistent findings in research relating to peak performance in sport.[2]

So what are some of the other benefits of having a high degree of self-confidence? To begin with, self-confident athletes/players are more likely to remain calm in pressure situations because they believe in their ability to do what is required to be successful. This is one of the reasons why team captains are often self-confident athletes/players – they must remain calm when there are three minutes to go and their team is two points/goals behind and stuck deep in their own half. They must be able to cope with this kind of pressure in order to make the correct tactical decisions to get their team down to the other end of the field/court and score (see also 'Coping with pressure' in Chapter 8).

In these situations, the ability to remain focused on the task is crucial, and confident athletes/players are able to do this. Their confidence allows them to focus on the task at hand, rather than worrying about the consequences of losing or playing poorly. In such situations, confident athletes/players will also be less likely to give up, and in fact they will increase their efforts to overcome the pressure because they believe they can do it.

So not only does confidence affect emotions (e.g. the ability to control anxiety), it can also have an effect on concentration, effort and decision-making (e.g. team strategies). Athletes/players and teams that play with confidence are more likely to adopt positive tactics that involve calculated risk-taking and taking control of their own performance rather than playing 'not to lose', which is often characterised by a more conservative and often tentative approach to sport (cf. succeeding v surviving in Chapter 2).[3]

Athletes/players who are not confident are afraid to make mistakes, don't take risks, and generally wait for things to happen rather than taking control of their own performance. This usually means that they wait for the opposition to do something rather than making something happen themselves. If they find themselves in a position where they have several options available to them, they will typically pick the most conservative of these, and often perform this option tentatively anyway, which increases the likelihood that they will make a mistake. If this happens their confidence can be further undermined, and a downward spiral begins to occur, with poor performance leading to less confidence, which in turn leads to further poor performance and so on. As a further consequence of this, the goals the athletes/players set for themselves are likely to be less challenging than if their confidence was high, therefore they are less likely to realise their full potential as a sportsperson. Confident athletes/players, on the other hand, set far more challenging goals, and are more likely to exert a great deal of effort in attaining these goals. Their confidence helps them to realise their potential as sportspeople (see Chapter 10, 'Goal setting').

In summary, then, not only will increased confidence lead to athletes backing themselves to attempt more skills, it can have an effect on their emotions, concentration levels, the amount of effort they put in, the types of game strategies they adopt, and the types of goals they set for themselves.[2] However, being confident doesn't mean these athletes/players never have any negative thoughts or self-doubts. It is normal to be nervous or apprehensive about an upcoming game or event, whether it is five minutes, one week or two months before the start! Confident athletes/players, however, are still able to believe in their ability to perform well, despite any self-doubts they may have.[2]

Despite the advantages of having a high degree of self-confidence, this skill alone will not guarantee success. Athletes/players need to have a realistic level of confidence that matches their ability levels. Those whose confidence exceeds their ability are likely not to succeed, and will continue to fail until their confidence is eventually brought down to a more realistic level. The danger here is that while they are overconfident not only does their own performance suffer, but that of their team also suffers as a consequence of their poor performance. By the same token, athletes/players who are underconfident, despite having the ability to perform well, are also likely to fail because their lack of confidence results in self-doubts, excessive nervousness, tentative performances, a lack of concentration, and conservative decision-making that restricts them from performing to their potential.

Developing self-confidence

So how do athletes/players develop a high level of self-confidence? Is self-confidence something that can be developed and improved upon? The best way to answer these questions is to look at the various sources of information that athletes/players use to assess their confidence levels, and the various strategies that coaches often use to boost confidence. Essentially there are four major sources of information that will influence your level of self-confidence.[1] These are:

1. Whether or not you have performed successfully in the past (performance accomplishments);
2. Watching other athletes/players perform the skill(s) (modelling or 'imitation');
3. Having other people tell you that you can perform a skill successfully (verbal persuasion);

4. How you interpret your physical and emotional feelings about an upcoming performance (activation levels).

Each of these sources of information can act to increase your confidence. The most powerful source of information about whether or not someone believes they are capable of performing a particular skill, not surprisingly, is whether or not they have been able to perform that skill in the past. For example, if a rugby player (no. 8) has been able to make the advantage line most of the time he/she takes the ball up from the base of the scrum during games, then he/she is likely to feel confident about doing it again in subsequent games. If, on the other hand, he or she has been consistently tackled behind the advantage line, then his/her level of confidence in achieving the advantage line from an '8-up' call is not likely to be very high. Similarly, if a netball goal-shooter has been consistently missing crucial shots at goal during the last quarter of recent matches, then her confidence about goal shooting is likely to be rather low. On the other hand, if her shooting percentage has been up over 80 per cent in the last few games, she is likely to approach future shooting opportunities with a lot more confidence. The message is clear – success breeds confidence, and vice versa.

The second source of information from which you can obtain confidence is watching someone else perform a particular skill successfully during a game or event, or demonstrating how to perform that skill during a practice (modelling). As the observer, you can learn how to perform the skill and gain confidence that you too can do it. Of course, this method of gaining confidence is nowhere near as powerful as knowing you have successfully performed the skill in the past, but it does work, especially if the athlete/player who demonstrates the skill is similar to you. For example, if Rick is only 1.80 metres tall, weighs 90 kg, and plays premier club rugby, he is more likely to believe that he can break the advantage line from the base of the scrum if he watches someone of a similar stature do it in a club game, rather than if he watches a video replay of Jerry Collins (1.9 metres tall, 110 kg) doing it for the All Blacks against South Africa. The message here is that the more similar the model is to you as the observer, the more powerful will be the influence on your confidence levels.

If Rick's coach is someone he trusts, and he tells Rick he is capable of breaking the advantage line from the base of the scrum, then Rick will gain some measure of confidence from his coach's words. In this case, Rick's coach has used verbal persuasion to try to instil some confidence in Rick about being able to perform this particular skill. Again, this kind of strategy is not nearly as powerful as actually performing the skill successfully, but it will have an influence if Rick believes his coach knows what he/she is talking about.

Finally, the way you interpret how you are feeling, emotionally and physically, about an upcoming performance will have an influence on your confidence levels. For example, if you get butterflies in your stomach every time you think about whether or not you will be able to successfully achieve the goals you have set for an upcoming event, and interpret these feelings as pressure or fear, then your confidence about being able to successfully perform the skills required may be much less than if you interpreted those feelings as ones of excitement and being 'fired-up' (see 'Controlling activation' in Chapter 8).

All these sources of information can be used to develop and further improve your confidence. Even though performance accomplishments are the most powerful source of information about confidence, all of these sources can be used by you and your coaches to develop and improve confidence, and different combinations of sources can also be used. But how exactly can they be used? To begin with, there is no substitute for actually performing a skill successfully, and the best way of accomplishing this is not during competition (although that is the ultimate aim) but on the training/practice field. Here, you and your coach can work together to build up the confidence to perform the skills required for certain games or events, certain strategies, and individual moves. You and/or your coach can use a combination of PST methods and general practice techniques that will influence all of the sources of confidence information. In general terms, the following strategies can be used to build confidence:

1. Performance accomplishments
2. Observing others performing successfully
3. Imagery
4. Acting and thinking confidently
5. Controlling activation levels
6. Preparation.

Performance accomplishments

Performance accomplishments are the most powerful source of information about confidence levels, and so situations should be created that allow you to experience success.[1] Consequently, striving to achieve performance and process goals in games and during practice can be a very effective way to develop self-confidence (see Chapter 10, 'Goal setting'). Another way to achieve success is to set up 'game/race simulation' drills in practice. The philosophy is simple: success increases confidence and leads to further success. Therefore coaches can set up situations that allow this to happen, and in this respect good practice structures are essential. Drills and techniques can be organised, taught, demonstrated and practised to ensure that athletes/players experience success, and these experiences can be reinforced through encouragement from coaches and other athletes/players. You will undoubtedly be more likely to feel confident about performing a certain move or a certain skill during a game or event if you successfully and consistently perform it in practice. This is also why practice conditions should often simulate the physical and mental requirements of actual competition. This can be accomplished if the coach sets up game/race-like scenarios during practice, so that the players experience performing the skills under the conditions they are likely to experience during an event. There is nothing more likely to build confidence than experiencing in practice what you want to accomplish in competition.[1]

Goal setting[4,7]

Focusing on achieving performance and process goals during competition will help you to stay focused on what it is you have to do in order to perform well (i.e., task orientation; see Chapter 3, 'Motivation for peak performance') and by doing this you will be better able to maintain your confidence (see Chapter 10, 'Goal setting'). This is important because athletes/players can often doubt their ability and lose confidence if they focus on the outcome and winning as the only goal, or think about how they would feel if they lose.

Observing others performing successfully

This simply involves making use of modelling and 'imitation' as a source of information about confidence.[1] For example, coaches can use athletes/players to demonstrate certain skills rather than do it themselves. In this manner, those whom the coach wants to acquire the skill will be more likely to believe they are capable of performing the skill if the person demonstrating it is more like them in terms of age, experience, height, weight, gender and ability level. Similarly, watching video replays of other athletes/players of similar stature, experience and ability will be more likely to instil a sense of confidence than only watching elite athletes/players play. However, the latter can sometimes be useful as an example of the execution of the skill at the elite level.

Imagery

The PST method of imagery is simply an extension of modelling (see Chapter 12, 'Imagery'). Instead of observing another person performing a particular skill, you can imagine yourself performing the skill. By imagining yourself successfully executing skills (for example, goal-shooting, passing, line-out throwing, tackling), or successfully shutting down opposition moves, you can approach an upcoming competition with more confidence. But imagery should not only be restricted to situations or skills in game or race settings. You can imagine yourself successfully performing practice drills, or making it through an especially hard training run or fitness session.

Acting and thinking confidently

Even if an athlete or player doesn't feel particularly confident, the more they act confident the more likely it will be that they will feel and perform with confidence. In addition, if they portray an image of confidence to others, then their opponents may begin to feel a little uneasy because they will feel as if they are playing against someone who seems totally calm and in control of the situation. This can sometimes cause opponents to lose some of their own confidence about being able to get on top of the athlete/player during the game. By the same token, if an athlete lets it be known that they have lost their confidence, either by negative body language or self-talk, this can have the effect of boosting their opponent's confidence since they will believe they have got the better of

them in the game. Portraying confidence, even if you are not feeling confident, can also act to lift your own teammates' spirits if they have begun to lose confidence. It may not help you to win the game/race/event, but it will certainly go a long way towards preventing the team from giving up and conceding defeat.

Similarly, coaches should maintain an air of confidence because this will rub off on their athletes/players. Confidence, like enthusiasm, is contagious. Coaches should keep their heads up, remain calm and focused, and when they have the chance to communicate with players during competition (e.g. at half-time) they should maintain that air of confidence. This can be accomplished by briefly emphasising the positive aspects of an athlete's or team's performance, making them aware of some of the things they may need to improve upon, and encouraging them to do some specific things in the next phase of competition. A coach who yells at her/his players during competition, and appears to be panicking, will go a long way towards successfully destroying their confidence.

'Tell someone they're brave and you help them become so.'

Athletes/players should also try to maintain a positive attitude during a performance (whether it is in practice or during competition). Negative thoughts can quickly undermine confidence, so athletes/players should actively encourage each other and themselves through the use of positive self-talk and affirmations (see Chapter 13, 'Self-talk'). If a mistake is made, it is no use getting down on yourself for making it; if you do, you should quickly replace the negative thought with a positive one (see also Chapter 15, 'CARS plan'). For example, if Nicky (a centre forward in hockey) misses a simple tackle or fires a poor pass during an attacking move close to the goal, rather than saying, 'You idiot, you couldn't catch a cold at this rate,' she should immediately refocus and say something positive like 'OK, hang in there, things will get better. Focus on the next job.'

Self-talk should either be motivational ('You can do it') or instructional (when kicking goals, Grant Fox used to say to himself, 'Head down, follow through'). It is self-defeating always to be judgemental. Besides, if the opposition hears a player getting down on him or herself, it will give their confidence a boost and probably mean they will lift their performance just that little bit extra because they think they've got the better of that player. The bottom line is that thoughts translate to action, and so players who are more positive in their thoughts and self-talk are more likely to be more confident and positive in their play.

Controlling activation levels

Your perception of your level of physical and emotional activation can directly influence your confidence levels.[1] Most athletes/players would admit to feeling apprehensive or nervous before competition, and this is a normal reaction. In fact, for many this is a desirable feeling to have because it means they care about the competition, want to do well, and are probably more focused on their own performance than if they were not feeling this way. However, these feelings are sometimes accompanied by feelings of tension in the muscles, a churning feeling in the stomach, sweaty palms, or wanting to urinate more than usual during the build-up to competition, and if you perceive these physical feelings as an indication that you are afraid, this can have a negative influence on your confidence levels (see also 'Controlling activation' in Chapter 8).

On the other hand, if you perceive these feelings as an indication that you are excited, 'pumped', or 'fired-up' for the event, this can sometimes increase your self-confidence because

you perceive it as a sign that you are ready to perform and eager to get out there.

So if you perceive these feelings as an indication of fear, how can you learn to control them and perhaps even change them to feelings of excitement and eagerness to perform so that your confidence is not undermined, but perhaps enhanced? One way is to bring your physical feelings under conscious control by learning how to reduce your activation levels (if they are too high and result in feelings of fear and anxiety) through PST methods such as relaxation, imagery and stress management techniques (see Chapters 11 and 12 for various relaxation and imagery techniques). Another method is to change your perceptions of these feelings altogether by training yourself to believe they are positive. This can be done through a number of PST methods including imagery and various self-talk techniques (see Chapters 12 and 13 for a description of these methods). On the other hand, if you feel as if you are physically too relaxed going into competition, then you can increase your activation levels via a number of techniques such as imagery, self-talk, or simply increasing your physical activity levels.

Mental preparation

Being as well prepared as possible for an event, or even a practice, will give you confidence that you have done everything you can to maximise your chances of being successful.[2] Going into competition with a well-prepared and well-practised game/race plan, with well-rehearsed moves and techniques (e.g. attacking moves, defensive screens) and with well-learned and practised individual skills can only increase your confidence about your performance. An integral part of this preparation is the preliminary training that you have done in terms of your off-season fitness training. Athletes who know that at the start of the season they are as fit, fast, strong and powerful as they could possibly be, will undoubtedly be confident in their ability to play at maximum intensity without fatigue, to handle the physical aspects of events, and to be able to focus on their own performance in competition without worrying about their lack of fitness, strength, pace or power.

A well-rehearsed pre-game mental preparation routine is also important (see Chapter 14, 'Mental preparation').[2] If you know the exact routine you will follow in the build-up to competition, in terms of what you will do and when you will do it, then you will be confident that you are as prepared as possible. For example, if Kayla (our netball player) knows that she should arrive at the stadium at least an hour before the start of the game, then follow a pre-set routine that allows her to physically and mentally prepare for the game, she will start the game knowing she has not left anything to chance in terms of her preparation, and will therefore be more confident about performing well. Coaches and players should be aware that every athlete/player has different preferences in terms of the way she/he likes to prepare for competition, and there should be enough flexibility in a pre-event routine to allow time for individual as well as team warm-up activities. These things should be discussed and agreed upon by the athletes/players and coaching staff early in the season (or ideally before the season begins), to allow the team and each individual the opportunity to prepare to the best of their ability.

Summary: self-confidence

Self-confidence is crucial for peak performance in sport. You need to develop a realistic level of confidence in your ability to perform the variety of skills needed during competition. This can be achieved in a number of ways,

most of which involve use of the four main sources of information that determine your level of confidence. PST methods such as goal-setting, imagery, self-talk, relaxation and mental preparation can all be used to develop, maintain and/or improve confidence levels. These PST methods, when used in conjunction with good practice and training habits, and hard work on fitness and physical skills, can have a significant impact on your levels of confidence.

You should always strive to have a strong level of self-confidence without being overconfident or arrogant. This will help you perform to your potential, and also help you cope with any slumps in performance.

PST skill: commitment

One of the most important 'tough stuff' building blocks for mental toughness is commitment.[4] This mental requirement is absolutely vital for consistent peak performance and the Ideal Performance State.

> 'I'm not just involved in tennis, I'm committed. Do you know the difference? Think of ham and eggs. The chicken is involved, but the pig is committed.'
>
> Martina Navratilova
> (nine-time Wimbledon champion)

The fully committed athlete/player is more determined, works harder, sets more challenging goals, and invests more time and energy in achieving peak performance than their less committed counterpart. Complete commitment to peak performance is not possible without a positive level of self-esteem and an assertive approach to life and sport. However, complete commitment does not mean becoming over-identified with sport as your only source of self-esteem. Complete commitment in sport means being committed to achieving peak performance in both sport and life.

Commitment as a psychological skill

Sport commitment is a psychological skill that represents the desire and resolve to continue participating in sport and to strive for peak performance.[4] We can look at it globally (commitment to sport in general) or specifically (commitment to a particular team or a personal goal).

The term commitment has been used by social psychologists to describe a set of factors that explain why people stay in or continue involvement in activities.[4] The concept of investment is a key one when trying to understand commitment. Your commitment to sport will be a combination of your satisfaction with your investment in sport, the attractiveness of the best alternative(s) to your sport, and your overall level of investment in the sport (e.g. time, effort, money).

> 'I can't believe this is all happening. Who would have thought I would ever have made it here after so much has happened? Dreams do come true. If you believe in yourself anything can happen.'
>
> Jennifer Capriati (US tennis player – commenting after she won the Australian Open in 2001 in her comeback season)

In 1992 a comprehensive study was completed on the 'amateur' All Black team, which looked at their motivation and commitment in considerable detail.[5] That study revealed that commitment was a key psychological skill for the players in the 1992 All Blacks. For example, when asked to offer advice to younger players, one All Black said, 'I'd sit him down and say to make a commitment to himself about being honest about his sport.'[5] Some of the key commitment themes that emerged were: enjoyment, sacrifice, desire to be the best, set your goal, love of the game, thrill of playing, and friendship.[5] The issue of sacrifice was found to be a very common theme for these amateur All Blacks: 'You've obviously got to enjoy doing what you're doing, but there's got to be sacrifice, you know.' 'If you have a desire to be the best, then it takes a lot of sacrifice, and sacrifice comes into time. Time just on skills, fitness skills – sacrifice, you know, sacrifice…'[5]

When asked, 'How important has commitment been to your success as a player?' the following strong answers were recorded: '… the over-riding reason for [my] success has been the commitment … [it's] the number one reason anyone is in this team…;' '… it's probably the greatest lesson you could learn in life… it's number one… it's the start of everything.' Some players went so far as to place commitment at the top of the list for rugby needs: '… overall 85–95 per cent of my success is [due to] … commitment.' 'The start and finish of sport at an elite level is commitment.'[5]

To summarise, sporting commitment can be described as a combination of sport enjoyment, the attractiveness of involvement in alternatives, personal investment in participation, the involvement opportunities afforded by continued participation, and social constraints to continue playing sport.[4]

Sport enjoyment is a positive emotional response to the sport experience, such as pleasure, liking and fun. Greater enjoyment is likely to lead to greater commitment. In an in-depth study of youth sport wrestlers a high correlation was found between seasonal enjoyment and desire for future participation in the sport.[6] Consequently, many sport psychologists consider enjoyment to be the cornerstone of commitment in sport. Knowledge of what makes the sport experience enjoyable and fun to the participant is the key to understanding and enhancing commitment.[7] So you need to ask yourself what it is that makes your sport enjoyable and fun – be very specific!

> 'The most important advice I can give is love the game. Enjoy and have fun playing it. Then put in the hard work and take it further. If you don't start with that love for the game you'll soon get sick of it, so just enjoy and play to your best.'
>
> Carlos Spencer (All Black 1996–), giving advice to young players

In a study of elite figure skaters, the following themes were found to represent sources of enjoyment: (a) social and life opportunities, forming relationships with new friends and coaches, broadening experiences outside the routine of sport life (e.g. travel); (b) perceived competence, belief that you are skilled and competent derived from your achievement in sport; (c) social recognition of competence, receiving recognition and praise from others for having sport skill competence, acknowledgement of your performances and achievements; and (d) physical exhilaration; sensations, perceptions, feelings of excitement and self-expression associated with the peak performance of sport skills.[8]

Involvement alternatives represent the attractiveness of the most preferred alternative(s) to continued participation in sport. So while your sport may be a lot of fun you may decide that another sport or maybe some form of recreation (e.g. hiking, skiing) is as much fun, is a more attractive option for your spare time, or offers a better opportunity for you to achieve your goals. The more attractive the alternative, the lower the commitment to your sport.

Personal investments are resources that you put into your sport which cannot be recovered if participation is discontinued. These include expenditures of time, effort and money. Increasing your investments creates greater commitment. The more you put into your sport the more you want to get back out of it; that is, you want a return on your investment and hopefully one with interest!

> 'Opportunity is missed by most people because it is dressed in overalls and looks like work.'
>
> Thomas Edison (US inventor)

Involvement opportunities are valued opportunities that are present only through continued participation in your sport. These may include such things as fun, the chance for sport mastery, the chance to be with friends, recognition by others of your skill and ability, or the chance to obtain extrinsic rewards (e.g. trophies, recognition, trips, money). Like investments in your sport, you may decide that the opportunities available are enough to keep you involved even when it may not be as much fun as it used to be – other opportunities (e.g. money, trips, recognition) may be enough reward for your investment of time, effort and money.

Social constraints are social expectations that create feelings of obligation to remain in your sport, such as feeling you have to play to please your coach, teammates, friends or parents. Sport commitment is likely to be higher when social constraints are high. However, this is a negative reason for remaining involved since you have no control over your level of commitment – it is dictated by the expectations of others. Things that we feel we have no control over often become major sources of stress. In turn, stress usually detracts from fun and enjoyment, so your level of commitment will likely suffer in the long run if you rely on social expectations and obligations to others for your level of commitment.

All these aspects of commitment are typically 'weighted' differently by each individual athlete/ player. For example, you may be highly committed because of the intense enjoyment you derive from performing the required skills of your sport, whereas someone else might be equally committed due to their great investment of time and energy, despite low levels of enjoyment.

All Black Jonah Lomu asked others to help him with the commitment needed to overcome his lack of fitness before the 1995 World Cup.[9] Supportive teammates were vital to Jonah's commitment: Lomu later admitted that at that point he considered accepting one of the several offers he had received from rugby league clubs. 'It seriously crossed my mind. What held me back were friends like Eric Rush who said the best way to deal with a situation like that was to prove them all wrong.' Lomu was enormously grateful to fellow All Black and rival winger Eric Rush for his support at that time. 'Eric's someone I knew I could trust. When you have to make a decision, it's great to have someone like him to turn to. He put my mind at ease, told me to believe in myself, told me to stick to my guns.'[9]

Jack's example

The peak performance profile for Jack, our golfer in Chapter 6 (page 46), revealed that at the start of the season he needed to commit himself fully to his golf and his training, take control of his own pre-round 'psych-up', sharpen up his concentration, and become smarter by improving his tactical skills with his caddy (he had to follow his game plan for each round of golf and communicate better with his caddy).

Jack was able to follow a PST programme that allowed him to improve his psych skill weaknesses. First he categorised his psych skill needs into foundation, performance and facilitative needs. These were: (i) commitment (foundation skill); (ii) pre-shot routine = peak activation (performance skill); (iii) concentration (performance skill), and (iv) coping with pressure (performance skill). Then,

based on this skill categorisation, he concluded that he first needed to identify some psych methods that would help him improve his foundation skill need for greater commitment. His first action was to complete a commitment self-assessment worksheet (see pages 66–7). As you can see, this process of self-assessment helped Jack to realise that he really loved the game, and that he was determined to enjoy his golf and start playing to his potential. In an effort to improve his commitment (a PST skill) Jack chose to use the PST methods of goal setting and self-talk. In addition, he and his coach developed specific goal achievement strategies to help him accomplish his goals. He reckoned that he could increase his personal commitment if he had a clearer picture of his goals and how to achieve them.

Enhancing commitment

Identify commitment characteristics

Use the peak performance profile in Chapter 6 to identify and rate the various aspects of your commitment to your sport – recognise these and consider how to use them to enhance your level of commitment.

Identify a team vision and team goals

For team sports, each team member must feel an investment in the team, its vision for the future, its goals for the season, and the required teamwork and team spirit (see also 'Team building' in Chapter 9).

> 'A journey of a thousand miles begins with a single step.'
>
> Chinese proverb

A wonderful example of the usefulness of developing a team vision was evident in Team New Zealand's triumph in the 1995 America's Cup.[10] They used a team management system that employed a 'vision-driven model' to organise the sailing and on-shore teams during the competition. As design manager Tom Schnackenberg pointed out, the use of a vision-driven model can achieve incredible results: 'We were dealing with normal, frail human beings; not super-beings by any means. And yet we achieved a super result.'[10] Use the 'team vision' worksheet in Chapter 9 (page 95) as a starting point for the process of helping your team sort out its own team vision. File copies of the team vision and team goals in your training logbook.

Use challenging, realistic goal setting

Use the goal-setting procedures outlined in Chapter 10 to identify and set difficult but realistic goals. The personal goals should also focus on achieving the commitment characteristics identified as part of the peak performance profiling process. Record these goals in your training logbook.

'Do not let what you cannot do interfere with what you can do.'

John Wooden (US basketball coach)

Use positive self-talk/ affirmations

Use the self-talk and affirmation procedures (i.e. personal self-confidence statements) outlined in Chapter 13 to focus your thoughts on positive outcomes and persistent effort in pursuit of your goals. Even corny wee sayings or clichés like the following quote/affirmation can be useful if they strike a chord with you and your goal commitment. For example:

'The dictionary is the only place where success comes before work.'

Anon

Michael Jordan's commitment[11]

Many successful athletes have encountered roadblocks early on in their careers and through hard work, setting goals, and being committed to those goals they have overcome those roadblocks. For example, at the age of 15, Michael Jordan (US basketball player; Chicago Bulls) was told by his basketball school coach that he was not good enough to play basketball and was dropped from the high school basketball team.

'For about two weeks, every boy who had tried out for the team knew what day the cut list was going to go up. I looked and looked for my name. It was almost as if I thought that if I didn't stop looking, it would be there. I had to wait until after school to go home. That's when I hurried to my house and closed the door of my room and I cried so hard.'

Jordan was embarrassed to be dropped from the team, but in hindsight it was one of the best things that ever happened to him. The embarrassment strengthened his resolve and commitment, and drove him to wake at 6 am each morning for practice sessions with his old high school coach.

'It was probably good that it happened. It was good because it made me know what the disappointment felt like. And I knew that I didn't want to have that feeling again.'

COMMITMENT SELF-ASSESSMENT: WORKSHEET

ENJOYMENT

Enjoyment is a positive emotional response to the sport experience, such as pleasure, liking and fun. Greater enjoyment is likely to lead to greater commitment. So you need to ask yourself what it is that makes your sport enjoyable and fun – be very specific!

PERSONAL INVESTMENTS

Personal investments are resources that are put into goal achievement in your sport which cannot be recovered if you stop pursuing your goal. These include expenditures of time, effort and money. Increasing your investments creates greater commitment. What is your investment in your sport?

INVOLVEMENT ALTERNATIVES

Involvement alternatives represent the attractiveness of the most preferred alternative(s) to continued pursuit of your goal(s) in sport. The more attractive the alternative(s), the lower the commitment to your sport goal(s). What are the alternatives and how attractive are they to you?

(Continued)

INVOLVEMENT OPPORTUNITIES

Involvement opportunities are valued opportunities that are present only through continued pursuit of your sport goal(s). These may include such things as fun, the chance for task mastery, the chance to be part of a successful team, or recognition by others of your skill and ability. What opportunities does pursuing this sport goal(s) provide for you?

SOCIAL CONSTRAINTS

Social constraints are social expectations by others that create feelings of obligation to remain in pursuit of your sport goal(s), such as feeling you have to pursue a goal(s) to please your coach, teammates, family or friends. What expectations by others do you feel obliged or constrained to meet?

OVERALL ASSESSMENT OF *YOUR* COMMITMENT

The above aspects of commitment are typically 'weighted' differently by each individual. For example, you may be highly committed because of the intense enjoyment you derive from performing the required skills of your sport, whereas another person might be equally committed due to their great investment of time and energy, despite low levels of enjoyment. What is your overall level of commitment to your sport goal(s)?

COMMITMENT SELF-ASSESSMENT: WORKSHEET

ENJOYMENT

Enjoyment is a positive emotional response to the sport experience, such as pleasure, liking and fun. Greater enjoyment is likely to lead to greater commitment. So you need to ask yourself what it is that makes your sport enjoyable and fun – be very specific!

I just love golf! It's a really 'fun' sport to play, I enjoy the club atmosphere and the challenge of being part of a team with my caddy that operates like a 'well-oiled machine'. It's also a real buzz to play in front of a vocal gallery of supporters in big tournaments. The challenge of matching up against elite players is also a lot of fun – trying to beat them one-on-one. Having a good game or doing something really well, like a big drive or a long putt, is just a great thrill and a buzz!

PERSONAL INVESTMENTS

Personal investments are resources that are put into goal achievement in your sport which cannot be recovered if you stop pursuing your goal. These include expenditures of time, effort and money. Increasing your investments creates greater commitment. What is your investment in your sport?

Golf, especially tournament golf, takes up a lot of TIME. That's time away from work, away from my girlfriend, my family, and my mates. The training required to make it to the top also requires time, but it really requires a heap of bloody hard work – all the practice, all the fitness work, the weights sessions for shoulder strength, and of course the skill training, and lessons with my coach. You have to be prepared to make big <u>sacrifices</u> if you want to succeed. Plus the cost – clubs, coaching, travel are all very expensive!

INVOLVEMENT ALTERNATIVES

Involvement alternatives represent the attractiveness of the most preferred alternative(s) to continued pursuit of your goal(s) in sport. The more attractive the alternative(s), the lower the commitment to your sport goal(s). What are the alternatives and how attractive are they to you?

One thing I really miss is skiing in the winter at Queenstown. I'm not much of a skier, but I really enjoy the thrill of hurtling down the mountain, barely in control! Skiing is also a great 'social' activity – good times and good people. Because elite golf is a year-round commitment I just don't get much of a chance to go skiing – but that can wait. I'd also like to have a crack at my old summer sport of cricket, but I just can't afford the time to play cricket. The other area of my life that I could devote my time and energy to, if I wasn't so involved in golf, is my job – I really like my job, I'm pretty good at it and the opportunity to expand the business is quite considerable, but I can't afford the extra hours for 'work' when I also need to do my golf practice, training etc. My career development will just have to wait until my 'serious' golfing days are over.

(Continued)

INVOLVEMENT OPPORTUNITIES

Involvement opportunities are valued opportunities that are present only through continued pursuit of your sport goal(s). These may include such things as fun, the chance for task mastery, the chance to be part of a successful team, or recognition by others of your skill and ability. What opportunities does pursuing this sport goal(s) provide for you?

I probably wouldn't have my current job as a sales rep for the computer company if I didn't have a bit of a public profile through my golf. Being an elite golfer opens a few doors. As I said before, golf is great fun to play and I got a real kick out of setting myself the goal of being a rep player and having achieved that goal – that's very satisfying! Also, I really enjoy the club atmosphere and all the mates I have made thru golf. The other thing is travel – I enjoy being a tourist and thru golf I've seen most of NZ and been on tour to Aussie and Asia.

SOCIAL CONSTRAINTS

Social constraints are social expectations by others that create feelings of obligation to remain in pursuit of your sport goal(s), such as feeling you have to pursue a goal(s) to please your coach, teammates, family or friends. What expectations by others do you feel obliged or constrained to meet?

I feel a bit of pressure from my club to play more club tournaments and to help with coaching of junior players. They have been really good to me – they helped me find my job and helped out with some spending money on my first tour with the rep team. I owe the club a big debt of gratitude. My parents have also been really supportive over the years and they get a kick out of coming to my rep tournaments. But probably the biggest obligation that I feel is to my coach – he's been my coach since I was a kid and he's helped me heaps over the years, I owe him a lot. I do feel that I 'owe' these people, but I figure the best way to pay them back is to play really well and give them something to be proud of – besides, I really enjoy playing for them as well.

OVERALL ASSESSMENT OF *YOUR* COMMITMENT

The above aspects of commitment are typically 'weighted' differently by each individual. For example, you may be highly committed because of the intense enjoyment you derive from performing the required skills of your sport, whereas another person might be equally committed due to their great investment of time and energy, despite low levels of enjoyment. What is your overall level of commitment to your sport goal(s)?

I am <u>110% committed</u> to achieving my goals in golf. It took a while to achieve my first goal of making the provincial rep team, but having to work hard just made it even more satisfying! My next goal of cementing a regular place in the starting team (rather than a reserve player) will also be a real challenge, but meeting that sort of challenge is what makes it so worthwhile and satisfying. Doing this 'Commitment Exercise' has made me realise just how much I love playing golf, especially at the rep level, and while there are some big sacrifices involved I reckon they are more than worth it. You're retired from the game for a long time, so you gotta make the most of it when the opportunity is in front of you!

MICHAEL CAMPBELL

'Confidence – lost and found'

New Zealand golfer: (3rd British Open, 1995; Winner, Johnnie Walker Classic, 1999; Winner, NZ Open 2000, Winner, Australian Masters, 2000)

The remarkable resurrection of Michael Campbell's golf career in 2000 is a lesson in tenacity and sporting self-belief. Campbell was close to the top with his third place at the 1995 British Open, but his world fell apart at the end of that year when a wrist injury put his game 'in the rough'.[1] His poor form continued with embarrassing struggles in Europe and he eventually lost his tour card. Campbell had to rebuild his golf swing, but most of all he had to regain his confidence. Golf is a sport that plays unforgiving games with your mind, and Campbell admitted that at times he had serious doubts about his future as a professional golfer: 'When I struggled for those last three years I thought, "Shit, I can't play this game any more".[2] [After missing the cut at the

1997 French Open] I chucked my clubs from one side of my hotel room to the other and just thought to myself "What can I do?" … But thanks to the circle of friends I had I've come through and now think it's possible I can be one of the best players in the world.'[3]

Campbell's progress in rebuilding his game took considerable time and commitment, but he started making cuts again. Still, the struggle wasn't over, as he would string together three solid rounds before faltering when victory was in his sights. His breakthrough came at the Johnnie Walker Classic in late-1999, with victory over an in-form Tiger Woods.[1] That victory was the 'tee shot' back to the big time for Campbell. His spectacular form in New Zealand and Australia in early 2000 confirmed that he was back at the top of his game and his career. By February 2000, Campbell was being mentioned in the same sentence as Tiger Woods, Greg Norman, Justin Leonard, and Ernie Els.[1]

Golf is a game where form ebbs and flows because there are so many variables: the individual, the course, the weather, a tough lie.[1] The margins can be so small, and yet so great. It can be the one centimetre difference between your ball resting in a divot or on the fairway, between a putt lipping out or dropping. For example, one week before he won the Australian Masters in 2000 Campbell missed the cut in Sydney – he realised that he had another opportunity and he wasn't going to let the Australian Masters pass him by. Second chances don't come too often at the top level.

Campbell's return to form is an inspiration to other New Zealand sportspeople. They could do worse than look at how Campbell handled himself during his slump, and how he worked hard to regain his confidence. It can be a long road back to the top, but it can be even more rewarding second time around.

PERFORMANCE PST SKILLS

PST skill: controlling activation

Controlling activation, or 'psych-up', is vital for peak performance (see Chapter 4). So how do you psych-up without psyching-out? There are a number of steps you can take to prevent over-activation, and to cure or control over-activation immediately before, during, and after competition. These methods and techniques take time and effort to learn correctly, they must be practised, and they need to be tailored to your individual needs. However, they are essential if you want to reach your peak level of activation or psych-up consistently.

Controlling activation: prevention or cure?

Although you should focus on minimising factors or situations in sport that might cause over-activation (i.e. prevention), you also need to learn psychological techniques to counter uncontroll-able factors (i.e., cure). Prevention is better than cure, but since sportspeople are not perfect there will always be a need for the 'cure' techniques.

Prevention — planning to avoid over-activation or reduce sources of stress

There are two major forms of 'prevention' coping: person factors (what you bring with you in terms of coping skills and abilities), and situational factors (what coping methods the situation allows you to use).

Person factors

Goal setting is a common PST method that players use to prevent over-activation. By setting 'performance and process' goals you can control the standards used to judge your success and give yourself a sense of control. This allows you to resist possible sources of pressure (see 'Coping with pressure', page 72). In setting goals you need to place less emphasis on the outcome and winning (see Chapter 10, 'Goal setting'). Try to match yourself with realistic task demands and goals (e.g., selection of performance and process goals for each game/race/event). If you can increase your self-confidence you will also reduce stress and anxiety (see 'Self-confidence', Chapter 7). Consequently, you should focus on personal best performances (PBs). Mental preparation strategies are effective methods for increasing confidence and reaching your 'peak' level of activation without becoming stressed (see Chapter 14, 'Mental preparation').

Situational factors

This is primarily the role of the coach and leader/captain. You can reduce pressure and stress by encouraging your coach and leader/captain to reinforce performance and technique goals. For example, many hockey, soccer and rugby teams are now developing match stats such as tackle counts, ball possession stats and turnovers, which can be used to set performance goals for the team and for individual players in each game. Encourage your coach and captain to emphasise doing your best, and encourage your coach to reward effort and goal attainment through the use of match stats, not just winning. This recommendation is designed to reduce the emphasis on the outcome. The outcome of a game or event – winning or losing – is clearly important, but you also need to emphasise effort and goal attainment, as these are aspects of the performance that are within your control. Control the controllables! That is, you can prevent over-activation by encouraging coaches and leaders/captains to focus on task goals and standards of success that you have control over.

> 'I'm not scared of how fast a bowler is, because the worst that can happen is I'll get hit and it will hurt… I honestly wouldn't give a toss if I got smacked right in the middle of the helmet, because I'm not out. But the fear of doing something wrong – that's what failure is to me. That's why I get nervous, even when I pull up outside my clubground.'
>
> Mark Richardson (NZ cricketer; opening batsman)

'Cure' methods to control activation

Like prevention, cure methods also include person factors and situational factors.

> 'You can't control the wind, but you can adjust your sail!'
>
> A sailor who has capsised

Person factors

Relaxation training is a PST method that you need to learn in order to control the mental and muscle tension that often results from pressure and anxiety (see Chapter 11, 'Relaxation and centring'). Thought-stopping is another PST method you can use to reduce negative thoughts by rationally eliminating stressful factors or cues, then focusing on positive thoughts (self-talk) and

performance goals (see Chapter 10, 'Goal setting').

Situational factors

Once again this is primarily the role of the coach and leader/captain. Both need to be good role models, acting confident and focusing on performance goals in discussing game/race strategy. The coach and leader/captain can also benefit from using relaxation procedures for themselves. Coaches can be very helpful if they are able to recognise your signs of over-activation, but unfortunately the research evidence shows that most coaches are poor at identifying their athletes'/players' levels of activation and anxiety.[1] The better coaches identified the following signs as useful in determining an athlete or player's levels of activation: changes in communication level (an athlete becomes more or less talkative than normal); changes in typical behaviour patterns; changes in facial expressions (especially eyes); excessive need to urinate; restlessness; and inattention.[1] The key to using these indicators of over-activation is to determine each athlete's individual pattern of indicators, and then to teach strategies that will help them regain their peak activation level.

The coach must also individualise her/his motivation techniques – not everyone needs an emotional pep talk. The coach may need to initiate and reinforce relaxation and thought-stopping techniques for certain athletes/players. Finally, it is vital that the coach and leader/captain focus on performance goals to establish a sense of control.

Specific methods for controlling activation

Most athletes/players use a number of psych methods, often using different methods to deal with different sources of over-activation.[2]

Considerable sport research shows that you need to learn your psych methods so well that they can be executed automatically.[2]

Mental preparation strategies

These are discussed in greater detail in Chapter 14, 'Mental preparation'. These techniques are useful for both prevention and cure of over-activation and pressure. The goal of mental preparation is to help you reach your peak level of activation; that is, to psych-up, without being psyched-out!

Self-talk

You need to identify the appropriate concentration signs or cues to focus on, and learn to maintain that focus (see 'Concentration and attention', page 76). The use of silent 'self-statements' can be useful for maintaining concentration (e.g., 'Watch the ball'), for increasing self-confidence ('I can do it,' 'I can do no more than give 100 per cent'), and for controlling activation levels ('Centre, stay calm, you are in control'); see Chapter 13, 'Self-talk', for more on this. Without a practised set of self-talk statements your self-talk can be negative and disruptive to your ability to control activation.

'Parking' (thought stopping)[3]

Practise stopping negative thought patterns by using silent instructions or 'triggers'; for example, 'Stop!' 'Park it!' or 'Bin it' (see Chapter 13, 'Self-talk'). Some athletes slap their leg or their equipment to mentally 'park' the negative thoughts somewhere else so they can refocus their concentration on the task at hand. 'Parking' is just like parking a car – when you don't need your car you park it in a carpark. So when you don't need or want a negative thought you can 'park' it somewhere and come back for it after the game or event!

Relaxation

Mental and physical relaxation procedures such as mind-to-muscle (centring) and muscle-to-mind relaxation are designed to decrease your heart rate, breathing rate, and muscle tension (see Chapter 11, 'Relaxation and centring'). Relaxation also demands a change of mental focus away from anxiety-producing thoughts; therefore it helps you cope with over-activation.

Imagery

Also known as mental practice, this technique can increase confidence and move your focus to task cues or thoughts (e.g., correct skill technique). Imagery allows you to cope with stress mentally before competition, so that you can develop ways to prevent or manage pressure situations during the game (see Chapter 12, 'Imagery').

> ### No Worries
> Ain't no use worrying about things beyond your control, because if they're beyond your control ain't no use worrying…
> …ain't no use worrying about things within your control, because if you have them under control, ain't no use worrying…
>
> Author unknown

Critical Action Response Strategy (CARS) Plan[4]

The CARS PST method is actually a combination of a number of the PST methods mentioned above (for examples of CARS plans, see Chapter 15). In designing your own CARS plan you need to choose a combination of PST methods that best suit the way you like to control over-activation. One person's CARS plan might involve a combination of imagery, self-talk and relaxation, while another's might include a mixture of self-talk and mental preparation (see CARS plans and the CARS plan worksheet on pages 152–8). CARS plans are designed to help you control your activation levels during a game or event.

PST skill: coping with pressure

Playing your sport with commitment and pride means that you must put pressure and stress on yourself to succeed and achieve your goals. This pressure can lead to over-activation, anxiety and stress (see 'Controlling activation' above, and also Chapter 4). In particular, anxiety and stress can cause problems with concentration and decision-making. All athletes/players, regardless of their sporting ability, must learn to cope with stress and pressure in order to regain or maintain their composure.[5]

> 'Winning the World Cup is all about handling pressure, and the team that does it best wins.'
>
> Imran Khan (former Pakistani cricket captain) previewing the 2002 Cricket World Cup.

Coping

Coping with 'pressure' means controlling stress, anxiety and adversity for peak performance.[5] Pressure, stress and adversity are part and parcel of competitive sport – you shouldn't fear them; indeed, you should expect them to be part of the sport experience. Thus, coping with these things becomes just another challenge posed by competitive sport; a challenge that you will gain enormous satisfaction from conquering. The effects of pressure, stress and adversity can be positive (e.g. reaching and maintaining peak

activation prior to and during competition) or negative (e.g. over-activation, anxiety, burn-out). Pressure and stress can be both long-term and short-term. Long-term stress is on-going and persistent; for example, the pressure that comes with a nagging injury or the pressure to retain your place in the starting team. Short-term stress is time-limited and temporary; for example, making a mistake during competition.

Coping with long-term as opposed to short-term stress in sport requires different PST methods. Long-term stress requires you to utilise coping resources such as PST methods, nutritional habits, lifestyle management, time management and social support,[5] and to develop other PST skills like self-confidence, self-esteem, motivation and commitment.

Short-term stress can negatively affect numerous psychological and physical skills such as concentration, motivation, effort, energy expenditure and peak activation.[5] If you experience a short-term stressor such as a major error or verbal abuse from an opponent, this can often create emotional turmoil and/or distract you from concentrating on the job at hand (i.e. the responsibilities and skills of your sport/playing position).[5] Short-term stress, then, is inherently negative for your immediate skill performance unless you have mastered appropriate coping strategies (see the CARS plan in Chapter 15 for examples of coping strategies).

In extreme cases, the inability to cope with repetitive short-term stress may lead to demotivation, unpleasant emotions, poor overall performance, and eventually to psychological burn-out and giving up competitive sport completely.[6] Thus, a useful strategy for ensuring success and enjoyment in sport is the development of PST skills and methods to cope with these common short-term stress events.

Successful coping requires you to be able to regain composure, to establish the proper mental set (i.e., the psychological readiness to respond to on-going skill demands), and to maintain your peak levels of activation and concentration. Managing short-term stress is primarily dependent on your self-control in a stressful situation – arguably, this is the most fundamental issue in coping with any stress.

Examples of short-term stressors in sport include committing a physical or mental error, experiencing pain, observing an opponent cheat, reacting to the sudden success of an opponent, contending with a poor call by the referee or umpire, an unfavourable game score, adverse weather or ground conditions, and receiving unpleasant comments from opponents (e.g. intimidating abuse), teammates (teasing or criticising), coaches (negative criticism) and others (e.g. booing).[7] Athletes/players frequently have to deal with unpleasant verbal abuse during competition, the purpose of which may be to provide your opponents with an outlet for their anger and frustration, or simply to intimidate, distract and annoy you. The coach represents another potential source of distraction if they serve up verbal criticism before the game/race, and unwanted advice from the sideline during it. Clearly, it is to your benefit to be able to ignore such verbal comments or abuse.

When we talk about coping effectively it is important to remember that pressure, stress and anxiety are not automatically bad. Some anxiety can be useful as it adds to your levels of activation and motivation (see Chapter 4). For example, many athletes report that the 'nervous butterflies' are a sign that they are going to be psyched-up for the event – in fact they get worried if they don't feel nervous before competition! Indeed, research has shown the positive effect that a controlled level of anxiety can have on motivation and commitment for peak performance.[8] To control anxiety you need to learn how to cope with the stress that causes it in the first place.

> 'There is more pressure on me here [NZ National Champs] than in international events. But it's cool. The pressure brings out the best in me. I use it to get the best out of myself.'
>
> Sarah Ulmer (NZ track cyclist; 2-time gold medallist at the Commonwealth Games)

To deal with the pressure and short-term stress inherent in sport, and to maintain peak performance, you must consciously use PST skills and methods – this is a process referred to as coping.

The process of coping

Coping refers to the process of using PST skills and methods to manage stressful demands that you perceive as pressure (i.e. exceeding your skills and ability).[5] Different types of stress often require different coping strategies or categories of strategy.[5] The most common categorisations of coping strategies are referred to as task-focused and emotion-focused coping.[5] These two types of coping strategy can each be further subdivided into approach and avoidance coping.[5] It is crucial that you understand these categories if you are determined to sort out the specifics of your coping needs and design coping methods that fit your personal needs.

Table 8.1 Coping			
Task-focused		Emotion-focused	
Approach	Avoidance	Approach	Avoidance

Task- and emotion-focused coping strategies

Task-focused strategies

Task-focused coping is the use of problem-solving, tactical decision-making, physical activity and extra effort to control the cause of the stress and achieve a specific task or skill objective (also referred to as 'problem-focused' coping). Task-focused coping can include methods like tactical changes, resetting goals, channelling your frustration into extra determination for your next skill (e.g. pass, tackle, shoot), seeking social support, becoming verbally assertive, or possibly deliberately avoiding the pressure situation. In other words, you get on with the game/event and don't dwell on the sources of stress and pressure. For example, a mistake or error during competition (a potential form of short-term stress) may require additional effort, determination and concentration to maintain a good performance. On the other hand, you may cope with unpleasant comments from your coach, captain or a teammate by attempting to distance yourself physically from that person. In another situation, you may cope with an opponent's verbal abuse by becoming increasingly assertive, vocally and/or physically. PST methods such as self-talk, imagery, the CARS plan and mental preparation can be particularly useful for task-focused coping by helping to increase effort and determination, and improve concentration. Task-focused coping is primarily directed at solving, changing or fixing the cause of the stress and pressure.

Emotion-focused strategies

Emotion-focused coping, on the other hand, consists of using thoughts to feel better about performing the task or skill and to cope with the negative and unpleasant emotions that result from the stress/ pressure. For instance, if you feel upset after committing a physical error during the game, PST methods such as positive self-talk (e.g., 'Keep at it', 'Concentrate on your job', 'Stay calm, nail it next time'), thought-stopping, blocking distractions, rational thinking, seeking social support, imagining successful skill execution and relaxation/ centring may be used to cope

and to reduce interfering thoughts and muscle tension. In general these emotion-focused strategies are designed to help you develop a mental readiness for any eventuality during competition. In this sense, readiness reflects a general confidence about your preparation for the game, and includes mental readiness, physical readiness, and performance expectations based on previous games or events. Research has shown that perceived readiness is a key issue in preventing stress and coping with anxiety.[9]

Emotion-focused coping is not focused on solving the stressful situation; rather, the focus is on dealing with the emotional consequences of feeling pressure and stress.

Approach and avoidance coping dimensions

Coping strategies can also be categorised into approach and avoidance categories.[5] An approach strategy consists of confronting the source of stress and attempting to reduce it deliberately – this can be achieved by using either a task-focus or an emotion-focus (or both). At times, however, avoiding pressure situations and their consequences is preferable to an approach strategy.[5] Each technique has its advantages and disadvantages.

Approach coping

Approach coping is preferable when: (a) the pressure situation is controllable; (b) the source of stress is known to you; or (c) there is a need to remain 'on task' after a period of inactivity following the stressor (e.g. after half-time or an injury break).[5] For example, one athlete ('Jason') may verbally abuse an opponent ('Jim') for the purpose of intimidation or distraction. Jim can ignore the abuse, using it as a source of increased effort and as an incentive for further action. However, given his control over the pressure situation and the high probability of continuous interaction with Jason during the game, an approach coping strategy (i.e., Jim using a task-focus to confront Jason) might be preferred. Avoiding or ignoring Jason may send the wrong message (i.e. feelings of fear and stress) which in turn may provoke Jason to continue abusing Jim.

Approach coping is more effective when direct action is required to deal with the cause of the pressure. In this sense, approach coping focuses on situation-relevant information (e.g. reading a defensive pattern), while ignoring any distracting and irrelevant information (e.g. dummy-runners, verbal comments or abuse from opponents).[5]

Avoidance coping

Avoidance coping is appropriate in some instances when the most effective coping response is to ignore or dissociate from the pressure situation. Avoidance coping is most useful when: (a) emotional resources are limited (e.g. low self-confidence/low self-esteem); (b) the source of stress is not clear; (c) the pressure situation is uncontrollable; or (d) when time is of the essence as the game or event 'moves on'.[5] For instance, you cannot afford to become distracted or demotivated if the ref makes a wrong call in situations in which play is on-going. Such uncontrollable sources of stress require an avoidance coping strategy because approaching the stressor will rarely improve the situation or the outcome – the ref won't change their call and the game has continued! The avoidance can be achieved by using a task focus (e.g. applying extra effort to the next job at hand) or an emotion focus (e.g. deliberately shifting your thoughts and concentration to other skills or to upcoming tactical options). If you are not able to avoid this type of pressure you will quickly become frustrated, angry and distracted, and although such emotions are a natural human response to stress they don't help you cope effectively. The most effective method of coping

with stressors that are outside your control is to ignore them or quickly forget them and mentally 'move on'. The game has carried on to the next phase and so must your thinking and concentration if you want to play well and enjoy yourself.

Using approach and avoidance coping techniques is not an either/or choice; you might use a combination of both techniques in an effort to cope with a particular source of pressure. Sometimes there can be a rapid switching between the two techniques, or certain aspects of a pressure situation can be avoided while other aspects are approached.[5] For example, if you are a rugby league player and you miss a simple midfield tackle you will likely feel frustrated and angry with yourself for letting yourself and your teammates down. In an effort to deal with the stress and pressure of such a major mistake you might attempt to cope by using centring and self-talk to *avoid* the stress and pressure that comes with the temptation to mentally criticise yourself for making such a basic error. If the game has carried on to the next phase this coping strategy is likely to be the most effective, since trying to solve your tackling problem by using *approach* coping would not be appropriate as you need to move on to your next job! However, at the next break in play (e.g. at a scrum or hand-over) you might also attempt to cope by *approaching* the cause of your mistake, quickly using imagery to 'replay' the situation in your head and figuring out what you did wrong in your defensive lines and your actual tackling technique. In this case, you have used centring and self-talk as emotion-focused techniques that *avoid* the source of pressure, but you have also used imagery as a task-focused technique to *approach* and problem-solve the cause of the mistake.

In competitive sport, avoidance coping may be more productive when performing continuous, on-going tasks such as decision-making during fast-paced play. Worrying about the causes of some stressors and dwelling on the unpleasant emotions will interfere with your concentration on the task at hand and your decision-making, thus resulting in a poorer performance. Instead, to be successful in your sport you must use PST methods to keep your activation levels under control and to help maintain your peak performance under adverse circumstances.

> 'Second, I refuse to yield to pressure. Some players wilt like lettuce when the heat is on. True competitors love the battle. Sure it gets intense and your nervous system is tested, but that's the most fun part of being a competitor. Ever wonder why Michael Jordan and Jack Nicklaus were so good in the clutch? Simple. They loved the spotlight and were inspired to reach another level of greatness by the need to accomplish.'
>
> Tiger Woods (US golfer).

Kayla's example

Our netball centre, Kayla, has a problem with pressure at the moment and she desperately needs to learn how to cope with the stress she is experiencing. As you can see from Kayla's peak performance profile on page 47, she currently needs to gain some self-confidence, learn how to cope with pressure, regain her concentration, improve her decision-making, and pick up her on-court communication. Based on the information in her peak performance profile, we categorised her psychological skill assessment as follows: (i) self-confidence (foundation skill); (ii) coping with pressure (performance skill); (iii) concentration and decision-making (performance skill); and (iv) teamwork and communication (facilitative skills).

Based on this classification of Kayla's psych skill needs, we picked some likely PST methods to match each skill. Following the logic of the PST programme, we worked on her foundation needs first. For example, we suggested to Kayla that a blend of goal setting, imagery and self-talk could be a useful way to enhance her self-confidence.

Once Kayla was happy that her self-confidence was starting to improve we would make some suggestions regarding PST methods for her need to cope with pressure. The likely PST methods here would be centring, self-talk, parking, and a CARS plan. Kayla's completed CARS plan for coping with pressure is shown on page 158. Kayla may wish to use imagery here as well, but the types of image would need to be a bit different to the imagery she used to improve her self-confidence. At the same time as she is working on her coping skills Kayla should also begin to work on her need for improved concentration and decision-making – see the next section for more information on concentration (likely methods here are mental preparation, self-talk and maybe a modified version of a CARS plan).

PST skill: concentration and attention

What is attention? Attention can be described as 'selective thinking'. We have a limited capacity for handling and processing (i.e. thinking about) information, consequently we need to selectively focus our attention on the information we decide is appropriate. This 'selection' is task related. For example, walking and talking at the same time is automatically achieved without a selected specific focus of attention. On the other hand, control of fine skills or movements (e.g., pistol shooting and talking at the same time) requires a very specific and selective focus of attention. We choose what information ('cues') to attend to and what information to ignore or disregard.

What is concentration? Concentration is the

ability to 'hold' the appropriate attentional focus for the required period of time. Distraction control or 'refocusing' is required to avoid disruptions to this focus of attention-concentration.

> 'Some intellectual attributes are particularly important for peak performance. Concentration is fundamental. Mistakes on the field almost invariably come from a loss of concentration. Ball handling errors and foolish penalties... all of these infringements come from players failing to think. Analysis is a skill that combines concentration, the ability to absorb information and organise it to reach a conclusion.'
>
> David Kirk (former All Black captain – 1987 World Cup Champions)

The concept of attentional style[10]

The concept of attentional style provides a useful description of the way players focus and control their attention during peak performance. The attentional style model describes attention-concentration in straightforward terms: (a) there are two key dimensions of attention; and (b) each individual has a dominant attentional 'style'.

Dimensions of attention

Breadth of focus (width)

Broad versus narrow focus of attention; this represents the *amount* of information attended to.

Direction of focus (direction)

External versus internal focus of attention; this represents the *location* of information attended to.

Four major attentional styles

'Broad-external'

This style is used to assess a situation rapidly; for example, 'reading' the game, especially in team sports. It is also used to develop and use anticipation; for example, reading the green before a putt or considering the wind before selecting a club in golf (assess).

'Narrow-external'

This style is required at the moment a response is given; for example, to focus (non-distracted) on one or two external cues such as hitting a golf ball or reacting to an opponent in soccer (perform).

'Broad-internal'

This style is used to analyse and plan; to develop game plans and tactics; to anticipate the future, and to recall past information. For example, the coach or caddy working out tactics and strategy with a golfer before or during a round (analyse).

'Narrow-internal'

This style is required to 'tune-in' and be sensitive to your body; to centre and calm yourself, to rehearse a skill or a move mentally (imagery). For example, this style is useful for activation regulation (rehearse).

Figure 8.1 Model of attentional style, Golf example

EXTERNAL

'Broad-external'	*'Narrow-external'*
To rapidly assess a situation.	Required at the moment a response is given.
For 'reading' the course and weather.	Focus, non-distracted, on one or two pieces
For 'reading' the greens.	of external info.
e.g., golf club selection	*e.g. hit the ball*

BROAD ———————————————————— NARROW

'Broad-internal'	*'Narrow-internal'*
Used to analyse and plan.	Required to 'tune-in' and be sensitive to your body.
To make plans for each round. Course tactics.	To centre and calm yourself.
To anticipate the future, and recall past info.	To mentally rehearse (imagery) shot.
e.g. course management. strategy for each hole	*e.g. control activation; centring, imagery*

INTERNAL

Attentional style: assumptions

The attentional style model describes attention in terms of trait and state aspects, a bit like trait and state anxiety. In this model a player's attentional style is a product of her/his trait 'style' and his/her perception of situational demands.[10]

Trait and state components

The attentional style is a trait characteristic of a person's personality. The trait style (e.g. primarily broad-external) is affected by situational demands or influences (e.g. increased activation from stress often leads to a primarily narrow-internal focus).

Individual differences

Individuals have preferred or dominant attentional styles (traits); they have individual strengths and weaknesses. These dominant styles may affect your choice of sport and have a major effect on your successful performance in that sport.

Attention-activation interaction

The ability to control attention and shift focus is related to activation; increased activation leads to a 'narrowing' of the attentional field (involuntary response). This in turn leads to a decreased attendance to peripheral cues (i.e. things seen out of the corner of your eye) and the athlete scans less (see Chapter 4, 'Anxiety, activation and peak performance').

Common attentional errors

These major styles can be both an advantage and a disadvantage.[10] Errors can occur if you are not able to voluntarily shift your attentional focus from one style to another as the situation requires (i.e. limited attentional flexibility). Some of the common errors are described below.

Broad-external

These individuals are often too busy reading and reacting to the situation to think about the specifics of 'here and now'. They make the same mistakes often, getting fooled by their opponent. Behaviour is externally controlled rather than

> 'The driver swing is the most physical act in all of golf. But there's a strong mental aspect to it, too. To consistently drive the ball long and straight, you need to be single-minded about what you're doing. You must be totally impervious to distractions and immune to thoughts that can make your swing fall to pieces. Because the driver swing is long and a bit violent in terms of the sheer speed you're trying to generate, timing is extremely important. If you allow something to break your concentration and upset your rhythm or tempo, you're in deep trouble... Staying focused can be a tall order for me, simply because there are large numbers of people very close by on virtually every drive I hit.'
>
> Tiger Woods (US golfer).

internally controlled. These athletes often become distracted by unimportant information such as crowd noise.

Narrow-external

These athletes often fail to adjust to changing situations. They get a plan, strategy or response in mind and stick to it no matter what. For example, an athlete might focus totally on the ball and fail to notice changes in positioning by teammates and opponents.

Broad-internal

These players often over-analyse and out-think themselves. They are inside their heads thinking about what will happen in the future or has happened in the past, rather than focusing on the game or race itself.

Narrow-internal

These individuals are often seen as 'chokers'. They sometimes become so focused on their own feelings that they can't function (i.e. 'paralysis by analysis'). For example, the centre in netball concentrating so hard on trying to control her activation and anxiety levels that she forgets to catch the ball!

Overloading

Attentional errors can occur from overloading either externally or internally. External over-loading happens when an athlete/player becomes confused by trying to concentrate on too many external cues at once. Internal overloading occurs when they become preoccupied with too much self-talk or 'internal coaching'.

Limited flexibility

The successful athlete is able to voluntarily shift their attentional style to match the situational demands. Over-activation, anxiety and stress often result in concentration being totally focused internally, so that the athlete/player is unable to shift attention-concentration voluntarily.

Training concentration-attention: PST methods[11]

Self-talk (see Chapter 13)

Effective use of self-talk helps you select and maintain the correct focus. Self-talk is also useful for shifting focus. Sometimes self-talk is described as attention 'cues', 'triggers' or 'signals' (e.g. golf 'swing thoughts' – 'watch the ball, follow through').

Mental preparation (see Chapter 14)

The use of pre-performance plans, performance focus plans and coping plans (distraction control) helps you to develop a clear understanding of the attentional demands of your sport or particular competition.

Relaxation/centring (see Chapter 11)

This is a way to decrease physical and mental activation. It is especially important given the interaction between activation and attention. If you can control levels of activation then you can control your attention shifts.

Imagery (see Chapter 12)

Mental rehearsal; rehearsal of coping skills. Learning to develop and control clear, vivid images of performances enables you to practise or rehearse your control of attention and attention shifts.

Summary: attention-concentration

Attention can be described as selective thinking; that is, thinking about the 'cues' or information that we attend to and use; what we 'focus' on. Concentration is the ability to hold or sustain the appropriate focus. Individuals have attentional styles that may or may not be appropriate for the particular attentional demands of the sport they are playing. Consequently, you need to assess the attentional demands of your sport (see Peak Performance Profile: Concentration on page 81, and Jack's example on page 82), then you need to identify your own personal style, and practise the PST methods designed to strengthen your attentional-concentration control.

Attentional style =
WIDTH ◄──► DIRECTION
(Broad-narrow)   *(External-internal)*

PEAK PERFORMANCE PROFILE: CONCENTRATION

List and rate the concentration/attention characteristics of your peak sport performance.
Rate yourself on each of the concentration qualities using the following scale:

	0	1	2	3	4	5	6	7	8	9	10
Current + Best:	Poor					Average					Excellent

Name: .... Sport: .... Date: ....

	Current (right now)	Best

Broad-external:

.... |..........| |..........|

.... |..........| |..........|

.... |..........| |..........|

.... |..........| |..........|

Broad-internal:

.... |..........| |..........|

.... |..........| |..........|

.... |..........| |..........|

.... |..........| |..........|

Narrow-external:

.... |..........| |..........|

.... |..........| |..........|

.... |..........| |..........|

.... |..........| |..........|

Narrow-internal:

.... |..........| |..........|

.... |..........| |..........|

.... |..........| |..........|

.... |..........| |..........|

PEAK PERFORMANCE PROFILE: CONCENTRATION

List and rate the concentration/attention characteristics of your peak sport performance.
Rate yourself on each of the concentration qualities using the following scale:

	0	1	2	3	4	5	6	7	8	9	10
Current + Best:	Poor					Average					Excellent

Name: Jack Robson   Sport: Golf   Date: 12/3/03

	Current (right now)	Best
Broad-external:		
'Reading' each hole – wind, hazards, distance	8	9
'Reading' greens	6	8
'Ignoring' distractions (crowd, opponent's play…)	4	7
Communication with caddy	8	9
Broad-internal:		
'Round' Plan for 18 holes (this course)	8	9
'Clubbing' – yardages, club choice	7	9
'Option-taking' within my Round Plan	6	8
'Hole' Plan for each hole	7	9
Narrow-external:		
Putting – long	4	7
Short Irons & Pitching	6	8
Long Irons	8	10
Driver & tee shots	9	10
Narrow-internal:		
Pre-shot Routine	5	9
Visualise each shot	8	10
'Centre' before each shot	5	8

SIR MURRAY HALBERG

'Courage and commitment'

New Zealand runner: Gold Medallist, 1960 Olympics; Gold Medallist, 1958 and 1962 Empire (Commonwealth) Games

Halberg won the 5000 m gold medal at the 1960 Olympics in Rome, held several world records and claimed two Commonwealth Games titles. But before all that he overcame a serious schoolboy rugby injury in 1950 that left his sports career in the balance and two months of hospitalisation.[1] His left shoulder was dislocated and veins and arteries were ruptured – serious blood clots formed and the nerves in his left arm were paralysed. There were concerns that he would never run again after an operation removed almost 1000 gm of congealed blood from around his heart, leaving him with a flagging pulse and in constant pain. He had to re-learn how to walk, dress, write and… how to run.[2] But he fought his way back to fitness, became a serious runner and in 1952 he joined Arthur Lydiard's training stable.

By 1953–54, Halberg began to run world-class times and

won a major mile race in the USA. However, his early international career was not all plain sailing.[2] In 1956, he made the final for the 1500 m at the Olympics, but finished a disappointing 11th.[3] Mentally shattered, he quit running and spent time tramping around the West Coast of the South Island of New Zealand before returning to Auckland. He later wrote that: '… the defeat [at the Olympics] seemed to make a mockery of my efforts [in training] … I and I alone had to convince myself that it hadn't been a total waste of time. Finally I did convince myself. Down there in the lonely splendour of the Southern Alps I made a decision… It was in me to do better [than my placing at the 1956 Olympics]. Yes, I was going to have another try. And this time nothing would stop me succeeding.'[4]

At the 1958 Empire (Commonwealth) Games in Cardiff, he won the gold medal in the 5000 m, and later that year he became the first Kiwi to run a sub 4-minute mile.[1] But his real goal, his dream, and his

destiny were to be realised at the 1960 Olympics in Rome.

The 5000 m finalists at the 1960 Olympics, as they do at all major track meets, warmed up outside the main stadium and then had to wait in a holding room before the race: 'We were kept in this room which wouldn't have been more than ten ft by ten ft, 12 of us, and there suddenly I realised that no one would look me in the eye. It passed through my mind that all I had to do was beat 11 scared men. It became that clear.'[2] He went on to win the gold medal in style, executing his race plan to perfection.

Despite his disability, Halberg was able to inspire a generation of New Zealand's finest athletes during the 1950s and 1960s. But it wasn't simply Halberg's efforts on tracks around the world that fascinated his fans.[5] It was something else. It was his burning desire to push back the boundaries of human endeavour and, having done so, to then react with humility.[1]

Halberg was a people's champion. Over the years he has put more back into his community than perhaps any other Kiwi athlete. Never having forgotten his own struggles as a teenager following his rugby injury, he launched the Murray Halberg Trust for Crippled Children in 1963.[1,2] Now simply known as the Halberg Trust, its mission statement reads: 'To honour sporting excellence and to encourage the inclusion of children with physical disabilities in sport and recreation.'[1] The Halberg Trust remains linked to New Zealand's premier annual sporting awards, but more importantly, raises millions of dollars to benefit children with disabilities.

Murray Halberg has shown us all how sport and commitment to one's goals can go beyond simple athletic feats and serve a purpose that touches everyday lives.

FACILITATIVE PST SKILLS

PST skill: communication

Understanding communication skills

Communication is a key facilitative PST skill; effective communication allows you to control the situation and attain peak performance. Communication is vital for you to have control. It is also the foundation of all teamwork, coaching and leadership. There are three dimensions of communication: (i) sending and receiving information; (ii) verbal and non-verbal communication skills; and (iii) content and emotion of the delivered information.[1]

> 'If the phone doesn't ring it's me!'
>
> Jimmy Buffett (song title)

Typical communication strengths are sending, verbal and content of information. Coaches and athletes/players are usually very good at sending verbal information to others that is high in content. On the other hand, typical communication weaknesses are receiving information (i.e. listening), non-verbal communication skills and control of the emotional delivery of information.

Since effective communication is a vital facilitative PST skill it is important that you identify your communication strengths and weaknesses. Effective communication is needed for you to be able to work on the other psychological aspects of peak performance, especially in team sports.

Enhancing communication skills[2]

Good communication skills are among the most important ingredients of peak performance in team sports, and also in coach–athlete relationships. There are several important strategies that athletes/players, captains and coaches can use to enhance the quality of their communication and deal with communication problems.[2] One of the biggest problems that athletes/players have in terms of communication is that we often expect other people to be mind readers.[3] We expect them to understand our thoughts and feelings without our ever expressing them. We expect teammates and coaches to understand our feelings from a simple gesture or an unspoken thought. Why doesn't he understand my feelings, my perspective? Why doesn't she respond to my needs? Why doesn't he know when I need some feedback or encouragement?

Mind reading

It is difficult to understand another person's feelings or appreciate their perspective if these things are never expressed clearly.[3] It is difficult, if not impossible, to respond to another person's needs when you don't know what those needs are. If you express your feelings and/or perceived needs, there is at least the possibility of someone understanding and responding. At least they have been made aware of your feelings, and therefore have the possibility of acting. The ability to express our feelings, to communicate clearly, and to criticise constructively is not easily acquired.[1] The communication skills of consistency, staying expressive, refined listening, clear speaking, and giving and receiving criticism need to be developed and refined over time.

Being consistent

Inconsistency in communicating with others destroys credibility.[2] Be consistent over time, and be consistent in your communications with different team members; that is, avoid having 'favourites' or 'scapegoats'. Also avoid double messages, which often have contradictory meanings and can result in confusion.[2] For example, avoid the confusion that can arise when you try to soften the blow of dropping or criticising a teammate by making complimentary comments only to follow them with the required criticism. While your goal of considering the other person's feelings is admirable, the double message ('You're a good player, but...') is often confusing to them and it may limit your credibility in their eyes.

Staying expressive

For a team to perform to its potential and to avoid players interfering with each other's psychological preparation before important events, you need to have open discussion with one another well before competition.[3] It is best if each member of the team (athletes/players, coaches and support staff) knows the pre-event needs and preparation idiosyncrasies of the others. Pre-game worries about what teammates are doing, or conflict between team members just before the start of the event, can easily result in a very strong team having a substantially lower performance. Do not let your teammates' varied ways of preparing affect your own preparation and performance. What is best for them in that hour before the start of competition is not necessarily what is best for you. Enabling each athlete/player to do what is best for them will allow the best team performance.

Staying expressive *within* the game or event is also very important in team sports. That means talking to each other and encouraging each other while playing the game. Calling out plays, giving each other verbal and physical support, and being genuinely positive (e.g., calling 'good play', 'we're in control', a clap of the hands, or a pat on the back) can help a team to achieve its goals. If staying expressive is important for your team, a team meeting should be held to clarify what is meant by staying expressive, to set some expectations for it to happen, to encourage each other, to indicate when it does happen, to rehearse it in practice, and to do it in games or events.

Giving criticism constructively

There is immense value in explaining the intent of your criticism *before* giving it.[3] Good examples are: 'I'm telling you this in the hope of improving our teamwork'; 'I need to get something off my chest that has been bothering me'; 'My intent is to help and not to hurt, regardless of how it might come out.' Explaining your intent *first* is probably the single most important thing you can do when giving criticism.[3]

Deciding to state your intent before you state your criticism forces you to think about your own purpose. This in turn should help you phrase the criticism appropriately. In addition, if you can think about how the criticised person is likely to react, it may also help you to phrase the criticism more constructively. Phrasing a criticism constructively includes expressing your intent and delivering your message in a clear, open and concerned way. In constructive communication there is never a desire to put the other person down or build yourself up, as often exists in power games.[3] A person delivering criticism has the most to gain if he or she can express it as constructively as possible, and if the criticism is face-to-face rather than behind the teammate's back.

'Stab each other in the stomach, not in the back.'

Receiving criticism constructively

A person receiving criticism has the most to gain if they can receive it as constructively as possible.[3] However, many athletes/players and coaches/managers are not that good at receiving criticism. They often interpret criticism as a personal attack, a put-down, rejection, or lack of appreciation for their good qualities. When you are being criticised, the anger or irritation that surfaces may result from a misperception or misunderstanding of the other person's intent. It is true that someone is pointing out what they perceive as an imperfection, and that, in this instance, they did not see you as as perfect or as skilled as you would like to be (or have them think you are). But why are they telling you this?

When criticism comes from a person who cares about you and your performance, the intent of that criticism is usually constructive or helpful, regardless of how it might be delivered.[3] The criticism is usually aimed at resolving a perceived problem, correcting a performance error, or improving a relationship. The hope is to make things better. Listen to criticism in this light. Learn from it instead of putting up protective barriers, and you will have a much better opportunity to gain from it, personally, interpersonally, and performance-wise.

In case criticism and advice still occasionally come through in a less constructive fashion, especially before or during competition, you should have your own plan to translate it into positive action (i.e. a CARS plan; see Chapter 15). For example, 'stop, breathe out, relax' (centring; see Chapter 11). Translate the message into what *you have to do* to set up properly for the particular skill. Take on that responsibility yourself. Run the correct image through your head several times. 'Feel it' going well. Then set

it aside. It should unfold as you imagined because you have focused on *what to do* and secured that message in your head through your repeated imagery (see Chapter 12, 'Imagery').

The more proficient you become at self-direction and self-criticism, the less you need to rely on the criticism of others. At times, however, direct, honest and objective criticism from another person can give you a perspective for improvement that you might not see in yourself.

Build credibility[2]

Become as knowledgeable as you can about all aspects of your sport. Be reliable, fair, honest and consistent in your dealings with others, and express warmth, friendliness and empathy towards them. Be spontaneous and open so that you demonstrate your 'trust' in others, which is vital for credibility. Trust is a two-way street, so you need others to trust you in order to establish credibility. In addition, you should own your messages by using 'I' as often as possible, and avoid using vague terms like 'we', 'they', or 'most people' when stating what *you* believe.

Send messages that are high in information[2]

Use specific information about 'how to do it' when talking to others. Focus on one message at a time to avoid information overload. Be knowledgeable or keep quiet. Separate fact from opinion; facts give a basis for opinion, so explain the facts first. For example, instead of just stating your opinion about a teammate's play, take the time to first outline the facts about the strengths and weaknesses of their play. This approach helps to avoid any misunderstandings or resentment.

Clear speaking[2]

When you speak to teammates, be sure to express yourself clearly. When your captain, coach or manager gives you instructions, how clear is the message? On more than one occasion I have heard coaches ask players to 'concentrate more' or 'pay attention'. What does that mean? How are you translating that into action? What are you supposed to do? I have asked athletes what they do when the coach says, 'Concentrate more.' Interestingly, many try to *look* like they are concentrating more, with a serious expression and a wrinkled forehead. Many do not have a clear understanding of what is being asked. It is best for a coach to say exactly what they want (e.g. 'Be more explosive onto the ball,' 'Take the pass earlier,' 'Focus on staying in synch with the rest of the backline.') If you are not getting this exact feedback ask your coach to be more explicit so that what you think the coach is saying and what the coach thinks he or she is saying are one and the same when translated into action. Can you encourage your coach to give you clarification when the message is not crystal-clear? Can you also attempt to express your own messages and suggestions as clearly as possible? Athletes/players are often unclear in their verbal messages too.

Develop non-verbal communication skills

At least 70 per cent of all communication is non-verbal.[2] Become aware of your body language, body motion, physical characteristics, touching behaviours, voice characteristics, body position (i.e. the space between you and others) and dress. Ensure that your verbal and non-verbal messages agree.

Refined listening

This is probably the most important communication skill, yet it is often the least developed. Listening involves your ears, your eyes and your heart.[3] What is this person *really* saying, and what are they really feeling? It is not always written on the surface. If you are not sure how someone is feeling about a decision or a performance, you may have to ask, 'How are you *really feeling* about this in your gut?' Becoming a keen observer also allows you to listen better.

To listen well, you should forget about how *you* see the situation and focus fully on how *the other person* sees it.[3] Don't interrupt; don't judge; let the other person express their feelings while you focus on listening and understanding. Eliminate the 'Yeah, but's'. Avoid challenging the speaker, and don't point fingers. Just listen and feel that person's perspective. Soak it in before responding.

Key words/phrases (see also Chapter 13, 'Self-talk')

These are essential for clear, controlled and unambiguous communication immediately before and during competition.[2] This is especially important between teammates, and between the coach and athletes/players during competition (for example, instructions relayed via the physio, or during injury time-outs and at half-time).

Improving your communication skills is a lifelong process. Like other skills it requires a plan, practice, reflections, and refinement. You will do yourself and your teammates a favour by beginning that process now.[2]

Media skills

Developing effective communication skills is also useful for dealing with the media.[3] If you are successful enough to reach an elite level of sport it is likely that you will be sought after by the media. Obviously, media exposure is necessary for raising the profile of your sport, recruiting new athletes/players, attracting sponsors, and marketing the sport. However, it is vital that you know how to express your thoughts clearly so that you are not misquoted or misinterpreted. Media exposure can become a major source of pressure and stress (see Chapter 4) if you do not have effective communication skills that allow you to express yourself without raising public expectations unrealistically or putting extra pressure on yourself.

PST skill: team building

Team vs group

A common cliché that is often applied to team sports is that 'a champion team will always beat a team of champions'.[4] A considerable amount of coaching wisdom is reflected in this claim – in interactive team sports where each player is totally reliant on her or his teammates (plus the coach(es) and the reserves bench) success requires a co-ordinated team effort. Consequently, a champion 'team' should indeed beat a team of 'champions' – the integrated, co-ordinated effort required to be successful in team sport can only be achieved by a high degree of teamwork. The second 'team' in this cliché (a team of champions) is more of a loose group of talented players than a real team.

This raises an interesting and important question – as a coach or captain how do you identify the key differences between these two types of team? As a leader how can you develop a champion team?[4] First, you need to understand some of the principles of 'group productivity' from the area of business/corporate team-building, and then you need to integrate these principles with findings from research on team performance in sport. Let's start by getting a handle on the principles of 'group productivity'.

The definition of a group

A group is defined as a collection of individuals who have connections with one another that make them interdependent to some significant degree.[5] The key requirements of a group are interaction, mutual awareness, interdependence, and continuity over time. In addition, groups are dynamic not static; they exhibit life and vitality, interaction and activity.[5]

A collection of individuals is not necessarily a group.[5] The defining characteristic of a group is that of interaction and mutual awareness; group members must all be aware of each other and be able to interact and communicate with each other.[5] Consequently, a collection of swimmers who swim for fitness during their lunch hour is not a group – they are not necessarily aware of each other, nor do they interact in a structured manner. On the other hand, a collection of competitive swimmers who meet for early morning swim training is a group – they have a shared purpose (training for competition), they are aware of each other (they belong to the same swim team/club), and they interact with each other (they pace each other and share coaches and training programmes).

What is a team?

A team is a special type of group. A team is a group of players who have a well-developed collective identity and who work together to achieve a specific goal or set of goals. This goal, or goals, makes the team members interdependent to some significant degree.[4] A team must have a shared sense of purpose, structured patterns of interaction, interdependence between teammates, team spirit, and a collective identity. Each team member must view membership of the team as being rewarding and satisfying, and believe that the rewards and satisfaction would not be attainable without membership of the team.[4]

A common assumption about team perfor-mance is that the best players/individuals make the best team. This assumed relationship between individual abilities and team perfor-mance is not always accurate. Simply summing the abilities of individual team members does not accurately describe the team performance. In order to understand team performance it is necessary to consider the team process as well as individual ability.[4] For example, team motivation, team cohesion and captaincy/leadership are all processes that have a significant impact on team performance.[4]

> 'Playing for yourself wins trophies; playing for your team wins championships.'
>
> Tommy Lasorda (manager of the LA Dodgers baseball team)

General observation of any team sport competition reveals that few teams consistently perform to their potential. On paper a team might appear to have the best players, consequently it is assumed that the team should perform well, but that is often not the case (i.e., they may not be a 'champion team'). Research into team dynamics focuses on explaining why teams do not always harness the individual abilities of their players effectively for consistent team performance.[4]

> 'Good teams become great ones when the members trust each other enough to surrender the 'me' for the 'we'.'
>
> Phil Jackson (coach of the Chicago Bulls basketball team, six-time winners of the NBA Championship; coach of the LA Lakers, three-time winners of the NBA Championship), outlining what he regards as the 'soul of teamwork'

A model of team performance[6]

A useful framework for explaining team performance in sport is expressed in the following equation.

**Actual performance =
Potential performance – Losses due to
faulty process**

Actual performance (or productivity) is what the team actually does. Potential performance is the team's best possible performance given the resources it has that are relevant to the task and the demands of that task. Process is everything the team does while transforming its resources into a performance.[6] In sport, process is basically each player's individual skill development combined with teamwork skills developed by the coach, including team tactics and strategies.

Faulty process is the ineffective use of available resources to meet task demands, and can result from two types of loss: co-ordination loss and motivation loss. Co-ordination losses include poor timing, teamwork or strategy. Motivation losses occur when all or some members of the team lack effort and desire.[6]

While this model is useful as a general description of team performance, it is the role of team leaders and coaches to decrease faulty process by developing and practising organisational strategies that reduce co-ordination losses (i.e. teamwork) and maintain high motivation levels (i.e. team motivation). As you are probably aware this is nowhere near as easy to achieve as it sounds! So why do teams not always perform up to their potential?

Team process and team performance

There is an aspect of team dynamics that is commonly referred to as 'social loafing'. Social loafing means that the average individual performance decreases with increases in team size.[7] Although the number of co-ordination losses may also increase as the number of people in the team increases, social loafing is usually not the result of co-ordination losses. Co-ordination losses may be part of the reason, but the key psychological reason seems to be motivation losses.[7]

Social loafing

Social loafing occurs when the 'identifiability' of individual performances is lost in a team performance, and performances decrease because of the diffusion of responsibility.[7] When the identifiability of individual performances is lost in a team performance ('It's not my job'; 'Not my fault') performances decrease because each player has less apparent responsibility for the overall performance.[7] If players believe that their own performance within the team can be identified (e.g. through individual statistics, tackle counts, video analysis) and that they will be held accountable for their contribution, then social loafing typically does not occur.[7] Therefore players need to have their individual performances monitored and they need to be made accountable for their personal contribution to the team performance.

As a coach or a captain you need to increase each team member's sense of responsibility for the team performance by increasing team interaction, commitment to the team goal(s), and task cohesion.[4] In addition, as a coach or captain you need to ensure that the team effort and team success is personally involving for each team member by developing a sense of team pride and a collective team identity.[4] Finally, you need to use systematic goal-setting for the team as a whole and for individual team members.

If monitoring individual performances can eliminate social loafing, then clearly other factors can increase individual effort in the team. The team can provide social incentives such as peer pressure and social support from teammates. For example, studies in swimming have found that when individual lap times were announced (high identifiability), individuals swam faster in relays than in individual race situations.[8] When lap times were not announced (low identifiability), individuals swam faster in the individual race situation than they did in the relays.[8] In many team sports you can develop and use 'match stats' as a means to identify, measure and reward each player's performance contributions to the team (see Chapter 10, 'Goal setting').

General implications for teams

Individual skill performance should not be the only factor for team member selection. For example, many team sports require high inter-action and communication skills that are not needed in individual performance. Motivation losses can be avoided by identifying and reward-ing the individual and teamwork behaviours that contribute to desired team performance. Contrary to the common coaching cliche, it may be useful to put the 'I' back into 'team' so that individual contributions are identified and desired teamwork behaviours (e.g. positive communication) are recognised, encouraged and rewarded.[4]

'With the talent and think power we had, we were able to open up the court and let one or two guys penetrate, then feed off of them. In the fourth quarter your leadership, your unity, your understanding of personnel, your fulfilment of roles – all those things come out. And I think that's the way we won.'

Michael Jordan (US basketball player, member of the Chicago Bulls, six-time winners of the NBA Championship)

Team motivation

While teamwork and team process are necessary, they are not sufficient to achieve peak perfor-mance in team sport. You also need to consider team motivation if a team is to consistently perform to its potential. The basis of team motivation is the team's goal(s) and each team member's desire for team success.

The fundamental factor to consider in developing team motivation is the identification of one single, unifying team goal; that is, a goal that all team members agree upon and commit themselves to achieving.[4] Your teammates have to freely agree to redefine their self-esteem to include membership of the team as being important to them as individuals.

> 'It's amazing what a team can achieve when no one cares about who gets the credit.'
>
> Anonymous coach

Increasing team motivation

First, emphasise a 'pride-in-team' approach.[4] With input from each of your teammates set a unifying team goal and objectives to achieve that single goal (see Chapter 10, 'Goal setting'). Second, ensure that the individual contribution of each of your teammates is valued and recognised by you as the coach or captain, and by other teammates.[4] Keep the reserves and substitutes involved as well; everyone needs to feel they have contributed, and that their contribution is noticed and valued. Third, place strong emphasis on good leadership from yourself as the coach or captain.[9] Fourth, actively work to encourage and develop team cohesion; that is, both social cohesion (team spirit), and task cohesion (teamwork). Fifth, encourage unified commitment to the team effort; teammates have to be prepared to invest time and energy to achieve the overall team goal.[4] Expect and reward the pursuit of high standards of excellence. Finally, it is vital that effective communication is utilised to keep all of your teammates informed and feeling 'part of the team' (see 'Communication' page 85).[2]

However, while you and each of your teammates need to feel a strong identification with the team, you also need to feel accountable. You need to accept the responsibility of playing your key part in the team's success in achieving its unifying goal. This sense of responsibility is related to the important issue of team cohesion.

Cohesion (team spirit, teamwork, team unity)

Team cohesion is the dynamic process that makes your team stick together and remain united in the pursuit of its goals.[4] Cohesive teams are able to ignore distractions and avoid disruptions, staying firmly focused on their team goal(s).[10]

There are two general dimensions associated with team cohesion. Social cohesion (interpersonal attraction) reflects the degree to which the members of your team like each other and enjoy each other's company.[4] Task cohesion reflects the degree to which your teammates work together to achieve specific and identifiable goals or tasks.[4]

Social cohesion = team spirit: you and your teammates need to respect each other, trust each other, and be willing to make sacrifices for each other and the team (e.g. give up personal time for fitness training, skill training, or extra team sub-unit practice).

Task cohesion = teamwork: synchronising the technical and tactical skills of every individual in the team requires a well-developed level of psych skills in each of the players, and in the leaders (captain, vice-captain) in particular.

Research into team cohesion involving New Zealand rugby teams has shown that for a professional rugby team (Super 12 team) task cohesion was very important for team success, but that social cohesion was not necessary for success on the field.[11] However, while social cohesion was not found to predict success during the game, there was a clear indication that it was a vital ingredient in creating a positive team environment for training, team practices and the travel that is a part of top-level team sport.[11] The clear implication from this research, and from the accumulated wisdom of New Zealand coaching identities such as Don Tricker, Tab Baldwin, Graham Lowe, Lois Muir, Brian Lochore, Graham Henry and Ruth Aitken, is that every team should put considerable time and effort into developing both task (teamwork) and social cohesion (team spirit).

Kayla's example

The peak performance profile for Kayla, our netball centre (page 47), shows that at the start of the season she needed to commit himself fully to her netball and her training, take control of her own pre-game 'psych-up', sharpen up her concentration, and be a more *cohesive team player* by improving her tactical skills (she had to follow the team's game plan). Kayla was able to follow a PST programme that allowed her to improve her PST skill weaknesses. She categorised her psych skill needs into foundation, performance, and facilitative needs; as noted previously these were: (i) commitment (foundation skill); (ii) pre-game psych-up = peak activation (performance skill); (iii) concentration (performance skill); and (iv) *team cohesion* (facilitative skill). After improving her 'commitment' (via goal setting and self-talk), she worked on some PST methods to enhance her performance skills of pre-game psych-up and concentration (via mental preparation, imagery and self-talk).

Finally, Kayla was ready to work on her *team cohesion* skills. She decided to use the PST methods of goal setting, imagery and self-talk to help her stick with the team's game plan and be a more cohesive team player. Kayla decided to use a variation on goal setting that focused on team goal setting – she convinced her coach and teammates to develop a team vision, team goals based on that vision, and then specific goal achievement strategies devised to accomplish those goals. In addition, Kayla talked her teammates into having some fun with a 'What if…' session (i.e., what if this happens or that goes wrong) called the 'Team Destruction Exercise' (see these worksheets on pages 98–9). Kayla's plan was that the act of sorting out the team's goals so specifically would help her as a player to identify her role and help her become committed to providing her contribution to the team's game plan. Finally, she used imagery to mentally rehearse the team's game plan and her role in it, and she practised self-talk to help her keep her concentration on the correct options within the team's game plan.

Make no mistake about it, the issue of team cohesion is a vital aspect of mental toughness for the individual players in team sports! In summary, the following acronym, 'PRIDE in the TEAM', serves as a useful review of a number of the key points in this chapter.

PRIDE	*in the*	**TEAM**
P Personal		**T** Together
R Responsibility		**E** Everyone
I In		**A** Achieves
D Delivering		**M** More
E Excellence		

'Now this is the Law of the Jungle –
As old and as true as the sky;

And the Wolf that shall keep it may prosper,
But the Wolf that shall break it must die.

As the creeper that girdles the tree trunk,
The Law runneth forward and back –

For the strength of the Pack is the Wolf,
And the strength of the Wolf is the Pack.'

Rudyard Kipling

TEAM GOAL-SETTING SESSION

OUTLINE

Team vision	(the *why* of this team; why are we together?)
Team goals	(*what* is this team aiming to achieve?)
Goal achievement strategies	(*how* are we going to achieve our goals?)
'Team Destruction Exercise'	(*what if* planning; coping with problems/weaknesses)

'The culture is bloody important. It's identifying the culture
and identifying the values. We call them Red and Black values
and it's what this team is all about. I think people who come
into this team really buy into it.'

Wayne Smith (coach of the Canterbury Crusaders,
Super 12 champions 1998–99)

'Do not let what you cannot do interfere with what you can do.'

John Wooden (US basketball coach, ten-time
National Collegiate Champion)

'There's no such thing as 'coulda, woulda, and shoulda'.
If you shoulda and coulda, you woulda done it.'

Pat Riley (coach of the LA Lakers 1981–89,
four-time NBA champions)

TEAM VISION

The *why* of this team.

Why are we together?

What team values do we want to emphasise?
(Values = 'How we do things around here')

Vision: ....

....

....

....

....

....

....

....

....

Values: ....

....

....

....

....

....

....

....

TEAM GOALS

What is this team aiming to achieve for the season?

Make the goals:

long-term & short-term, specific & measurable, positive, tied to a deadline.

1. ....
....
....
....

2. ....
....
....
....

3. ....
....
....
....

4. ....
....
....
....

GOAL ACHIEVEMENT STRATEGIES

How are we going to achieve our goals?

Be very specific:
precisely what do we need to do in order to achieve each of our goals?

Goal 1. ....

....

....

....

....

Goal 2. ....

....

....

....

....

Goal 3. ....

....

....

....

....

Goal 4. ....

....

....

....

....

'TEAM DESTRUCTION' EXERCISE

Imagine you are part of the management team for our main opponents
– your mission is to send a saboteur or spy into this team for the season
in order to *sabotage* and *destroy* their season.

What would your instructions be? What would you get the spy to sabotage?

What would you get the spy to do in order to destroy
our team and stop us achieving our goal(s)?

1. ....
....

2. ....
....

3. ....
....

4. ....
....

5. ....
....

6. ....
....

7. ....
....

8. ....
....

TEAM DESTRUCTION:
'COUNTER-ATTACK' OPTIONS PLAN

What plans can be put into place to prevent these problems/issues
happening or cope with them if they arise?

1. ....

....

2. ....

....

3. ....

....

4. ....

....

5. ....

....

6. ....

....

7. ....

....

8. ....

....

PST METHODS

PART FOUR

PST METHOD: GOAL SETTING

Goal setting is a very effective method for developing a number of PST skills such as self-confidence, self-control of activation, and motivation. In addition, your goals are linked to your levels of motivation, anxiety, stress, and self-confidence. For example, when a player is solely focused on the outcome and winning (i.e. outcome goal orientation: see Chapter 3), unrealistic and unattainable expectations often result. This leads to lower self-confidence, increased mental anxiety (therefore increased activation), decreased effort, and consequently poor performance. You need to select your goals by identifying the 'qualities' from your peak performance profile (see Chapter 6) that you believe to be the most important or give you the most room for improvement.

> 'Setting goals for your game is an art. The trick is setting them at the right level – neither too low nor too high. A good goal should be lofty enough to inspire hard work, yet realistic enough to provide solid hope of attainment.'
>
> Greg Norman (Australian golfing legend)

What is a goal?

A goal is an aim, objective, target or dream. More precisely, a goal is a specific standard of performance, usually to be attained within a specified time limit.[1]

Why set goals in sport?

Achieving goals helps to create and maintain motivation by reflecting improvement. In addition, your goals are linked to your levels of self-confidence, activation and motivation in sport – appropriate goal setting will help you maintain optimal levels of each of these psychological skills.[1] Goal setting also helps you to make key decisions about how you should manage the time you have available for training. You need to make the most efficient and effective use of your training time – goal setting will help you prioritise the use of that time.

> *Goal setting and time management:*
> **'Time is nature's way of making sure everything doesn't happen at once.'**

The process of goal setting will also help you to identify your strengths and weaknesses, which is the ideal starting point for designing a training plan. Goals provide direction and force you to prioritise your needs.[1] Goal setting is like a roadmap; the long-term goal is the destination, while the short-term goals are pitstops along the way. The goal achievement strategies (i.e. training methods) are the choice of route you take to your destination.

> 'Goal setting definitely works. I've found that if you write down your goals and what you've done, see what you've achieved, you feel your goals are more attainable.'
>
> Zinzan Brooke (All Black 1987–97)

What types of goals should you set?[2]

Set performance and process goals (i.e. task orientation; see Chapter 3, 'Motivation for peak performance') rather than outcome goals.[2] These performance and process goals should be based on the peak performance needs identified in your peak performance profile (Chapter 6). In competitive sport there is enormous pressure from many sources, especially the media, to set outcome goals (e.g. winning, beating an opponent). Indeed, coaches often emphasise and teach outcome goals. However, outcome goals are not fully within your control; consequently they can become a major source of pressure and anxiety, which in turn can lead to poor performance.[2] Therefore, rather than just setting outcome goals, you should also set performance and process goals as your main focus for motivation and self-confidence.

Performance goals

These goals differ from outcome goals in that they focus on a 'task' definition of success (see Chapter 3).[2] That is, performance goals are all about mastering specific tasks or skills. The nuts and bolts of playing well and being successful depend on doing these basic tasks and skills correctly (e.g. passing, kicking, tackling, shooting). If you succeed in performing these tasks well then you are likely to achieve the 'outcome' that you are seeking. Consequently, performance goals encourage you to focus on 'how to win', rather than winning itself. The beauty of these goals is that you have control, because they are based on measuring your mastery of specified tasks or standards of performance (e.g. increasing your first serve percentage in tennis by 10 per cent over the next two matches). With performance goals the criteria for success is being better at the specified task than you were last time (e.g. the number of first-time tackles in rugby league; goal-shooting percentage in netball) or better than a standard you set yourself for a task. So, rather than determining your success solely by comparing yourself with your opponent(s), performance goals allow you to make a comparison with your own previous performance.

You have more control over performance goals, and they are also a very honest and demanding way to measure success. For example, even when you win easily against poor opposition, your performance goals will provide a more demanding evaluation of your 'real' success on the day. Conversely, when you lose to a good opponent you still have a measure of success that provides you with information about performance improvements and the effectiveness of your training. Outcome goals are just too crude and imprecise to be useful as the sole measure of success.

Process goals

These goals are a variation on performance goals – the focus of achievement is placed on the actual 'process' of playing well, as opposed to the resulting 'performance'.[2] You need to break down complex skills into the key components or actions that combine to produce successful execution of the skill. This provides you with a primary focus for attention and effort – a focus over which you have more control.[2] For example, a process goal for a goalkicker might be to maintain balance on the non-kicking foot and have a full follow-through on every kick at goal. This process goal helps the player to concentrate on good kicking technique – on 'just doing it!' A performance goal for the same player may have been to succeed with 90 per cent of all kicks at goal within a range of 40 metres.

Process goals should form part of your technical and tactical skill development and eventually lead to the automatic execution of your tactical and technical skills.[2] The skills become second nature so that you barely need to think – you just do it.

The process goal focuses on how to do something, while the performance goal focuses on the objective success or failure at the task. Both types of goal utilise a task-goal orientation, but with a distinct difference in emphasis. Both are useful for motivation, self-confidence and concentration, and many athletes/players utilise both types of goal at the same time.

Set long-term and short-term goals

'Goals should be out of reach, but not out of sight.'

A long-term goal is a 'dream' goal. It is the ultimate objective, and it provides direction for your season and for your training. Short-term goals allow you to see on a regular basis how much you have improved, and can increase your intensity of effort in training and games. Achieving short-term goals is also useful in that it allows you to reward yourself for effort and hard work in training and games.

The 1976 US Olympic swimming gold medallist John Naber provides an excellent example of the process of breaking down a long-term goal into a set of short-term goals. In 1972, he decided that he wanted to win a gold medal in the 100-metre backstroke at the 1976 Olympics. Using previous times, he calculated what time it would take to win the gold in 1976 (a performance goal), and determined that to achieve his performance goal he had to drop four seconds off his personal best time in four years. Now, four seconds is a lot of time to cut from any sprint event, but Naber didn't stop

there. He broke the goal down further into one second per year, one-tenth of a second per month (with a two-month rest/break), one-hundredth of a second per day, and one-twelve-hundredth of a second per hour of training. Naturally the goal of improving one-twelve-hundredth of a second per hour of training seemed much more achievable and easier to grasp than the long-term goal of improving by four seconds – especially given that it takes five-twelve-hundredths of a second to blink your eyes! He could now believe that he could improve that much every hour, and he set about doing just that. His plan worked, he achieved his performance goal (i.e. a personal best race time), and to top it off he won the gold medal.[3]

Set specific, measurable goals

Specific, numerical goals are easy to measure and thus make it simple to determine whether or not you have achieved them. These goals need to be very specific to the skill you are trying to improve. You also need to write down a detailed description of each goal so that you can see whether or not you have attained it.

Examples of 'poor' goals and 'good' – i.e. specific, measurable – goals:

Poor goal: I want to be faster.
Good goal: I want to reduce my average time for five 40-metre sprints by 1 second by the end of a four-week training phase.

Poor goal: I want to be more accurate in my passing in netball.
Good goal: I want to be able to hit a 30-cm-square target, on the run, nine times out of ten after receiving a pass from another player.

Set positive, not negative, goals

Instead of saying to yourself, 'I will not blow my cool every time a refereeing decision goes against me,' say, 'Whenever a refereeing decision goes against me I will remember to remain composed and stay focused on my game.' Or instead of saying, 'I will not miss any more than 10 per cent of my first serves in tennis,' say, 'I will strive to hit 90 per cent of my first serves.' That is, instead of focusing on 'I won't fail', focus on 'I will succeed'.

Examples of areas in which to set goals

Physical goals: health and fitness goals
(for example, improving endurance, power, strength, flexibility, weight, diet, sleep patterns)

Technical goals: related to performance of the particular skills of your sport
(for example, keeping shoulders relaxed when sprinting; passing accurately with both left and right hands; following through when goal-kicking)

Tactical goals: related to an understanding and appreciation of appropriate tactics, attacking and defensive strategies, and game plans
(for example, improving ability to 'read' the opposition defensive pattern (hockey/soccer) and quickly identify the best point of attack; improve ability to read the right 'lines' to run in support)

Psychological goals: psych skills and methods
(for example, planning to practise mental preparation techniques; practising imagery of performance in pressure situations; coping with poor refereeing)

Goal-setting staircase

This involves the steady progression through short-term goals to reach your ultimate long-term goal. You should make up a staircase for each long-term goal. For an example, see fig. 10.1

Prioritise goals. Choose the key areas in your peak performance profile (Chapter 6) that need improvement. (i) Set long-term goals for each area; (ii) set short-term sub-goals for each long-term goal. Each key area has its own staircase of sub-goals.

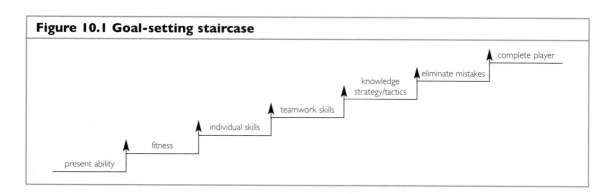

Figure 10.1 Goal-setting staircase

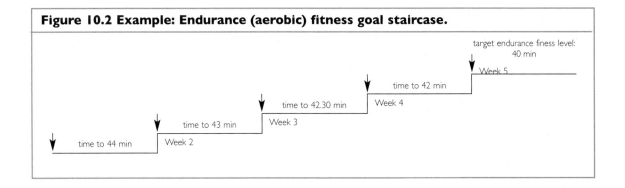

Figure 10.2 Example: Endurance (aerobic) fitness goal staircase.

target endurance finess level:
40 min

Week 5

time to 42 min

Week 4

time to 42.30 min

Week 3

time to 43 min

Week 2

time to 44 min

How to set SMART goals[4]

Talk to your coach. However, before you talk to your coach about the results of your peak performance profile (see Chapter 6) make sure you have asked yourself some key questions regarding your sport performance.[4] These should include: Where am I now? Where do I want to be in one week, next month, six months, two years? What are my strengths and weaknesses?

Select key areas: prioritise needs. Using your coach's advice, set long-term and short-term goals for each area. Then, based on these priorities, use the SMART(S) system to actually 'set' your goals.

SMART(S) goal setting

S = Specific   M = Measurable
A = Adjustable   R = Realistic
T = Time-referenced   S = Strategy to achieve
                             goal(s)

Specific

Set specific goal(s). These need to be difficult to reach, but still realistic. They should be performance and process goals, stated positively. You should write a detailed description of the goal so that it can be measured.

Measurable

Set numerical goal(s). When goals are stated in readily measured, numerical terms, it is easy to determine whether or not you have achieved them.

Adjustable

Goals and goal schedules may need to be adjusted or changed. Sickness or injury may interfere with progress towards your goal, or the goals initially selected may be too hard or too easy. You must be prepared to modify and change goals, strategies and target dates as required. Like any activity that you attempt for the first time, it will take time to develop effective, accurate and realistic goal setting.

Monitor your progress regularly, and check your target dates. Record these in your training logbook (see Hodge, Sleivert, & McKenzie, [1996] for sample logbooks)[5]. They may need to be adjusted according to how well you are progressing towards your goals. Finally, your training methods/strategies should also be reviewed periodically with regard to their effectiveness. Remember, setting goals in itself does not improve performance; the hard work and training detailed in the strategy(s) is what allows for goal achievement and subsequently improves performance.

Realistic

Set goals that are difficult, but realistic. Know your own limitations, but aim to stretch your capabilities. Remember, goals must be out of reach but not out of sight! Make sure they are achievable if you put the work in. If you set goals that are unrealistic and too hard to achieve then you are virtually guaranteeing failure, rather than increasing your chances of success.

Poor goal: I want to make 90 per cent of my goal shots from the edge of the circle (netball).

Good goal: Because I'm only currently making 50 per cent of my shots from the edge of the circle, my goal is to average making 75 per cent of my shots from the edge of the circle over the next five games.

Time-referenced

Set target dates for achieving goal(s). Again, these should be difficult but realistic. If you don't set a target date, you can always use the excuse that you're still working towards achieving the goal if somebody asks you how you are progressing. But if you have a target date set, then the closer to that date you find yourself, the more effort you are likely to put into making sure you achieve the goal.

Strategy

Outline a strategy of training methods to achieve the goal(s) (be specific). For example, goal strategy for improving punting accuracy (kicking for touch in rugby/rugby league):

> 'I will practise an extra 50 kicks punting for touch after training on Mon/Wed/Fri, and ask for an extra hour of one-on-one coaching each week.'

Complete the goal achievement worksheet

To help you think through the key questions mentioned above you should fill out the worksheet on pages 108–9. This will help you 'think through' your goals in depth as you strive to express yourself by filling in the worksheet. Make sure the goals you set are specific and numerical, with specific target dates for goal attainment, and with a specific strategy of training methods to achieve each goal (record these in your training logbook).

Ensure your commitment to your goal(s)

You must have the desire, motivation and commitment to pursue your goal strategies. Writing a 'contract' with yourself can be helpful (see the worksheet on pages 108–9). Social support from significant people in your life is also vital (e.g. teammates, parents, partner, friends, boss). Make sure you inform these significant people about your goals and training plan. They can't support you if they don't know what you are trying to achieve and why it matters to you!

Self-monitor your commitment to your goal setting

To ensure your commitment to your goals and your training plan you should do the following.[1,4]

Write down your goals

Write out both long-term and short-term goals (see fig. 10.3 below). Write down at least one goal achievement strategy for each short-term goal. Use the 'Goal Achievement Worksheet' on pages 108–9 to record this information (photocopy extra worksheets as you need them). Write down target dates as well; deadlines provide added incentive

Figure 10.3 Goalsetting

Skill/area needing improvement	Specific goal	Goal achievement strategy(s)	Target date evaluation
Goal-kicking accuracy (rugby league).	I want to be able to consistently make 8 out of 10 shots from all angles within the 40 m.	1. Before practice I will spend 30 minutes practising my kicking, taking at least 30 shots at goal (Tuesday and Thursday). 2. I will take extra instruction once a week (Sundays) from a goal-kicking expert (45–60 minutes).	8th May, fourth weekend of the season. Then reset goal to 10 out of 10 by 12 June.

and help you plan the time frame of goal achievement. Finally, the goal evaluation procedures should also be recorded for use with a training log (see Hodge, Sleivert and McKenzie [1996] for examples of training logbooks).[5]

Remind yourself of your goals

Maintain a training logbook.[5] Other options include making a wall poster as a visual reminder of your goals, target dates and overall training plan. Write your goals on index cards and stick them somewhere obvious, such as on your mirror or on the fridge door.

Question yourself periodically

Ask yourself periodically: 'What did I do today to become a better athlete/player?'

Monitoring is your job, not your coach's

Self-monitoring and self-evaluation lead to self-motivation. Be organised, be responsible, be committed and be assertive. Have the attitude: 'If it's to be, it's up to me!'

Common goal-setting problems

- Goals that are not specific or measurable.
- Goals that are not realistic.
- Setting too many goals at one time.
- No goal achievement strategy.
- Poor goal monitoring/evaluation.
- Lack of commitment.

Summary: goal setting for peak performance

Once you have identified your peak performance needs and written them out as performance and/or process goals you will be on your way to improving motivation, commitment and self-confidence. You need to choose the appropriate training methods to develop or improve the performance qualities identified in your peak performance profile. Goal setting is the first step in prioritising your needs and becoming fully committed to success in sport.

GOAL ACHIEVEMENT WORKSHEET

Name: .... Date: ....

My 'DREAM': ....

Statement of my goal: ....

....

....

Target date: ....

What is the *'payoff'* from achieving my goal? ....

....

....

What are the *consequences* of not achieving my goal? ....

....

....

What is my *strategy* to achieve my goal? ....

....

....

....

....

....

Possible *obstacles* in the way of my goal achievement: ....

....

....

(Continued)

Strategies for *overcoming* the obstacles: ....
....
....
....
....
....

What *excuses* do I usually make? ....
....
....
....
....

Is it *worth* the time, effort, and commitment to reach my goal?   Yes .... No ....
Why? ....
....
....
....
....
....
....

Goal Setting Contract

I .... hereby do solemnly swear that I am committed to achieving the goal that I have set out above. I will achieve this goal by following the goal achievement strategy that I have developed and outlined above.

I am fully committed to this goal and my achievement strategy.

Signed: .... Date: ....

BOB BLAIR

'Courage, commitment and team spirit'

In 1953 there were two things which turned the second cricket test in Johannesburg into an open-air melodrama.[1] The first was the lively pitch, the second was a train wreck in New Zealand that cost nearly 150 lives (the Tangiwai disaster, Christmas Eve, 1953).

There was a great deal of theorising about the pitch after the match.[2] Whatever the cause, the effect was remarkable. Fast bowling on a length would frequently get the ball up head high – it was a difficult and dangerous situation in which to bat.

The first news of the Tangiwai train disaster reached the New Zealand team on the second morning of the match. The team's manager woke some of the older members of the party in the early hours to tell them that Bob Blair's fiancée had been one of the victims. At the ground that morning, the New Zealand and South African flags were at half-mast as a measure of the players' sympathy for Blair and his fiancée's family.

The New Zealand team left for the ground the morning after receiving news of Tangiwai, with Bob Blair left behind grieving for his fiancée.[5] It was another morning of intense heat, and there was a crowd of 23,000 to greet the New Zealanders. During the lunch interval, it was announced that New Zealand batsman Bert Sutcliffe had been medically advised not to bat again after receiving a severe head injury and collapsing on the pitch. Sutcliffe had collapsed for a second time while being x-rayed at the hospital.[5] However, as the match wore on the lively pitch led to a New Zealand batting collapse and the situation became desperate.

It was Bert Sutcliffe who eventually walked out to bat, and the Springboks joined in the tremendous applause that greeted him. Sutcliffe took guard, bent his bandaged head to make his mark, and faced the fast bowling. He batted on bravely through the session, losing batting partners until finally the last batsman was caught out with the score at 154. Since New Zealand had no batsmen

left everyone assumed that that was the end of the innings.[2]

Indeed, the players turned away and began to walk off the field, but the crowd was puzzled when suddenly they stopped. Out of the tunnel beneath the stand, into the bright sunlight, Bob Blair walked slowly, fumbling with his gloves, and as one the spectators in the huge stand stood for him, standing in complete silence. John Reid, the New Zealand captain, recalled the incident: 'The crowd stood as one. In silence. This was the most unforgettable moment in my life. Tears streamed unchecked down the cheeks of those around me, and down my own. To be hurt physically and return to fight I can understand. To be so deeply bruised mentally and emotionally, and return, took a kind of courage which passed understanding.'[5]

As Blair approached the wicket, Sutcliffe went to meet him and put an arm around his comrade. All the New Zealanders had taken hard knocks in this match, but Sutcliffe's courage was excelled only by that of Blair.[2] Facing his first ball, Blair hurriedly passed a hand across his eyes. The silence was immense as the bowler moved in to bowl. But Blair kept him out.

Then it was Sutcliffe's turn for more heroics, moving into a ball on his leg stump he sent it soaring over the boundary at mid-wicket, and the crowd regained its voice. Its roar had not died away when Sutcliffe, two balls later, drove for another six. Two balls later again, he repeated the shot. Blair was left to face the last ball of the over. Down it came, and Blair put his foot down the pitch and hit a towering six to mid-wicket, the ball dropping far over the fence among a mass of frenzied spectators.[5] The over cost South Africa 25 runs, and was a counter-attack on a Hollywood scale.[4] In the next over, Sutcliffe hit two graceful fours, but he lost the strike and Blair was stumped off the next ball. Together they had scored 33 runs in 10 minutes, with Sutcliffe finishing on 80 not out.[2]

So Sutcliffe and Blair left the field to sustained and tremendous applause, which lasted long after they had disappeared, arms about each other, into the depths of the tunnel. This was indeed a triumph from tragedy, a great and glorious victory over misfortune and despair and a wonderful example of team spirit.[3]

PST METHOD: RELAXATION AND CENTRING

> 'I'm quite relaxed before games. This is another aspect of finding the right balance. Once upon a time, before test matches I used to think you had to sit in your room getting yourself all worked up and tense about it… But then I thought, what is this actually doing for me? It wasn't doing me any good at all. I feel I'm ready to play better if I'm relaxed, not tense, beforehand… I think that the ability to relax and keep your balance mentally could be the X-factor that lets you perform better than your opposition.'
>
> Zinzan Brooke (All Black 1987–97)

To many people, competitive sport has traditionally been associated with a group of 'fired up' players/athletes going out onto the field or court and giving their all for their school, club, province or country. Indeed, there is a long-standing myth that athletes/players have to be as psyched up as possible in order to play well. In fact, this has led to many athletes being 'over-psyched' and playing poorly as a result (see 'Controlling activation' in Chapter 8). Consequently, you will often hear coaches, commentators and players comment that a team or athlete took 20 minutes or more to settle down and start playing according to the game plan, and to their ability.

As we have seen in Chapter 4, every athlete/player, every game, and every situation within a game or event requires a slightly different level of activation in order for the athlete to perform optimally. Your ability to control your level of activation is therefore an important skill to master. For most athletes/players, the problem lies not so much in being able to 'psych

themselves up' for a particular game or event, or a particular situation within a game, but in preventing themselves being 'psyched out' by being too activated for the situation.[1] They are unable to cope effectively with the pressure of the situation, and may experience not only a decrease in performance, but actual physical illness (some players have been known to vomit before games) and mental distress.[1] It is their inability to control their activation levels effectively that is the problem. Their limited control seems to be entirely in one direction – they can easily raise their activation level, but have a problem lowering it when required.

Therefore, given that (a), controlling activation is a key skill in maintaining peak performance through peak activation, and (b), most athletes/players need to lower their activation levels rather than raise them, the ability to relax physically and mentally is an important weapon in an athlete's arsenal. If you are aware of what it feels like to be totally relaxed, then you are more likely to recognise when you are over-activated. In addition, if you also know how to relax, there will be less chance of your becoming even more activated when a teammate or your coach tells you to 'relax'! This often happens when athletes/players are told to relax, or told not to panic, and don't know how to calm themselves down. The instruction often has the opposite effect to what was intended because the athlete/player thinks 'There must be something to panic about,' or 'I must be too uptight.' Because they don't know how to deal with the situation, the problem simply intensifies. Players/athletes who know how to relax, on the other hand, can simply perform a relaxation procedure and lower their activation to a more appropriate level for the task they are about to perform. Consequently, they play better!

What is relaxation?

Knowing when and how to relax allows you to become physically and mentally free from uncontrolled activation, tension, anxiety and negative thoughts before, during and after games or events and practices.[1] An athlete who is relaxed might describe the feeling as one of ease, looseness, and readiness to perform. This involves both physical relaxation and mental relaxation – calm the body and clear the mind.

Purposes of relaxation training

The most obvious purpose of relaxation is to calm the body physiologically by decreasing muscle tension, as well as decreasing your heart rate and breathing rate. In addition, relaxation can also help to shift your concentration from anxiety-provoking thoughts to a more relaxed and focused mindset (i.e. to the Ideal Performance State) by helping you to reach your peak level of physical and mental activation, before and during an event.[1]

Being able to relax can also help you sleep the night before a major event, which can be a common problem for many sportspeople. It is also used as a mechanism for helping to develop other PST skills and methods (e.g. peak concentration, imagery).

Relaxation techniques

There are a range of relaxation techniques that you can use, and I will only describe some of the most common here. It is useful to become

proficient in a number of techniques, because not all of them will be appropriate in every situation.[1] For example, a technique that takes several minutes to perform is of no use during a game/event when you only have a few seconds between the end of one passage of play and the start of the next, but it might be very useful as part of your pre-match/race preparation. On the other hand, a technique such as 'centring' can, with practice, be performed in a few seconds or less, and therefore might be useful as a means of reducing activation levels during a game or event.

Centring

Centring is a relaxation and concentration exercise where you focus on your breathing in a particular way; that is, on breathing from your 'centre of gravity', which is just behind the navel/stomach for most of us. Centring combines the use of abdominal breathing and key words, and is described as a mind-to-muscle relaxation technique.[2]

How can centring help you? In the martial arts, centring is used as a method to reduce unwanted tension and to increase concentration powers for body control. Likewise, you can use centring to stay loose under pressure and to focus attention on your centre of control. Remember that whoever controls the centre of gravity controls where the body moves. If it is your opponent, they control you! Learning to 'centre' helps you keep in control.

Physical effects of centring

The physical effects of centring include decreased heart rate, decreased breathing rate, increased oxygen to the muscles, decreased negative tension, better control of hips, and better balance.[2] Movements that are initiated and controlled from your centre of gravity generate better timing and better co-ordination.[2] This can help your sport in a number of ways, ranging from the simple act of running more efficiently, to being better able to tackle, pass, jump and push! For example, a rugby scrum that is made up of eight players who are each able to effectively control and initiate power and force from their centre of gravity will potentially be able to exert more pressure on their opponents due to their superior body control and co-ordination.

Psychological effects of centring

Players who are able to centre effectively may feel stronger, more confident, and more in control of their actions on the field.[2] Their attention will be focused on their centre of gravity and therefore on body control, rather than on negative thoughts or other distractions.

Training centring skills

Everyone can centre to at least some degree right now. However, like all psychological abilities, centring under the pressure of a game requires practice. For example, it may be appropriate for you to relax yourself before shooting a free throw in basketball or before throwing into a lineout in rugby, but if you don't know how to do that, and if you haven't practised doing it beforehand, it can lead to a poor performance. The following two-phase learning process is designed to help you learn and practise centring.

Phase 1: breathing skills and centring of attention

Focus on a point just behind your navel. Concentrate on this point, then feel your entire body in relation to it. Remind yourself that your strength, power, balance and control all come from this point.

The easiest way to learn this technique is to lie down on your back with your legs uncrossed.

- Place one hand on your stomach just below your navel and rest the other hand on top of it.
- Breathe in through your nose so that your stomach and your hand rise as you inhale. Breathe out through your mouth so that your stomach and hand fall as the air goes out. Keep breathing in and out in this manner with your attention totally focused on your breathing and nothing else.
- Try to make the inhalation and exhalation last the same amount of time. The transition between the two should be very natural and unforced.
- Every time you breathe out say the word 'one' silently to yourself. If your mind drifts just refocus on your breathing and your concentration word (eventually replace the word 'one' with a word that is meaningful to you). It can also help to visualise each muscle group loosening up (like light bulbs being turned off one by one).
- At first, spend about ten minutes on this exercise each day. Eventually decrease the time to three to five minutes and change your position from lying down to sitting, then to standing. Eventually practise the exercise in a position that is relevant to your sport (for example, settling into your stance for a golf shot, waiting to receive a penalty corner in hockey, waiting for the ball to be thrown into a lineout in rugby).

Build in a mental cue for centring. As you breathe in, say a cue word to yourself (e.g. 'centre') to remind yourself to centre, and as you exhale say another cue word (e.g. 'relax') to remind yourself to stay loose. At the end of one breathing cycle many players like to cue their attention towards their opponent or the next task while staying centred; a word like 'concentrate', 'focus' or 'action' works well. See the 'Training Log for Centring' on page 119; record your centring practice on this log sheet.

The entire sequence might be:

Breathe in (nose) → Breathe out (mouth)
Centre' → *'Relax'* → *'Focus/action'*

Phase 2: centring during practice or training

Practise centring between drills or between periods of practice. Later, make it a habit to centre before each 'set piece' in your sport (e.g. settling into your stance for a golf shot; at each centre pass/restart in netball).

Use cue words to reinforce the centring drill. As your skill improves, try centring in low pressure games, gradually working up to more important games or events. The more automatic your centring skills become, the more they can be used in important games. The better-centred athlete/player will have more strength, speed and balance, and better timing, concentration and confidence. Centring helps you switch on your 'automatic pilot' and the Ideal Performance State.

Centring example

Whenever you are feeling too uptight or are distracted from your present task, use the centring procedure.

1. Stand comfortably with your feet shoulder distance apart and your knees slightly flexed.
2. Consciously relax your neck, arm and shoulder muscles. Smile slightly to reduce the tension in your jaw.
3. Focus on the movement of your abdominal muscles. Notice your stomach muscles tightening and relaxing.
4. Take a slow, deep breath using the diaphragm. Notice you are extending your stomach.
5. Consciously maintain the relaxation in your chest and shoulders. There should be minimal chest movement and absolutely no hunching or raising of the shoulders.

6. Exhale slowly. Let yourself go. Feel yourself get heavier as all your muscles relax.
7. Focus on the job that you have to do right now. Use your game focus plan or coping plan to find the correct focus point. 'All I've got to do now is…'.

Progressive muscular relaxation (PMR)

PMR is a physical relaxation exercise that might be necessary if you are unable to control your activation levels effectively with centring alone. PMR also allows you to relax to a much 'deeper' level than centring; this depth of relaxation is useful for controlling insomnia (sleeping problems) and can also be useful as a lead-in to an imagery practice session.[2] There are four phases to learning PMR effectively so that you can progress to using centring before or during a practice or game. Use the PMR relaxation training log sheets at the end of this section to record your PMR practice.

Phase 1: tense-relax cycle

This learning phase relies on the overshoot principle – when a muscle is tensed it will then relax below the initial level of tension. Allow 15–20 minutes to do this exercise. You may wish to record the following 'script' onto an audiotape to use with a walkman. See the 'PMR Relaxation Phase 1 Training Log' on page 120.

1. Lie down and relax your entire body. If you hear noises don't try to block them out, but focus on your breathing: inhaling, then exhaling slowly. If you want to move slightly, that's okay. Close your eyes, take it easy and relax. Focus on your breathing. Breathe in through your nose and out through your mouth.

2. Tense the muscles of your right lower leg and foot by pointing your toe. You'll tense for five or six seconds and then relax. You should be able to feel the tension in the foot and the calf and then totally relax. When you relax feel the warmth in the muscles as the tension drains away. Focus on the differences between tension and relaxation. Repeat this procedure with the right leg and then do it twice with the left leg.

3. Think to yourself 'loose' and 'relax' every time you release the tension. Focus on your breathing again as you do so.

4. After tensing and relaxing the lower leg and foot, tense (for five seconds) and relax the thigh and buttocks region (twice for each leg). Tense the buttocks and thighs by pushing down with your butt.

5. Tense and relax the forearm and hand by making a fist. Do this twice for each arm.

6. Tense and relax the biceps of each arm by bending at the elbow and pretending you are doing a chin-up. Do this twice for each arm.

7. Tense (for five seconds) and relax the back muscles by arching the back up. Tense and relax the back twice.

8. Tense the stomach and chest muscles by breathing in deeply and releasing/relaxing. Do this twice.

9. Tense the neck and shoulders by shrugging your shoulders (pulling them upwards) then releasing them and relaxing. Repeat this twice.

10. Tense the face and forehead by gritting your teeth and pulling your eyebrows together, then relax. Do this twice.

11. When this sequence is completed mentally check your body for any tension. Release it if you find any. By now you should be completely relaxed (after 15–20 minutes of tense/relax). Focus on the feelings of ease and looseness in your muscles, the deep breathing cycle you are in, and the calm, focused thoughts of your mindset. To a degree your peak level of activation should also represent a calm, semi-relaxed state.

This script is a general example of a PMR sequence. You should modify the sequence of muscle relaxation to suit your personal needs and preferences.

Phase 2: relax-only cycle

Relax the same muscle groups without tensing. Begin to use a cue word or phrase to signal relaxation (e.g. 'loose and easy', 'calm and ready'). Allow 10–15 minutes each time you practise this phase. Progress to a sitting then a standing position, and finally to a position that is relevant to your playing position. See the 'PMR Relaxation Phase 2 Training Log' on page 121.

Phase 3: full-speed relaxation

Begin to add speed by learning to relax the muscle groups more quickly. You can start by dividing the body into fewer parts. The ultimate goal is to learn to relax deeply in the time it requires to take a deep breath, and to use your cue word/phrase (i.e. the centring procedure). Practise this about ten times a day. See the 'PMR Relaxation Phase 3 Training Log' on page 122.

Phase 4: utilisation stage

Begin to use PMR relaxation in anxiety-provoking situations. Practise first in low-stress conditions (e.g. practice), then under moderately stressful conditions, and finally in highly stressful situations. See the 'PMR Relaxation Phase 4 Training Log' on page 123.

The time frame for moving through these four phases depends on your ability to master each phase and the time you have available to practise.

Additional techniques for lowering activation levels

1. Physical stretching, relaxing music, and the use of schedules/routines (e.g. mental preparation; see Chapter 14), imagery and self-talk are other examples of techniques that can be used to relax yourself before and, in some cases, during a game. In addition to these techniques, there are a number of other methods that you might be able to use to help you stay relaxed during a game.[1,2]

    Smile when you feel you are becoming too tense. If you think about it, it is hard to become upset or mad if you are smiling, so by doing this you can effectively reduce the anxiety of a particular situation. It might also distract your opponents if they see you smiling in a tense situation!

2. Focus on enjoying the game/race/event. After all, one of the main reasons you play sport in the first place is because it is enjoyable! By focusing on enjoying the experience of playing, without being too concerned about the outcome, you will go a long way towards reducing the anxiety you feel during a performance. Many athletes become too concerned about whether or not they are going to win a particular game or event, rather than focusing on how they are going to achieve that goal. In most cases, the 'how' is achieved by successfully executing the moves and strategies that you have practised. Most athletes experience a great deal of satisfaction and enjoyment when they successfully perform a particular skill, pull off a great tackle, make a good run with the ball, or set up a goal for one of their team mates. So why not focus on these aspects of the game – the enjoyable aspects – and let the outcome take care of itself? Of course it's enjoyable to win, but winning happens when you perform these different aspects of the event well. Doing them well is enjoyable, and can give you and the rest of the team confidence, and therefore reduce the anxiety you may have been feeling. Consequently, focusing on enjoying the various aspects of the event that make up a complete performance can be seen as an effective relaxation strategy.

3. Set up pressure situations in practice. By practising your responses to simulated pressure situations you can become accustomed to playing under pressure, and will be less likely to become too anxious or uptight when these situations occur in a game/race/event. For example, during a soccer team practice, your coach or captain may set up a situation where the team is told there are two minutes left in the game, you have been stuck deep in your own half for the past five minutes, you are one goal down, but have a penalty in centre field. What are your options? How will you approach this situation? Once a decision is made, you should then practise that response. The idea is that if that situation arises in a game, the team will not get too anxious because they have experienced it before (even if it was in practice) and know they have a strategy in place to deal with it.

4. Slow down and take your time. Players/athletes often rush things when they are anxious and uptight, because they think the easiest way to cope with the pressure is to get it over with. As a consequence, their execution of a particular move or skill is often poor, which makes them even more uptight. They'll drop a pass, fumble a catch, kick the ball off the side of their boot, get offside, or get into a poor body position! One of the ways to prevent these things happening is to have an established and consistent pre-performance routine (e.g. before each shot in golf) that incorporates some form of relaxation

procedure (e.g. centring). See the CARS plans in Chapter 15.

5. Stay focused on the present. What do you have to do right now? You will become even more uptight and anxious if you dwell on a mistake that you have just made, how it will feel if you lose (or win) the game, or what the opposition might try to do in the second half. These types of thoughts can only distract you from your immediate task, and can often lead to mistakes because you weren't totally focused (see also 'Concentration' in Chapter 8). This can cause you to become even more uptight, and a vicious cycle begins to take place. Remaining focused on the present will prevent these types of thoughts increasing your anxiety because your attention will be taken up by what it is that you have to do at that moment. One way to remain focused on the present is to use the referee's whistle to stop play as a cue to ask yourself the question, 'What do I have to do now?' In addition, you might like to think about each stoppage in play as a chance to regroup, to analyse the last play, and to plan for the next play (see Chapter 15). The whistle to restart play should be considered as an opportunity for you to perform well. For example, a hockey player who has missed a number of tackles should use the whistle that signals the end of a passage of play as a cue to mark the end of a poor performance. Rather than use the time in between plays to dwell on how many tackles they have missed, they should analyse why those tackles were missed, and then treat the whistle to start play again as an opportunity to perform better. This can help the player keep focused on the present.

6. Make sure you and your team have a well-prepared game plan. In addition, make sure you know what that plan is in terms of the overall strategy of the team and exactly what you have to do in your particular position to make sure the game plan is followed. If you are not exactly sure what to do, then you are more likely to become uptight and anxious. In a team sport you will be faced with literally hundreds of situations that will require you to make a decision about what to do (what line should I run, which opponent should I be marking, should I hold on to the ball or pass it, etc.), so having a well-developed, specific and well-practised game plan will make the decision-making process a lot easier. As a consequence, your reactions and responses will become quicker, which will help you to perform better. This in turn will help you become more confident, and will mean you are more likely to remain focused and relaxed (see also Chapter 14, 'Mental preparation').

Summary

Relaxation and centring are effective PST methods for all athletes/players to learn; however, they require sustained practice. You need to create the right physical and mental environment to develop your ability to relax: a quiet setting; a comfortable position; the use of a mental cue word, phrase or trigger; and a positive attitude. The length of time you take to learn to relax quickly will depend on your individual ability and the time you have available to practise. However, it is also important to remember that the same relaxation training procedure is not best for everyone. You should try the techniques described, then modify them to suit your personal needs and style. The additional techniques described at the end of the section also require practice and modification to suit your personal needs and style, and should not be attempted during events until you have developed them to a level where you trust your ability to use them effectively.

TRAINING LOG FOR CENTRING

Use a scale from −10 to +10, where −10 = extremely tense and +10 = extremely relaxed, to show your level of relaxation before the centring exercise and afterward.

Practise on five consecutive days. Each session should last only ten minutes.
Before training or before bedtime is a popular time.
Practise in a quiet, warm environment where you will not be disturbed.
Give yourself the opportunity to relax.

	Date of practice	Time of practice	Level before relaxing	Level after relaxing
e.g.	May 8	10 p.m.	−7	+5

After three days of centring training, try putting your new skill into practice at work or in social situations. When you feel yourself getting physically tense, your thinking rushed, or your emotions gaining control over your thoughts, stop and centre. Drop your shoulders, relax your facial muscles and focus on your stomach breathing. Close your eyes if you can. Remember, centring, like all PST methods, needs consistent practice.

PMR RELAXATION PHASE 1:

TRAINING LOG

Use a scale from −10 to +10, where −10 = extremely tense and +10 = extremely relaxed, to show your level of relaxation before and after the phase 1 PMR relaxation exercise.

	Date of practice	Time of practice	Level before relaxing	Level after relaxing
e.g.	May 30	6 p.m.	−8	+9

1. What physical changes did you experience as you practised?

....

....

2. What mental changes did you experience as you practised?

....

....

3. In what situations would you use PMR?

....

....

PMR RELAXATION PHASE 2:

TRAINING LOG

Use a scale from −10 to +10, where −10 = extremely tense and +10 = extremely relaxed, to show your level of relaxation before and after the phase 2 PMR relaxation exercise.

	Date of practice	Time of practice	Level before relaxing	Level after relaxing
e.g.	June 9	6 p.m.	−8	+9

PMR RELAXATION PHASE 3:

TRAINING LOG FOR RELAXING ON CUE

When you discover a cue word/phrase (or cues) that works for you, begin to use it with centring by thinking of your cue as you breathe. Remember that relaxation takes time to learn. The successful association of cue words with relaxation also takes time and practice.

Practise your trigger cues with centring for ten minutes daily.

Use the scale from −10 to +10, where −10 = extremely tense and +10 = extremely relaxed, to show your level of relaxation before the centring/cue word exercise and afterward.

	Date of practice	Venue of practice	Level before relaxing	Level after relaxing
e.g.	June 22	During training; after each set of physical drills	−7	+3

When your level of relaxation after the centring/cue exercise has consistently reached +7 or better, then move to phase 4 instructions.
This usually takes three to four practice sessions.

My cue word or phrase is ....

PMR RELAXATION PHASE 4:

RELAXING BEFORE AND DURING THE GAME/RACE/EVENT

By the time you are ready to move on to phase 4 you should be able to initiate PMR relaxation by centring and in places other than a quiet room without lying down or closing your eyes. You should also be able to achieve the relaxed state in much less than one minute.

Pick a situation in which you feel relaxation will be useful; for example, on the way to a game, prior to beginning your warm-up, or before critical moments in the game. Initially you may want to close your eyes for the brief centring exercise; later you may be able to centre with your eyes open but not focused on anything specific.

- First, centre with stomach breathing
- Next, visualise each muscle group loosening up (like light bulbs being turned off one by one)
- Next, use your triggering cues to relax further
- Next, check for any spots that are still tense
- Continue centred breathing to flow the relaxation to those spots.

Relaxing before the game/race/event

	Date of practice	Venue of practice	Level before relaxing	Level after relaxing
e.g.	July 10	Club game	−10	+7

PST METHOD: IMAGERY

Have you ever imagined yourself wearing your country's colours and performing alongside your heroes? After major televised sports events it is not uncommon to see young kids playing in backyards and neighbourhood parks reliving the exploits of their heroes. What are you and these kids doing with your imagination? You are using your imagination to recreate the atmosphere of the game and the performances of your idols. You are using imagery to make these things come alive. So what exactly is imagery, and how can you use it to help you with your performance in sport?

What is imagery?

Imagery is a PST method that involves the ability of an athlete/player to mentally recreate objects, persons, skills, experiences and situations, while not actually being physically involved in these situations. It can also be used to create new experiences in our minds.[1] Usually, a player/athlete will generate an image from a memory of an experience or situation, much like creating your own 'instant replay'. That image can then be manipulated to create a new one, or simply used as a recreation of a past event or experience. For example, a player could re-create the image of their performance in their last game, then manipulate that image to create a new image of themselves performing more successfully in the same situation. It must be remembered, however, that imagery is not 'daydreaming' about the great athlete/player you would like to be. It is a specific psych method that can be used to improve your

performance, but it requires consistent practice to be used effectively.

Imagery has at various times been called visualisation, mental practice, or mental rehearsal. However, imagery is more than just visualisation ('movies in the mind'). It can and should involve all the senses, so that a clear and vivid image will involve the player being able to see the image, hear it, smell it, taste it, and feel it. It is a mental and physical 'blueprint' of a sporting performance. In addition, the emotions associated with re-creating or creating a sporting experience in the mind are an important part of the imagery process.[1] For example, a player/athlete might imagine their thoughts and feelings during a particularly poor game in an attempt to understand how their level of anxiety may have hurt their performance.[1]

In summary, it must be remembered that imagery:

- involves creating or recreating experiences and events
- involves using all the senses
- Can take place without any external stimuli (you don't have to be holding a ball or bat, wearing your playing gear, or physically going through the movements of the image you are trying to create).

How does imagery work?

There is a great deal of evidence to show that the use of imagery can enhance performance in a variety of sports.[1] Many elite athletes have reported that imagery has helped them to perform at the highest levels. Perhaps the most well-known of these is golfer Tiger Woods.

> 'I like to visualise the ball flight – where I want the ball to start and finish – then commit to it …I use that same preshot routine today. It doesn't matter what your individual preshot routine is, just as long as you do it the same way every time and you don't hold up play… Great players operate 'in the moment'. In other words, they never get ahead of themselves. And they never, ever appear overwhelmed by any situation. One of the reasons I'm able to hit good shots is because I go through the same routine… If you notice, my preshot routine doesn't vary and it is uniquely mine. It helps me remain calm and in the present, prepared to execute a shot to the best of my ability.'
>
> Tiger Woods (US golfer).

In addition, there is also a great deal of scientific evidence in support of imagery's use as a means of enhancing performance in a variety of sports and skills, ranging from basketball,[2] cricket bowling,[3] golf putting[4] and rugby.[5]

In simple terms, imagery allows you to practise physical skills without actually having to perform them; it is thus a form of mental practice. Imagery also gives you a chance to deal with a problem or event in your mind before being physically confronted with it. In essence, imagery provides a mental blueprint of the performance, skill or situation.[1]

Key issues in learning imagery

There are a number of key considerations that need to be taken into account when using imagery to help you with your sport, and that can affect how well it is able to help you with your performance.[1]

1. Imagery perspective[1]

When you practise imagery, you will usually notice that your images are either external or internal. External imagery is when you see yourself playing as if you were watching yourself on video, whereas internal imagery occurs when you experience the image from inside your body, as if you were actually performing. It has been demonstrated that top-level athletes are more likely to use internal than external imagery, although many athletes/players are able to switch between imagery perspectives depending on what they are using their imagery for! If an athlete wants to conjure up the 'feeling' of performing a particular skill (e.g. tackling in soccer), then an internal image is more likely to accomplish this. On the other hand, a soccer player who wants to replay a particular team move might use an external perspective to get an image of how the move might have looked from the sideline or from above (to see the lines the players involved in the move might have run). It simply depends on what type of image you want to produce.

2. Mental practice and physical practice[1]

Imagery (i.e. mental practice) should never take the place of physical practice; it should be used in combination with physical practice, not as a replacement. It can be used as a substitute for physical practice if players/athletes are injured or unable to train for any other reason (e.g. illness, fatigue, or when practice fields are unavailable because of bad weather), but whenever possible, athletes/players should use physical practice as well as imagery.

3. Skill level of the athlete/player[1]

Although much of the research on the effect of imagery has indicated that more experienced athletes get the greatest performance gains from using this technique, both inexperienced and experienced players/athletes can improve their performances by using it, whether for rehearsing moves, building confidence, creating peak activation levels, or learning and practising specific sport skills.

4. Imagery ability of the athlete/player[1]

It makes sense that those players/athletes who are better able to develop clear, vivid and controllable images will gain the most benefit from using imagery to improve their performance, and the research has supported this notion. However, it is important to remember that, like any skill, the development of good imagery ability takes time, and thus you should be prepared to persist with your practice. A study conducted on Olympic athletes found that even these elite-level performers did not initially have good control over their ability to develop strong images, but through persistent daily practice they were able to develop their imagery ability to a high level.[6]

Uses of imagery[1]

Imagery can be used to improve both your physical and your psychological skills. As well as being useful for learning and practising specific sport skills and strategies, you can use imagery for setting and achieving goals, controlling your emotions and activation levels, coping with unexpected events or problems, developing self-awareness and self-confidence, and coping with pain and injury.

The advantages of using imagery to improve your sport skills are numerous. To begin with, imagery is a very efficient way to practise; it is not physically fatiguing, you can't injure (or re-injure) yourself (which is useful when practising contact skills in sports such as rugby; e.g. tackling, scrummaging and rucking/mauling), you can practise imagery anywhere and at any time, and it offers a change of pace that can help to break the monotony of physical practice.

Key issues in training imagery[1]

If you are not familiar with using imagery, it is important that you select the right setting when you begin to practise the technique. Distractions should be avoided, so you might want to practise in a quiet and relaxed setting. Just before going to sleep at night, or just after waking up in the morning, are often good times. Start by using the exercises included here, then create your own imagery 'script' based on the instructions in this section. You may even want to record the script onto an audiotape and use your walkman. Remember to stay relaxed but alert when learning imagery. Later on you will be able to use the technique during practices and at some stages during games, but in the beginning you should practise in a relaxed state. You also need to be realistic and patient, and persist with your imagery practice. Imagery works but it takes time, effort and practice.

When developing your imagery skills, you should focus on three basic types of exercise. First, you should work on developing clear and vivid images in order to strengthen your ability to create the sights, sounds, smells, tastes and feelings of playing and practising your sport. Second, you should learn how to control your images, so that you are able to imagine yourself performing the way you want to. Third, you should improve your ability to become more self-aware when practising imagery. Awareness of your thoughts and feelings during good and poor performances is important to incorporate into your imagery in order to make your images as close as possible to the real experience of playing.[1]

Basic imagery practice exercises

(The following exercises are adapted from Roberts et al., 1986, with permission.[7])

1. Focus on the ball

- Open your eyes and focus on every detail of this ball; look at the shape and colour (pause).
- Close your eyes and imagine you are still looking at the ball – see all of the detail, the brand name, stitching, and the colours (pause).
- Now open your eyes and compare your image with the real ball (pause).
- Close your eyes again and see the ball with its colour and detail (pause).

2. Developing clear, vivid images

- Now imagine your house – you are standing in the front yard looking at your house – notice the colour and the detail (pause).
- Walk to the front door – notice how the house seems to grow larger as you get closer (pause).
- Open the door and walk into your house – and walk to the doorway of your room (pause).
- See the colours of the walls, the furniture, the curtains, the floor (pause).
- Notice all of the details as you look around your room (pause).
- Now turn around and walk back to the front door of your house (pause).
- Open the door and walk out into the yard – turn around and look back at your house (pause).

3. Controlling your images

- Make your house get larger – make it grow bigger in size (pause).
- Now make your house get smaller and shrink back to its normal size (pause).
- Make your house shrink smaller until it is half its regular size (pause).
- Now make your house get bigger – back to its normal size (pause).

4. Using all the senses in your images

- Now imagine a beautiful warm summer day and that you are standing on an ocean beach.

You feel the warm, gritty sand between your toes (pause).

- Lie down on the beach on a towel and feel the warm, soft towel you are lying on and the penetrating warmth of the sun as you lie quietly (pause).
- Hear the ocean waves as they break on the shore, and feel a slight cool breeze blow over you as you lie on the sand – you feel warm and relaxed (pause).
- Imagine the blue sky with a few white clouds skidding slowly across the sky (pause).
- You feel warm and relaxed (pause).
- Stand up and walk down to the water, wading in to knee depth – feel the cool, wet water on your legs. Cup your hands and scoop up some water – taste the saltwater and spit it out; focus on the bitter, salty taste (pause).
- Walk back up the beach and lie down on your towel again. Feel the penetrating warmth of the sun. You feel light-headed, and sleepy (pause).
- Now open your eyes and sit up, slowly.

Advanced imagery practice exercises

Vividness exercises[1]

(These examples are for the team sport of soccer; adapt them to your sport as appropriate.)

1. Imagine you are in the changing room before a game, and that your coach is giving the team talk. Visualise the coach as clearly as possible. What is he/she wearing? What type of build is he/she? What mannerisms, facial expressions, distinguishing features does he/she have? Imagine as many details of the person as possible. Imagine that the coach is walking around the changing room as he/she speaks, and that s/he has stopped in front of you and is talking to you directly. How do you feel

about your coach and what he/she is saying? What emotions do you feel towards him/her – friendship, respect, anger, admiration? Try to imagine this scene from an internal perspective – from inside your own body.[1]

2. Think of the ground or venue on which you have played most of your sport, or the one that you are most familiar with. Imagine you are standing in the middle of that ground, and that there is nobody else there. Notice how quiet and empty it is. Look around you and pick out as many details of the ground as possible. Does it have a particular smell about it? What can you see as you look around? Now imagine that you are at the same ground, but this time you are in the changing room getting ready for a game. It is 15 minutes before start time. Try to imagine the scene as if you were inside your own body. Your teammates are all around you getting themselves prepared. Hear the clicking of their shoes on the floor as they jump around in nervous anticipation. Listen to the voices of those who are in the changing room, as well as the noise of the crowd outside waiting for the event to get underway. Try to imagine the smell of the Deep Heat and Vaseline that the players are rubbing into their muscles as they warm up, and listen to the physio tearing off bits of tape to strap up the various joints and muscles of the athletes. Recreate the feeling of excitement and nervous anticipation as the time ticks down to start time. How do you feel?[1]

3. Think about the game ball, and imagine you are sitting in the changing room turning it over in your hands before going out onto the field. Examine every part of it – the texture, the colour, the smell of the ball, the writing on it, the feel of it in your hands.[1] Now imagine that you have the ball at your feet and you are dribbling towards the opposition goal. You have about 15 metres to go before you can take a shot and there is only one player to beat. See yourself from behind your own eyes, and then switch to watching yourself as if you were on television. Switch back to being inside yourself performing, and continue towards the opposition goal. What sounds can you hear? Is anyone close in support calling for the ball? Can you hear the crowd roar? Are you dribbling the ball with your left or right foot? How does it feel against your foot? Put the sights and sounds together and imagine how it feels to be that close to the goal with only one person to beat.[1]

4. Pick a fundamental or simple soccer skill, such as trapping and passing the ball, leaping to head a ball, running upfield with the ball at your feet, or making a side-on tackle.[1] Imagine yourself performing that skill over and over again in your mind, from an internal perspective. Focus on how it feels to perform that skill. How do your muscles feel as they contract? What does it feel like when contact is made with the ground, the ball, or with another player? Make sure you imagine yourself performing this skill perfectly, and concentrate on the feeling of the movement. Now combine all these sounds, sights and feeling, and try to put together the total experience of performing the skill. Don't concentrate too hard on one sense, just try to recreate the whole experience as clearly and as vividly as possible.[1]

Controllability exercises[1]

1. Imagine that your coach is walking around the changing room as your team is getting ready for a big game. Focus specifically on the coach's face and pay particular attention to his/her features. Now watch the coach walk around the room talking to the players. Imagine that he or she stops and talks to various players individually. Keep watching as s/he walks up and begins speaking to you.

Imagine the conversation you might have with your coach at that time.

2. Choose a particular skill, move or technique that you have had trouble performing. Imagine you are practising that skill over and over, and that you are seeing this from inside your own body (internal perspective).[1] If you make a mistake, stop the image immediately and start again. Try to perform the skill successfully every time. You might also want to watch yourself performing the skill from an external perspective, as if you were watching yourself on video, to see if you can pick up what you are doing wrong when you make a mistake. If you can identify where the error occurs, try to imagine yourself performing successfully, then revert back to an internal perspective and imagine what it feels like to perform this skill well. Practise that image over and over again.[1]

Self-awareness exercises[1]

1. Try to remember one of your best-ever games. It doesn't have to be a game your team won, but one in which you played particularly well. Using all your senses, try to recreate that experience.[1] What were you feeling while you were playing that game? Were you confident, excited, nervous, relaxed, elated? Can you remember what your body felt like as you performed that day? What could you hear, see, smell, taste? Try to identify what it was that made you perform so well that day. If you manage to work this out, try to figure out why those factors were present during that game. What did you do that might have caused those things to occur? Think back – how did you prepare for that game? What thoughts and feelings did you have prior to going out onto the field? What specific things did you do leading up to the game, during the warm-up, or during the game that might have caused you to perform so well?

Sometimes imagery is helpful in gaining an insight into why a peak performance might have occurred. Often players will over-analyse a poor performance and try to figure out what went wrong, but get too caught up in the excitement and celebration of a peak performance to bother trying to figure out what went right! If you want a peak performance to occur again, then using imagery to help you try to figure out 'what went right' is often a good idea (see also peak performance profile, pages 44–5).

Now go through this same exercise, but this time imagine a particularly poor performance on your part.[1] Again, it doesn't matter whether your team won or lost, but it should be a game in which you performed badly. Try to stay relaxed as you remember this performance, but recall how you reacted to certain things that might have happened during the game (e.g. poor referee's decisions, making simple errors, the coach's comments before the game and at half-time, opponents' behaviour, the feeling before the game, etc.). Think back – how might your thoughts and feelings have interfered with your performance that day? Run the image of the game through your head and try to find some answers to these questions.

2. Think back to a situation in which you were extremely anxious.[1] It might have been before or during a game or practice, or it might have been a team meeting before a game or practice. Recall what you were thinking and feeling at that time. Pay particular attention to those feelings of anxiety. What caused them, and how did you react to that feeling? Were your muscles tense, did you sweat, were your hands clammy, did you fidget, did you feel like you had to go to the toilet all the time? Recreate that situation as clearly and as vividly as you can. Conjure up those thoughts and feelings

again, as if you were there right now! Now try to release all of that anxiety and let your body relax.[1] Imagine that all the tension is being drained away by being pulled into your lungs and exhaled from your body. With each breath out you get rid of more and more of that anxiety and tension. Keep going until you feel completely relaxed. Now repeat the exercise using a situation in which you recall being extremely angry.

3. Think back to a situation during a game when things were going well until you made a bad mistake.[1] There might be more than one occasion when this happened, so try to recall several of these times. Recreate the situations in your mind and try to identify what it was that caused this mistake (e.g. a distraction, focusing on the wrong cue, an opponent's remark). Once you have identified the things that might have caused this poor performance, go over the situation again in your mind. Try to figure out a strategy to deal with these factors, and then implement that strategy when you replay the image of that situation. See and feel yourself using the strategy to prevent the negative factors interfering with your performance, and imagine yourself performing well in that situation. Imagine also how it feels to be able to control these negative factors and to perform well. Using imagery in this way can also be incorporated into a CARS plan (see Chapter 15).

Stages in sports imagery development

Begin with guided practice

Use an instructor (e.g. a sportpsych consultant, coach or teammate) to guide the imagery session. Use the imagery exercises outlined in this chapter. Have the person take you through these exercises or record them onto your walkman. Remember to develop sensory awareness, and to focus on all the senses, not just the visual. Develop vivid and clear images – hear the crowd, smell the linament, feel the ground, feel the movement, feel the contact.

Practise self-directed imagery

Develop your own imagery 'script', record it onto an audiotape and use a walkman to practise it. Base the script on the imagery exercises in this chapter, but develop a script that is relevant to your position in the team. Use the 'Imagery Training Log' on page 133 to record your imagery practice and to evaluate your improvement. Aim to be able to develop clear, vivid and controllable images. Eventually you should progress to practising without the use of the tape and walkman. Practise controlling your images – start with simple skills and move to more complex ones, making sure you can imagine yourself correctly executing these skills. Controlling your images is very important, as uncontrolled imagery (e.g. 'seeing' yourself fail or make errors) can increase anxiety and stress.

Use imagery during training or practice

Once you have been able to develop clear, vivid and controllable images in a quiet and relaxed setting, progress to using imagery during training or practices. Use the 'Imagery Training Log' on page 134 to record this level of imagery practice.

Begin using imagery before and during competition

Now that you have become more skilled at using imagery, you should start to include it in your pre-event mental preparation, for developing the right frame of mind to play, or for rehearsing specific skills/moves such as a pre-goalkick routine in rugby, a putting routine in golf, a penalty flick in hockey, an attacking move formation in netball, running good 'lines' in attack and defence in soccer and as a defensive pattern option (use the Imagery Training Log on page 134).

Imagery guidelines

- When learning imagery, you should use short practice sessions (about five minutes). Consistency and quality are more important than length of practice.
- Imagine good performances and positive outcomes.
- Use all your senses to create the image.
- Follow images of incorrect performance with images of correct performance.
- Use triggers to strengthen the vividness of imagery (e.g. cue words/phrases, the colour of your playing shirt/jersey, your shoes/boots, the smell of linament).
- Practise, practise, practise…

When to use imagery[1]

Although imagery can be used at almost any time and in a variety of situations, there seem to be some specific times when it is most useful.[1]

1. Before and after practice

Either before you get to practice, or in the changing room before you go out to start your warm-up, it can be useful to go over the drills, techniques and moves that you are likely to be rehearsing at practice. After practice, it is also useful to review the session using imagery.

2. Before and after games/races/events

Before a game or event, and as part of your mental preparation for it, you should create a clear and vivid image of exactly what you want to achieve and how you want to play during the competition. After the event you should replay the things that you did well, as well as trying to analyse why certain things might not have gone as well as you would have liked.

3. During breaks in competition

Every time the umpire's or referee's whistle blows there is time for you to quickly create a clear and vivid image of what you should do at the next passage of play/competition. If the break in play is long enough, you might even have time to review the last passage of play in your mind, and analyse what has just happened, before creating an image of your role in the next part of the game/race.

4. During personal time

Players/athletes can practise their imagery at home, at work, or at any other time during the day when the opportunity presents itself. Remember, imagery practice does not have to be very long; five minutes may be all that is required!

5. When recovering from injury

Imagery can be useful for rehearsing skills that players are physically unable to do while they are injured (see also Chapter 17). This imagery training can help them to return more quickly to the level at which they were able to perform prior to their injury. Developing powerful positive images of the healing process (e.g. bones and muscles knitting together, damaged tissue becoming healthy) has also been shown to aid the recovery process.[8]

Summary

Imagery can be a very valuable tool for every sportsperson. It can improve your competition performance by not only helping you to learn and practise skills, but also by improving your concentration and self-confidence, and by helping you to maintain an optimal level of activation. Remember, imagery should never be used as a substitute for physical practice, but can be used in conjunction with it whenever possible. Like physical skills, imagery requires practice to be effective. When learning imagery, it is best to practise in a quiet setting and to be as relaxed as possible. However, after a time you should begin to use imagery in practice situations and eventually be able to use it during events. Make sure you develop clear, vivid and controllable images using all of your senses, and incorporate the appropriate emotional responses into those images.

IMAGERY TRAINING LOG

Practise your imagery script regularly and record your imagery 'ability' using the following rating scales. Rate your imagery vividness and your imagery control.

Practise on five consecutive days with the same imagery script. Then change the script to a more difficult one. Each practice session should only last about ten minutes. Before training or before bedtime is a popular time to do this. Practise in a quiet, warm environment where you will not be disturbed.

Use a scale from 1 to 5, where 1 = low vividness/control and 5 = high vividness/control, to show your level of imagery.

	Date of practice	Time of practice	Vividness level	Control level
e.g.	May 30	6 p.m.	3	2

1. What vividness changes did you experience as you practised?

....

....

2. What control changes did you experience as you practised?

....

....

IMAGERY TRAINING LOG

Practise your more difficult imagery 'script' for ten minutes daily.

Use the scale from 1 to 5, where 1 = low vividness/control and 5 = high vividness/control, to show your level of imagery.

	Date of practice	Time of practice	Vividness level	Control level
e.g.	June 9	6 p.m.	4	4

My personal imagery script is:

....

....

....

....

....

....

....

....

....

IMAGERY TRAINING LOG:

IMAGERY ON CUE

When you discover an imagery cue word/phrase (or cues) that works for you, begin to use it with imagery by thinking of your cue as you image. Remember that imagery takes time to learn. The successful association of cue words with imagery also takes time and practice.

Practise your trigger cues with imagery for ten minutes daily.

Use the scale from 1 to 5, where 1 = low vividness/control and 5 = high vividness/control, to show your level of imagery.

	Date of practice	Venue of practice	Level before relaxing	Level after relaxing
e.g.	June 22	In the clubrooms; after training	5	4

When your level after cue-imagery has consistently reached 4 or better for both vividness and control, then move to using imagery before/during a game/race/event.

My imagery cue word or phrase is ....

PST METHOD: SELF-TALK

13

'The demons are just the little voice in your head telling you that you'll get out, telling you that you're no good. It has been one of the biggest influences on my career – the head chatter.'

Mark Richardson (NZ cricketer; opening batsman)

What is self-talk?

Self-talk may be described as conscious thinking, as an inner conversation, or as intentional thinking.[1]

Self-talk/thoughts → feelings → behaviour

Your level and type of self-talk is clearly linked to your motivation and self-confidence.[1] Confident athletes/players think they can, and they do! They imagine themselves being successful, they focus on positive things, on successfully mastering a task rather than worrying about performing poorly. Self-talk is also a useful method for developing the performance PST skill of concentration.

On the other hand, athletes/players with low self-confidence think they can't and invariably they don't. The effect of positive versus negative self-talk will be obvious to you if you complete the following exercise.

Self-test: positive versus negative self-talk

Have a friend read the following instructions to you.

'Close your eyes. I am going to ask you to NOT think about some things, so whatever you do DO NOT think about them. First, DON'T think about an orange. Second, DON'T think about a white soccer/rugby/cricket/netball. Finally, DON'T think about a nice cold glass of your favourite drink on a scorching hot summer's day.'

Most people listen to the instructions, tell themselves NOT to see the object mentioned (i.e. orange, ball, glass), but end up seeing or imagining the object anyway! Negative self-talk can become a self-fulfilling prophecy. Imagine the consequences of negative self-talk if you give yourself instructions like: 'Don't panic!' 'Don't worry about the weather or ground conditions,' and 'Don't worry about your hamstring injury.' Too often athletes/players and coaches use the word 'worry' incorrectly; such as, 'All I have to worry about is playing to our game/race plan.' The correct word to use would be something like think or focus. Using words like 'worry' indicates to the athlete/player that there is indeed something to worry about!

Intentional thinking is the basis of controlled self-talk. You can learn to replace negative, self-defeating thoughts with positive ones; that is, thoughts that build confidence and expectations of success. Positive thoughts and expectations can become self-fulfilling prophecies; that is, if you think positive, you will likely play in a positive manner.[1]

Self-talk does not mean having a long conversation with yourself during a game; self-talk words and phrases need to be brief and precise, short and sharp. Self-talk is like having your own CD player in your head; you make your own 'CDs' and then play them when you need them! Self-talk is designed to enable you to create and maintain your Ideal Performance State; good self-talk helps you switch on your automatic pilot.

Uses of self-talk[1]

Skill learning

Self-instructional talk or 'cue words' are very useful in learning and practising physical skills. For example, 'Head down, follow through,' (e.g. for a golf swing, or rugby goal-kicking) or 'Hit the dartboard,' (lineout-throwing in rugby). Keep it brief, but precise, and work towards automatic execution of the skill(s). Automatic use of self-talk is necessary for you to play in the Ideal Performance State.

Attention control

Use a specific set of self-talk cues to 'hold' the appropriate focus on the task at hand (i.e. in the present tense). For example, 'Here and now!' 'Watch the ball into your hands,' 'Run good lines,' 'Watch the zone defence.'

Creating 'mood'

Use words or phrases with a clear, specific, emotional message. For example, 'Go' or 'Explode' (e.g. sprinting out of the blocks for a 100-metre runner), 'Smooth', 'Easy', 'Oily' or 'Rhythm' (e.g. golf swing).

Controlling effort

Use phrases to maintain energy and persistence – for the direction of effort and sustaining that effort. For example, 'Go for it', 'Push it', 'Pick it up', 'Guts it out', 'Hold onto it'.

Coping with distractions

Self-talk phrases can be very helpful when you need to hold your concentration in the face of an external distraction (e.g. an opponent) or an internal distraction (e.g. negative thoughts about failure or mistakes). See the section on 'Parking' on page 138.

Mental preparation

Use cue words or phrases to assist with mental preparation pre-game, during the game, or when refocusing after the game (see Chapter 14, 'Mental preparation').

Affirmations for building self-confidence

'Affirmations' are self-statements that reflect positive attitudes or thoughts about yourself. You are only able to do what you 'think' you can do, or in other words: 'To be an achiever, you have to be a believer!' Affirmations help you believe in yourself and develop self-confidence. For example, 'I'm the greatest!' (Muhammed Ali), 'I play well under pressure.'

Identifying self-talk

The first step in gaining control of self-talk is to become aware of what you say to yourself. Surprisingly, most athletes/players are not aware of their thoughts and their impact on performance. It is especially important to identify and eliminate negative and self-defeating thoughts. For example, 'I always struggle against this opponent,' or 'I never play well in the rain.'

How do you identify self-talk?

Retrospection

By recalling past situations of good and bad performances, and trying to recreate your thoughts and feelings (e.g. use the 'Self-talk Log' on page 140; see also peak performance profile on pages 44-5).

Imagery

By 'reliving' past performances through imagery; record the recalled thoughts, phrases and self-talk from good and bad performances.

Self-talk log

Keep a daily diary or self-talk log of thoughts used during games and practice (over a period of weeks). For example, ask yourself: 'When do I have negative thoughts?' 'What seems to cause negative thoughts?' 'When and why do I have self-doubts?' Record the frequency and content of both positive and negative thoughts. See the Self-talk Log worksheet on page 140.

Techniques for controlling self-talk[1]

Once 'awareness' of negative thoughts and feelings is heightened, you need to learn techniques to deal with the negative thoughts, and to focus on positive thoughts.

Key word or phrase list

Develop a list of key words and phrases that have specific purposes (e.g. self-instruction, creating mood, holding attention, affirmation/confidence statements). See the Self-talk List worksheet on page 141, and the sample Self-talk List for a rugby first-five on page 142.

'Parking' (thought stopping)[2]

Practise stopping negative thought patterns by using silent instructions or 'triggers'. For example,

'Stop!' 'Park it!' or 'Bin it.' Some athletes/players use imagery to mentally write the negative thought on a piece of paper then throw it in the rubbish bin (i.e., 'bin it') or set fire to it! Others mentally write the thought on a whiteboard then wipe it clean. Some players slap their leg or their equipment to mentally 'park' the negative thoughts somewhere else so they can refocus their concentration on the task at hand. 'Parking' is just like parking a car; when you don't need your car you park it in a carpark; so when you don't need or want a negative thought you can 'park' it somewhere and come back for it after the game/race![2] As mentioned earlier, self-talk phrases can be very helpful when you need to hold your concentration in the face of an external distraction (e.g. opponents verbally taunting you as you get ready to take a shot at goal in netball/basketball) or an internal distraction (e.g. negative thoughts about a mistake you made when you took a difficult shot at goal earlier in the game). You might want to get your coach to initiate 'parking' and thought stopping during training, for example by asking, 'Where is your head – past, present, or future?' or stating 'Here and now!' Parking can also be very useful as part of a CARS plan (see Chapter 15).

> 'I've developed a little habit where, when I say something negative to myself – and every batter does it – I pretend it's a little man on my shoulder and so I brush him off. There are times when people must think 'this guy's a lunatic' because I'm standing out in the middle flicking my shoulder every second ball.'
>
> Mark Richardson (NZ cricketer; opening batsman)

Changing negative thoughts to positive thoughts[1]

You need to make a list of typical negative and self-defeating thoughts (use your completed self-talk log), then design a substitute positive thought for each negative thought, as in the examples below. Couple this process with relaxation and centring.

Negative thoughts changed to positive/coping thoughts:

> 'I don't want to fail; I don't want the responsibility for this shot (netball/ basketball).'
> '… Relax… all you can do is give your best effort; accept the responsibility; enjoy the challenge!'
>
> 'I can't believe it's raining, I never play well in the rain.'
> '… Relax… no one likes playing in the rain, but it's the same for them as it is for me; I can handle it better!'
>
> 'This umpire is useless, she's picking on us!'
> '… Relax… the umpiring/refereeing is not in my control; focus on my job and playing well, then the standard of officiating won't matter.'

Reframing irrational thinking[1]

Following are a number of common irrational thought patterns: perfection is essential; worth = achievement ('Unless we win I'm not a good person'); fallacy of the 'fair deal' (the umpire/ref isn't being fair to us); polarised thinking (either/or thoughts – absolute terms); catastrophising ('What if …'); personalisation ('MY fault!'); blaming ('It was the ref/weather/conditions'); and one-trial generalisations ('I missed that shot at goal, now I'm going to miss for the whole game!'). You need to practise recognising these thoughts as irrational and reframing them into rational, positive thoughts (see also Chapter 15, 'CARS plan').

Personal affirmation statements[1]

You need to construct a 'success list' of your strengths, skills, and qualities. Create positive action-oriented self-statements; for example, 'I have trained hard, I deserve to succeed,' 'I play well under pressure,' 'I am an excellent defender,' 'I always make my short putts.' It can be useful to print these on index cards and carry them in your gear bag or stick them to your mirror as consistent visual reminders of your affirmations.

Coping and mastery self-talk tapes[1]

Create an audio tape or CD with affirmation statements, cue words, and refocusing or coping statements. Repeated listening to positive self-talk tapes/CDs helps programme your mind for positive thoughts during training and performance.

Summary: self-talk

Your self-talk is linked to your concentration, self-confidence, and stress. Self-talk is not an in-depth conversation with yourself or a long list of self-instructions. Effective self-talk is short and precise; that is, the minimal amount of thought required to correctly complete a skill or affirm confidence in yourself. Self-talk = inner conversation, self-statements, intentional thinking.

**Self-talk/thoughts →
feelings →
behaviour**

'Confident players "think" they can, and they do!'

> The following examples may help you with the self-talk list on page 141.
>
> **Focus words/phrases**
> e.g.
> 'Pass in front at chest height.'
>
> 'Head down, follow through.'
>
> 'Hit the dartboard' (lineout throw in rugby).
>
> **Mood words/phrases**
> e.g.
> 'Calm and relaxed,'
>
> 'Strong & aggressive,'
>
> 'Feelin' fine.'
>
> **Positive self-statement**
> e.g.
> 'I have trained well, I deserve to play well.'
>
> 'I'm ready.'

SELF-TALK LOG

Positive self-talk	Negative self-talk

SELF-TALK LIST

Statements I will use	When?	Purpose?
Focus words/phrases		
Mood words/phrases		
Positive self-statement		

SELF-TALK LIST

Statements I will use	When?	Purpose?
Focus words/phrases		
'Pass in – chest height.'	Before a miss-2 pass; especially to my right.	To help me avoid having negative thoughts: I sometimes doubt my ability on these 'miss' passes.
'I.C.E.' (Intensity, Concentration, Effort)	Concentrate and focus my attention when I'm setting up at 1st phase ball.	To help with my 'mental prep' during the phases of the game.
'Smooth follow through.'	Technique reminder for goalkicking.	I have to resist the tendency to 'self-coach' myself during my goalkicking – I need simple self-talk to help me to 'trust' my technique.
Mood words/phrases		
'Calm and relaxed' or 'Smooth & easy.'	At the start of my goalkicking routine.	To set the 'pace' and 'mood' for each and every goalkick.
'Boots on, switch on.'	15 mins before kick-off.	To help kickstart my 'kickoff countdown' prep plan.
'Chop down the tree.'	Facing a big 2nd five on a 1-out defence.	To help me focus on good tackling technique against the 'big boys'.
Positive self-statement		
'I've worked bloody hard, I deserve to play well.'	During my pre-game mental prep.	To remind myself of one of my sources of self-confidence – all my training!
'I'm ripped and ready.'	During the 'kick-off countdown' part of mental prep.	To 'gee myself up' for physical contact (I'm just a wee guy!).
'Stay in the PRESENT!' or 'Start your CARS.'	After a mistake or a loss of concentration.	To cope with pressure and keep my concentration.
'P.R.I.D.E.' (Personal Responsibility in Delivering Excellence)	'Kick-off countdown' part of mental prep; & when I need to use my CARS plan.	To fizz on 'my' contribution to the team; play with pride and guts.

PST METHOD: MENTAL PREPARATION

14

What is mental preparation?

Mental preparation is a useful method for developing the PST skills of optimal physical activation, optimal mental activation and optimal attention (see Chapter 8). Quality mental preparation has been identified as a key element of sporting success.[1]

Mental preparation is used to organise a consistent and systematic 'psych-up' period before a game or race – helping you to 'psych up' without becoming 'psyched out' (i.e. over-activated). Its purpose is to help you consistently reach your Ideal Performance State of optimal activation and mental readiness.[2]

Mental preparation strategies

The strategies used in mental preparation include mental plans, self-talk, centring/relaxation, and imagery. We have already discussed the basics of the latter methods, so now let's look at mental plans.

Mental plans

Mental preparation needs to be individually designed to suit your needs and your optimal level of activation. There is no one perfect mental preparation plan; it depends on your needs and preferences, and the particular situation in which you are competing.

Performance plans

There are three types of performance plan to help you achieve optimal mental preparation.[3]

These are pre-performance plans, performance focus plans, and coping plans (distraction control). There are planning sheets for developing these at the end of this chapter, which you can photocopy and use to write out your ideas and plans.

To develop these plans you need to ask yourself the following questions. What kind of preparation do I like – how much, when and why? What do I like and dislike about events leading up to competition day, 24 hours before competition, and during the competition itself? Do I already have a routine for competition day – how, when and where do I warm up? Do I have a clearly defined competition strategy (e.g. a game plan of tactics) going into each competition? What, if anything, makes me anxious and uptight before competition? How disciplined am I about my mental preparation and my concentration focus for each competitive performance?

You may be quite happy with your current mental preparation plans. If this is the case, then follow the old saying: 'If it ain't broke, don't try to fix it!' However, I encourage you to use the mental plan sheets at the end of the Chapter to write down your current plans – that way, if you have any problems with your mental prep in the future you will have a record of what has worked for you in the past.

You can also compare your mental prep with the written plan to check for any subtle changes that might have crept into your pre-performance and performance routines. Athletes often get a little lazy about following their pre-performance and performance plans, and the small changes they make inadvertently can have major effects on their mental preparation and performance.

Once you have developed mental plans that you are happy with, be prepared to adjust and modify them as your sporting career progresses. Like many things, mental plans can become a bit boring unless you keep looking for ways to keep them fresh and meaningful. Be wary of the danger of hanging onto a good mental plan that has worked well for you, but that has lost some of its meaning – if you go through the motions during your mental preparation you will likely perform the same way!

You should also be prepared to tinker with your mental plans for quite some time. Like any new skill, it takes time to get it just right. Write out your best guess, then try it out, make changes, try it again, and modify it some more until you are happy that you have developed a set of mental plans that will allow you to get into your Ideal Performance State regularly.

Finally, be wary of letting your mental plan(s) become a superstition. If you get too attached to a detailed plan you are guaranteeing yourself some stress in the future – one day your 'superstition' will be upset by some hassle (e.g. you lose your walkman, the batteries go dead). When that day comes, your mental plan becomes a source of stress rather than a way to create a calm, focused period of mental preparation. So, while it is important to have a structured mental plan, be careful not to overdo it and create superstition. This is where coping plans are vital!

Pre-performance plan

Plan, organise and structure your thoughts, actions and behaviour on the day of competition. That is, develop a mental warm-up to go with your physical warm-up. This is often referred to as 'segmenting', since you organise your mental warm-up in distinct 'segments' that give your mental prep a sound structure, like a checklist to go through before competition. See the pre-performance planning sheet on page 146; I have

also included an example of a pre-performance plan for rugby (page 147).

You should also have a short pre-performance plan (two to three minutes long) for use in situations where you don't have as much time as usual for your mental preparation; this should be linked with your coping plan. Situations where having a short plan is vital include: (i) after half-time; (ii) after a time-out; (iii) after an extended injury break, and (iv) when you have go on 'off the bench' as a substitute, reserve, or injury replacement. You must have a plan to help you psych-up without being psyched-out or over-activated in these time-pressured situations (see also Chapter 15, 'CARS plan').

> 'More than anything my pre-ball routine has helped me most in the first half hour of an innings. In between balls I assess how I'm feeling. I've got strategies to use if I'm overkeyed or underkeyed. If I'm overkeyed, I'll slow myself down, slow down my breathing; then when the bowler's at the top of his mark I get back in my stance and say the cue words that are critical for the conditions – "play it straight, get forward", or "get in behind it". Then when the bowler gets into his delivery stride I say "now" – my cue to look for the seams on the ball.'
>
> Mark Richardson (NZ cricketer; opening batsman)

Performance focus plan

Plan and organise how you want to think, feel and focus during the event or game. If your sport allows such a structure, it often helps to do some segmenting so that you have a structure to organise your thoughts during performance. For example, you might segment your game or race into the first few minutes, first 100 metres, first half, first innings, etc. See the performance focus planning sheet on page 148.

Coping plan (distraction control)

Plan and organise methods, strategies and thoughts that will help you deal with hassles and distractions before, during and after the event or game. For example, you might choose to include self-talk, imagery, relaxation or centring as part of a coping plan. Thought-stopping procedures like 'Park it' and 'Bin it' can be very useful as part of your coping plan. See the coping plan sheet on page 149.

> 'On the bus to the stadium I will try to switch off, just watch the world go by and save my intensity for when it is needed. This doesn't get any easier, but you can cope. This doesn't get any easier; my own expectations are higher, other people's are higher. I just know what a disappointment it would be to under-perform, to fail yourself.'
>
> Jonny Wilkinson (England rugby player) describing his relentless pursuit of perfection.

Summary: mental preparation

Mental preparation is vital to the development of the PST skills of optimal physical activation, optimal mental activation and optimal attention. Mental preparation strategies are needed to organise a consistent and systematic 'psych-up' period that does not cause you to become 'psyched-out' (i.e. over-activated).

Mental plans are used to help you reach the Ideal Performance State of optimal activation and mental readiness. They need to be individually designed to suit your needs and the situation in which you are competing. You need to develop a pre-performance plan, a performance focus plan and a coping plan (distraction control) in order to be fully mentally prepared.

PRE-PERFORMANCE PLAN

Write out your pre-game or pre-race plan in the sequence in which you want it to occur at the performance/competition venue. List your physical warm-up in note form, and develop a mental warm-up to go with it. List stretches, drills, activities, self-talk, self-suggestions, imagery, centring, etc. in the sequence in which you intend to do them.

'General' warm-up: physical and mental (approx. 45–60 mins)		'Start' preparation: physical and mental (approx. 5–10 mins)	
Physical	Mental	Physical	Mental

PRE-PERFORMANCE PLAN

Write out your pre-game or pre-race plan in the sequence in which you want it to occur at the performance/competition venue. List your physical warm-up in note form, and develop a mental warm-up to go with it. List stretches, drills, activities, self-talk, self-suggestions, imagery, centring, etc. in the sequence in which you intend to do them.

'General' warm-up: physical and mental (approx. 45–60 mins)		'Start' preparation: physical and mental (approx. 5–10 mins)	
Physical	*Mental*	*Physical*	*Mental*
FRIDAY NIGHT: Video or movies.	Keep my mind off the game: 'Don't play the game on Friday night.'	30 min: Grids with team, – upper body stretches.	Psyching-up: focus on 'my' goals & 'my' standards.
SATURDAY MORNING: Read the paper. Go for a walk. Pre-game meal. Check gear, mouthguard.	Think over my 'goals for today'; focus on 'standards'.	KICK-OFF COUNTDOWN 15 min: 2nd pee stop, – recheck gear & mouthguard, – put boots on: 'Boots on, switch on.'	Think ➤ MUST DOMINATE my opponent, be physical, but be smart – stay focused on accurate technique; do MY jobs 100% effort every time.
AT THE GROUND: 60 min: Team talk – coach/captain.	Take it in, but keep psych-up under control. Build psych-up toward kick-off.	12 min: Jogging on spot & stretches, – stay warm & loose.	Use imagery & self-talk to replay key 'jobs' to be done: back-row moves, line-outs, 2nd phase.
50 min: Change gear – strapping, – rub down, (1st pee stop).	Think a/b opposition – their weaknesses & strengths, – our game plan against them: back-row moves, 'runners', etc.		Use imagery to 'psych-up' if needed; OR use centring to 'calm-down' if needed. Avoid talking to others until on the field: 'Stay inside my bubble.'
40 min: Stretching – hamstrings, – neck & shoulders at same time. – calves, – groin.	'Scrum thinking' – back-row moves, – running lines from scrum in attack. 'Line-out thinking' – jump selection, – support of '5' jumper, – line-out defence.	5 min: Last pee stop. 4 min: 'Stay warm & loose,' – stretches/jog. 2 min: Take warm-up gear off.	Enjoy the adrenaline! Briefly review general game plan. After the toss; focus SOLELY on my first job at kick-off.
35 min: Jogging on spot for 3–5 mins.	Support play & 'lines' – accurate lines, – speed & urgency, – back-line 'targets'.		'Keep the fizz.' 'Be focused & disciplined.'

PERFORMANCE FOCUS PLAN

Write out your segmented plan of tactics, strategies, thoughts, cues, self-talk, imagery, centring, activities, etc. as you intend to use them during the performance or competition.

First five minutes/period/innings:

Last five minutes of the half/period:

First five minutes of the second half/period/innings:

Focus points or critical moments, such as before set plays, actions:
(e.g. free throw, scrum, serve, pitch)

COPING PLAN

Write out the coping plans you intend to use if you are faced with distractions before and during your performance. Identify possible things that could go wrong, then develop possible solutions to help you deal with them – to help you cope and refocus. List stretches, drills, activities, self-talk, thought-stopping, self-suggestions, imagery, relaxation, centring, etc. in the sequence in which you intend to do them to help you cope.

Below are some possible sources of problems/distractions –
use these as a basis for developing your coping plan(s).

Pre-performance distraction:

Change in start time (earlier or later):

Non-ideal ground, court, weather conditions:

Not psyched-up enough:

(Continued)

Being over-psyched (i.e. over-activated):

Early mistake or error in your game or race:

Loss of ideal focus in game or race:

Repeated mistakes or errors during the game or race:

Poor performance (e.g. first half/heat):

Poor overall performance (i.e. need to cope and refocus for next game or race):

PRE-SHOT ROUTINE: GOLF WORKSHEET

Name: .... Club: .... Handicap: .... Date: ....

1. Before each shot

Physical routine: (e.g. stance; 'dry' swing)

Psychological routine: (e.g. self-talk or 'swing thoughts': *'strong leg action', 'still head'*)

2. Between each shot

Physical routine: (e.g., place club in bag, walk quickly/slowly to ball)

Psychological routine: (e.g. mentally evaluate last shot then plan next shot; or evaluate last shot then think about 'nothing' until I get to ball)

CRITICAL ACTION RESPONSE STRATEGIES (CARS) PLAN

15

This is a specific psych method that all players/athletes will benefit from working on. It is designed to help you cope with pressure. While it is in some ways similar to the coping plan discussed in Chapter 14, the CARS plan is much more specific. It is designed to help athletes/players cope with the stress and pressure associated with critical actions in a game/race/event – critical actions (either skills or moments) such as defence and tackling, goal shooting/kicking, your own mistakes, mistakes by teammates, umpiring/refereeing decisions, adverse weather conditions, physical/verbal intimidation by opponents, and coming on as a substitute.[1] This stress and pressure is one of the major challenges of playing top-level sport – as an athlete you need to relish and enjoy that challenge. If you do not have effective action-response strategies for these challenges you will not be consistently successful at this level of sport.

CARS plans are also designed to help you maintain your skill level in the eight 'Cs': **C**ommitment, **C**onfidence, **C**ontrolling activation, **C**oping with pressure, **C**oncentration, team **C**ohesion, **C**aptaincy and **C**ommunication.

Why you should develop a CARS plan

The CARS psych method is particularly important for continuous, interactive sports like soccer, netball, hockey, basketball and rugby, where stress and pressure must be dealt with 'on the go'.[2] Typically there are no lengthy breaks in play (other than quarter/half-time or the occasional injury break), thus you need a quick (i.e.

5–20 second) method to help you cope with the stress and pressure you may encounter during the game. As you move up through the grades to elite sport the pace of the game increases substantially. As the pace increases the time available for decision-making drastically decreases, so you must be able to think more quickly and be mentally tough!

CARS is actually a combination of a number of PST methods. In designing your own CARS plan you will need to choose a combination of PST methods that best suit the way you like to deal with the pressure that is part and parcel of top-level sport.[2] One athlete's CARS plan might involve a combination of imagery, self-talk and centring; another's might include a mixture of self-talk, parking and mental prep (see the CARS plan worksheet on page 157 and the example of a CARS plan on page 158). Your CARS plan needs to be so well-practised that it becomes second nature and an automatic action-response to critical moments and skills in the game/event. This is absolutely essential, as you will have little time to think through your response during the event – you have to 'just do it!'[2]

'Start your CARS!'

Many athletes/players invent their own personalised labels to help them remember and use the CARS method – some imagine their CARS to be a 4WD truck, others imagine a sports car, etc. Such labels may sound corny, but they work because they help you remember the key aspects of the CARS plan that you have planned and practised using.

For example, you can use your CARS plan at

the following 'breaks in play' as a means to refocus attention/effort and cope with any stress and pressure: penalties/corners in soccer/hockey; scrums, lineouts and kick-offs in rugby; half-time and injury breaks.

The nature of your CARS plan will vary depending on the type of critical 'action' you will be dealing with. In general, there are two types of critical action that you will encounter: (i) critical moments – a time-referenced critical stage of the game/event when you need to have total concentration and confidence (e.g. after making a major mistake, after an injury break); and (ii) critical skills – common team skills (e.g. scrums, lineouts in rugby) and individual skills (e.g. tackling, passing in soccer) that can happen at any time during the game/event, and are repeated many times during a game/event.[1]

Critical moments in the game/event

Critical moments are a time-referenced critical stage of the game/event when you need to have total concentration and confidence. For example:

- after you have made a mistake
- when a teammate has made a mistake
- after you or your opponents have scored a goal/try
- after a refereeing/umpiring decision
- during adverse weather/changes in ground conditions
- physical/verbal intimidation by your opponents
- coming on as a substitute or injury replacement
- the first five minutes of the game
- the last five minutes before half-time
- the first five minutes after half-time
- the last five minutes before full-time
- after an injury break.

CARS plan for dealing with mistakes

One of the most common critical moments is after a mistake has been made. Mistakes are part of sport – for you, for your teammates, and for umpires/referees. Most of these mistakes are small (e.g. a missed pass in soccer/netball), but there are some major errors that can drastically affect the course of the game (e.g. missing a simple tackle and letting in a goal, giving away an avoidable penalty, or not passing to an unmarked player and 'bombing' a goal in hockey/soccer).

You need to have a CARS plan to cope with the emotions that typically come with making a mistake. How you deal with a mistake is often more important that the consequences of the mistake itself.[2,3] You don't want to spend a lot of time thinking about making mistakes, but you do need to be prepared to handle them. Having a CARS plan for dealing with mistakes is not negative thinking; it's a positive approach for coping with an inevitable part of sport.

Keep this in mind: representative coaches and selectors often hope the players they are watching will make a few mistakes or face some other pressure so that they can judge the player's ability to cope with mistakes and maintain their performance level.[3]

Sometimes the game will stop after you have made a mistake (e.g. for a free kick or corner in soccer; for a scrum or lineout in rugby) – if that is the case you will have a few moments to use a CARS plan (see the example on page 158). However, often the umpire or referee will apply the 'advantage rule' in sports like soccer, rugby and netball, and the game will continue after your mistake – if that is the case you need a quick CARS plan that allows you to 'let go' of the mistake and the emotions surrounding it (see the example on page 158). You need to keep your head 'in the game' and not get stuck thinking in the past about the mistake.

'I realise that a poor shot is just a swing away. I also realise that once I've hit a poor shot my only recourse is to hit a better shot on the next swing. In other words, I've learned how to hit it and forget it. There's no sense dwelling on a mistake. You can't hit the shot again, so forget about it. The same thing applies to my occasional emotional outbursts. They're no more than a release and once I get it out I'm fine.'

Tiger Woods (US golfer).

Here are some ideas for a CARS plan for coping with mistakes.

Game has stopped for a few moments: you might choose to use a combination of a number of PST methods, like centring, imagery and self-talk (e.g. 'parking'). It might also help to talk to one or more teammates since we often get 'internal' with the anger that comes with a mistake. Communication can help relieve the anger and pressure, and it can also help you identify or sort out the cause of the mistake – for example, a missed tackle may have been partially due to a lack of communication among the defenders ('Whose player was it?').

Game has carried on: you must be able to shake off the anger and frustration immediately. You might choose to use just one or two PST methods, like centring and one self-talk or 'parking' phrase (e.g. 'Stay in the game;' 'Do my next job.').

Once you have designed your CARS plan for mistakes you need to practise it diligently during your individual training, but especially during team training. Mistakes and errors are inevitable at practice as you and your teammates strive to improve various sub-unit skills (e.g. zone defence in netball/basketball, lineout options in rugby), attacking strategies (e.g. triangle offence in basketball, backline attacking moves in rugby), and defensive strategies (e.g. zone or one-on-one in netball/basketball, one-out defence in rugby). As you attempt these new skills and strategies you and your teammates are bound to make mistakes as you come to terms with the demands of the situation. These mistakes are opportunities for learning more about the game and for practising and fine-tuning a CARS plan for dealing with the emotions that come with mistakes and errors. It is vital that you get to the stage of being able to execute your CARS plan automatically – you want it to become almost second nature, just like your fundamental physical/technical skills have become an automatic action-response.[1,2]

A mistake can either be a stumbling block or a stepping stone, it depends on your approach to mistakes – your subsequent reaction is the key.[3] We all make mistakes, but not all of us deal with them effectively and learn from them. Indeed, some of us continue to make the same mistakes over and over again. You must take the attitude that mistakes are the stepping stones to success. Learn from your mistakes and practise a CARS plan to cope with the pressure that comes with the error. The easiest way to be a mistake-free athlete/player is to seldom attempt anything risky or 'have a go'; but the nature of continuous, interactive sports like soccer, hockey, netball and rugby requires that we take calculated risks if we wish to score points and be successful.

Critical skills in the game

Critical skills are common team skills (e.g. corner kicks in soccer, scrums in rugby) and individual skills (e.g. tackling in soccer, goal-shooting in netball) that can happen at any time during the game and are repeated many times during a game. While they are 'common', they are no less critical and important than critical moments.

Individual skills = individual player task demands. For example:

- passing
- tackling
- goal shooting
- goal kicking
- kicking for touch (from penalty/free kick in rugby).

Team skills = team-related or sub-unit-related roles/jobs.
For example:

- team defensive pattern(s)
- team attacking move(s)
- scrums and lineouts in rugby
- fast breaks in basketball.

CARS plan for 'playing on the bench'

We all play sport because we want to play our sport, but we can't all take the field or court in every game – when you play a team sport you have to expect to spend your share of time as one of the 'back-up' players. Lack of playing time is one of the hardest mental challenges you will face.[3] In order to cope with this challenge you need to keep your confidence up, even though the coach has picked someone else ahead of you. You need to maintain your motivation to train and play, even though you are getting limited opportunities to play. Finally, you need to maintain a peak level of concentration and activation 'on the bench' in case you go on as a substitute or an injury replacement.

If you are in a team where your role is that of a back-up player you need to develop your motivation and commitment with that role in mind.[3] You might not like being a 'back-up player', but someone has to fill the role, and you must be ready to perform when you do take the field or court as a sub or an injury replacement.

If you are not able to take your chance when it comes you might not get another one – coaches want performance, not excuses about having come on from the bench. You need to take the approach that you will show the coaches they can't leave you out of the starting team in the future.

Summary

The CARS PST method is specifically designed to help players cope with pressure. CARS plans are designed to help players cope with the stress and pressure associated with critical skills and moments in the game. Stress and pressure make up one of the major challenges of playing top-level sport; as an athlete/player you need to relish and enjoy that challenge. If you do not have effective action-response strategies for these challenges you will not be consistently successful at this level of sport.

Example: CARS critical moment (a rugby example for dealing with mistakes)[1]

Rob plays right wing for a 1st Division NPC rugby team. He has played for this team for the past four years, and is an exceptional attacking player and a solid defensive player. He has had a taste of higher honours as a back-up player for a Super 12 team, but he hasn't progressed higher, mainly because his form is a bit inconsistent.

Rob is playing a mid-season 1st Division game against one of the team's traditional rivals. Thirty minutes into the first half, Rob knocks on a regulation pass from his centre – it's his third knock-on in the game. The mistake happens as his team is swinging onto counterattack after weathering a period of sustained defensive pressure. If Rob had held the pass he would have had the fullback unmarked outside him with a clear path to the goal-line. After shrugging off the first two knock-ons as bad luck, Rob is now very frustrated because he can't work out why his normally safe hands are letting him down (three knock-ons in 30 minutes!). He's also annoyed with himself for not putting the fullback in the clear. The ensuing scrum is set 20 metres in from the right-hand touch, on Rob's 10-metre line. Rob has lost some confidence in himself, and he's still thinking about the third knock-on, and 'what might have been', as the scrum is being set.

The opposition halfback sees Rob's negative body language as he slowly trudges back into position, head down, shaking his head in disbelief, and with his back turned to the play. The halfback decides to attack Rob's wing while he's distracted; he calls up the loosehead side of the scrum and makes the call for a simple 8–9 flick on the blindside to give himself room to bang up a high box kick right on top of Rob's wing. Rob is slow to react, he barely gets to the ball on the full and ends up knocking it on. He retrieves the ball, but is tied up by the opposition no. 8 and buried in a tight maul 15 metres in from touch, just out from his own 22-metre line. The ref calls the knock-on and sets a scrum on the 22-metre line. Rob climbs out from under the collapsed maul and quickly jogs back into position anxious to make up for his mistake, muttering under his breath and bitching at himself for spilling a simple catch (he would have had a simple 'mark' just inside the 22 metres). He's really annoyed with himself and now he's also angry at his fullback and 1st five who are telling him to 'sort himself out and show some guts under the high ball!'. Rob is angry, anxious and distracted as he returns to his position on the right wing.

The opposition no. 8 (who made the tackle on Rob) sees that he is visibly angry and that he's not paying attention to his defensive respons-ibilities as the ensuing scrum is forming. The no. 8 calls out to cancel the planned backline move on the open, and makes the call for a simple 'Lefto' back-row move on the blindside to attack Rob's wing once again. The back-row move ends up being run as an 8–9–11 move with the left wing cutting back behind the halfback, looking like he's going to link with the blindside flanker. The halfback dummies to the left wing, but Rob doesn't 'see' the move and buys the dummy – he moves in quickly and tackles the left wing ferociously, determined to make up for his two recent knock-ons. The halfback is quick enough to be outside the loose forward defence and he now has a clear run down the left-hand touch. He draws the fullback, who is across in cover, and puts the no. 8 in the clear on the inside. The no. 8 scores in the corner in the tackle of the cover defending 1st five. Rob is left lying on the ground in the post-tackle tangle of bodies back on the 22-metre line. Now he's not just angry, he's angry and depressed – and it's not even half-time![1]

Rob needed a 'method' to help him cope with the frustration, anxiety and loss of concentration that occurred after the third knock-on, and the blind anger, loss of confidence and almost complete distraction that occurred after he knocked on the high kick. Rob is a good player, he's a tough player, and he doesn't give in or give up; but he didn't have the right skills to be mentally tough enough to cope with the consequences of the pressure in this game. He tried hard, but didn't have the psych skills needed for an effective action-response.

Rob needed a CARS plan, one that he had already practised until it was second nature, and he needed supportive teammates who could have made the call to him to 'Start your CARS!' See the example of the CARS plan on page 158 that Kayla (our netball centre) used for dealing with mistakes as part of her PST.

CARS PLAN: WORKSHEET

Name: .... Position: .... Date: ....

Critical moments: (e.g ...., ..., ...,)

[Moment = a time-referenced critical stage of the game]

PST skills: (circle all that apply) Commitment   Confidence   Control   Coping

                                                  Concentration   Captaincy   Cohesion   Communication

PST methods: (circle all that apply) Goal setting   Self-talk   Parking   Centring

                                                  Imagery   Mental preparation

CARS plan:

Critical skills: (e.g ...., ..., ...,)

[Individual skill = a repetitive individual task demand; Team skill = a repetitive team or sub-unit role/job]

PST skills: (circle all that apply) Commitment   Confidence   Control   Coping

                                                  Concentration   Captaincy   Cohesion   Communication

PST methods: (circle all that apply) Goal setting   Self-talk   Parking   Centring

                                                  Imagery   Mental preparation

CARS plan:

CARS PLAN: WORKSHEET

Name: Kayla McHugh   Position: Netball Centre   Date: 16 / 7 / 03

Critical moments: (e.g My mistakes   , Umpire decisions   , After they score   )
[Moment = a time-referenced critical stage of the game]

PST skills: (circle all that apply) Commitment   Confidence   (Control)   (Coping)
                                       (Concentration)   Captaincy   Cohesion   Communication

PST methods: (circle all that apply) Goal setting   (Self-talk)   (Parking)   (Centring)
                                        (Imagery)   Mental preparation

CARS plan:

At critical moments like these I usually get really annoyed and I often 'lose my cool' and struggle to stay calm and concentrate on the job at hand. I need to 'park' all my negative thoughts and plug in some positive thoughts instead. I also need to combine this with 'centring' to calm me down (control of activation), cope with the pressure, and clear my thinking; as well as use some 'imagery' to rehearse the correct performance of my skills in the next phase of play. If there is enough time after the 'critical moment' I might use self-talk and imagery to quickly look at the cause of the mistake/problem and try to sort out how to do it correctly next time – if there isn't time (e.g, play has moved on as the umpire plays advantage) I will need to 'park' any thinking about the mistake/critical moment and think 'in the present' about my next job on the court.

Critical skills: (e.g A 'centre pass restart'   Feeding GA & GS   , One-on-one defence   )
[Individual skill = a repetitive individual task demand; Team skill = a repetitive team or sub-unit role/job]

PST skills: (circle all that apply) Commitment   (Confidence)   Control   (Coping)
                                       (Concentration)   Captaincy   Cohesion   Communication

PST methods: (circle all that apply) Goal setting   (Self-talk)   (Parking)   Centring
                                        (Imagery)   (Mental preparation)

CARS plan:

I often find that my 'confidence' is pretty shaky with attacking moves run to my left where I have to pass off my left hand. Also I've recently had problems with my feeding into the circle and I've lost almost all confidence in my ability to bounce pass into the circle. With critical skills like these I usually get really nervous and worry about screwing it up for my teammates. Often I struggle to stay focused and concentrate on the job at hand; sometimes I get quite nervous, my heart rate and breathing races and my timing slips as I feel tight. I need to 'park' all my negative thoughts and self-doubts, and use 'self-talk' to cope with this self-imposed pressure; then I need to plug in some positive thoughts instead about correct skill technique. I also need to combine this with a quick 'mental prep' plan to calm me down, clear my thinking and help me prepare my thoughts for these repetitive critical skills. Finally I need to use some 'imagery' to rehearse the correct performance of these skills – reminding myself that I've done them correctly hundreds of times before.

PST IN ACTION

PART FIVE

TRAINING MOTIVATION

16

Sportspeople at the elite level of sport typically spend far more time training than they do competing. This training requires a huge amount of dedication, commitment, time, effort and motivation. As you reach an elite level of performance there are greater demands placed on you in terms of reaching your peak physical and mental condition.[1] These increasing demands mean that you will have to spend hours outside of team/squad training situations completing your own personal training sessions (i.e. training fitness, strength and individual skills). These training demands require a huge amount of motivation, and this training motivation will be influenced by a variety of factors.

> 'My goal – and it may be unattainable – is to groove my swing to the extent that I play my best golf all the time. There is only one way that's going to happen: practice and more practice. Long ago, I committed myself to the idea that there are no shortcuts to improvement. The best way to ingrain the correct movements and positions is through repetition. Some players look at practice as drudgery. I happen to love it… My workout regimen is one designed specifically for golf, with emphasis on strength, flexibility and endurance. I've learned a great deal about nutrition and human physiology in general. My understanding of sport psychology has made me a better golfer emotionally and intellectually.'
>
> Tiger Woods (US golfer).

In order to survive in top-level sport you can't rely on 'natural flair and talent' alone. Fitness, strength and skill training are key factors in your peak performance 'recipe'. However, it is apparent that there are players/athletes, even at the elite level, who do not consistently adhere to their training programmes and show poor levels of training motivation. There is little value in a coach or trainer developing a training programme for you to increase your skills, fitness and strength if you are not committed to persisting with your training throughout the season.[1]

Rugby is an example of the demands of elite sport, where in the age of professionalism there are increased demands and pressures on players to be fitter, stronger, faster and to perform better.[1,2] Tana Umaga (All Black 1997–2003) emphasised this point when he commented: 'When I was younger I used to rely on my natural talent a lot and they [my family] were the ones that convinced me that I'd have to put in the hard work if I was to enjoy any kind of success in rugby… It's not going to happen unless you commit yourself.'[3] Soon after rugby turned professional in 1995, Eric Rush (All Black 1992–96) concluded that, 'As amateurs, the odd bad performance could be tolerated, but rich pay packets mean that the players must be more consistent.'[3] Despite these comments, adhering to structured fitness training programmes is a relatively new concept for many players in rugby and in many other sports.[4]

Recent research in netball, rugby and swimming has shown that players who adhere to their fitness training programmes do so for a number of reasons. These players have been found to be highly self-motivated, enjoy their training, have a positive attitude towards their training, and view training as part of the role they play for their team.[5]

This research has indicated that, like other aspects of motivation in sport, your training motivation will be influenced by both your personal motivation for your sport and training (e.g. individual goals) and by situational factors (for example, team climate, coach feedback).[5]

A New Zealand case study

A recent New Zealand study examined the factors that influenced elite rugby players' motivation to train for their sport, with a particular focus on identifying reasons for an individual's motivation to train or not train.[6] 'Training' was defined as the individual training sessions a player completed outside of team training situations; this primarily involved fitness and strength training, but also involved skills or technique training. Eight players from an elite professional rugby team were interviewed during the 2000 Super 12 season.[6] Each of the players took part in three interviews, performed at three different stages of the season: pre-season, mid-season, and immediately prior to the end of the season. The players had an average of 17 years' playing experience (range 10–21 years).

Six consistent themes emerged to explain training motivation among these elite rugby players.[6] These were: (1) life skills; (2) training ethic; (3) social support; (4) social environment; (5) extrinsic factors; and (6) commitment. These themes were verified by the team fitness trainer. I have integrated these 'themes' with themes/ results from training motivation research in other sports (such as netball and swimming) in order to provide the following practical implications for your training motivation. These recommendations will also be useful for coaches and fitness trainers working with serious/elite sportspeople.

Practical implications

A variety of factors influence your training motivation, but there are six consistent factors that need to be taken into account in developing or strengthening your motivation.

Life skills

There are a number of life skills that you need to develop in order to strengthen your training motivation. These include time management, organisational skills and knowledge of training principles. In general, athletes/players who have good time management and organisational skills (i.e. they have other commitments in their lives such as a job or tertiary study and use a diary and/or a training log) are also 'good' trainers. This is in contrast to 'poor' trainers (relatively speaking) who have no commitments other than their sport and training.

In the study of elite rugby players, it was those who had 'taken control' of their lives and had a balanced lifestyle (i.e. they had some other outlet or interest outside of rugby) who had adhered to their training programmes over several seasons and had high levels of training motivation.[6] Time management skills are clearly an important issue in determining your training motivation and adherence.

If you are at the elite level and virtually a full-time athlete, it is obviously difficult to maintain full-time work or full-time tertiary studies; however, it would appear that you need something other than a sport-only focus. This is important not only for training motivation but also for your life 'after sport' (see Chapter 18, 'Retirement and lifestyle management'). If you were to sustain a major injury, for example, you would have little else to fall back on.

Training ethic

If you have a 'task-mastery' focus towards your training you will strengthen your motivation (see Chapter 3, 'Motivation for peak performance'). That is, your focus should be on improving your performance as your primary motivation for training. In general, 'good' trainers want to succeed in achieving their training goals. They view training as an important and enjoyable task that allows them to set and accomplish goals. In addition, they have a clear understanding of the link between improved training accomplishments and improvements in their game/race performance. 'Good' trainers explicitly monitor the influence their training has on their game/race performance, specifically checking for training benefits reflected in performance during competition. In contrast, 'poor' trainers tend to view training as a means to an end (i.e. a chore); that is, they 'have to' do it if they want to play. 'Good' trainers have typically developed a training ethic of 'wanting to' train, and they view the challenge of achieving goals in training as a rewarding and satisfying task in itself. You need to be a 'good' trainer!

Social support

Social support from a number of sources has a powerful influence on training motivation. These sources include two key groups of people: (i) management support/guidance, and (ii) training partners.

Management support and guidance

If you are fortunate enough to be in a team or squad with a team fitness trainer then they are likely to have a powerful influence on your training motivation.[6,7] Training programmes provided by trainers generally have considerable variation and include aspects that prevent boredom. Good fitness trainers will make a concerted effort to educate you as to why you are doing your training, how this relates to your sport and how it will help your game/race day performance. The role and input of coaches also has an important influence on your training motivation. The coach's influence can be both positive and negative, depending on the feedback you receive from them (or the lack of feedback!). Athletes who are 'good' trainers typically indicate that if their coaches are supportive and respected, then they don't want to let them down and are consequently prepared to train hard for them. Good trainers also mention that their coaches give them good feedback on the areas they need to work on at training; in turn, this gives the player/athlete a clear focus and direction for their training. Many players also indicate that receiving feedback from coaches is 'motivating' as the feedback indicates that the coaches are watching them and taking an interest in their training and development.

Training partners

Athletes/players have different needs in terms of training support for different training sessions. In general, 'good' trainers prefer to train with training partners. Nevertheless, there will always be exceptions, and indeed some good trainers have indicated that they prefer to train on their own if they feel that training with others will 'hold them back'. Some players like variation in their training partners. They like to mix up who they train with so that the training does not become too routine, making them feel they are just 'going through the motions'. On the other hand, some athletes/players do not like training one-on-one with a partner as they do not like competition with a training partner. Some athletes like to better their own times or weights rather than compete with someone else. Others prefer to train with a training partner as they can push themselves harder and are more motivated when the 'competition' with a training partner is present. You need to be proactive and decide for yourself what your preference is regarding training partner(s). For team sports especially, group fitness training also appears to help with training motivation.[6]

Social environment

'Good' trainers typically mention that the training and team environment influences their training motivation in both a positive and a negative way. Some players indicate that their motivation changes between team training sessions and fitness sessions. Some may be more motivated for team training as this is more sport-skill specific, is with the team and the coaches, and they therefore have to be more focused. Other players, however, may be more motivated for their fitness training, as this is more focused on their own performance and what they specifically need to work on. 'Good' trainers in both team and individual sports indicate that the 'team/squad' environment (especially team spirit) is a factor that has the potential to influence their training motivation.[5] Make sure you contribute positively to the team spirit within your team/squad. For some players the team's win–loss record also has an influence on their training motivation, although this can affect people in different ways. Some players train harder when the team is losing in order to rectify the situation, while others find that team losses cause them to lose motivation, as they are not enjoying their sport as much.

External factors

There are a number of external factors that influence training motivation. These typically include: (a) tangible benefits; (b) seasonal factors; and (c) playing/making the team.

Tangible benefits

Many players indicate that tangible rewards such as recognition and praise from others, trophies, medals, social status, travel, scholarships and money can have a positive influence on their training motivation. While such benefits may not be your primary reason for training, they can provide a convenient 'reward' that you can focus on as extra motivation to complete training sessions.

Seasonal factors

Factors that change over the course of a competitive season can also have an important influence on your training motivation. These factors may only be apparent at one stage of the season, but may change during another stage of the season (i.e. being on tour, semi-finals, off-season, end of season, club competitions vs regional or national competitions, a big game/race).

A number of players find that the off-season has the potential to influence their training motivation. Some athletes find that the off-season has a negative influence on their training motivation as there are no games/races to train for and training often consists of long, monotonous aerobic sessions to develop base fitness conditioning. In contrast, other athletes/players find the off-season offers them a chance to have a break from structured training and they enjoy the opportunity to 'do their own thing', which might not always include traditional training methods.

Playing/making the team (in team sports)

Making the starting line-up each week also has an effect on a player's motivation to train – both positively and negatively. In some team sports, players report that selection or non-selection, and feeling there is competition for their position in the starting line-up, can influence their training motivation. Team selection has the potential to influence the training motivation of those selected as well as those not selected. For some players non-selection can have a negative effect on their training motivation, especially if they are training hard and not getting selected; they spend much of the season in the reserves, or they get dropped from the team after being selected for games beforehand.

Some team athletes/players view being on the bench as both a positive and a negative influence on their training motivation. Some players find that being on the bench makes them train harder, as they have to keep up their match fitness via training since they are not playing games to get match fitness. For others, being on the bench might have the potential to decrease their training motivation. If they aren't playing, some athletes/players feel they are not contributing to the team. If these players spend too long on the bench their training motivation will decrease, as they start to feel their training is a waste of time given that they are not playing regularly.

Commitment

Commitment to training is a key issue for 'good' trainers (also see 'Commitment' in Chapter 7). Commitment issues include: personal investment; lifestyle alternatives, and social expectations/ obligation.

Personal investment

Like most serious or elite sportspeople you will have invested a considerable amount of time and effort (and money) into your training over the years. This 'investment' will likely have a positive influence on your training motivation, as you seek to get a 'return' on your investment! Some athletes/players believe that by pursuing their sport goals they also create a lot of

opportunities both during their sports career and post-sport. Many serious/elite sportspeople believe that being involved in sport at the elite level leads to opportunities that would not have been available if they did not play elite sport. These might include making friends, overseas travel, overseas playing contracts, making a living from sport, paying for their education, developing a network of business/employment contacts, and enjoying their job if they are professional athletes. Make sure you take some time to consider the benefits your 'investment' in sport is providing for you – the realisation that the hard work is worth it will help strengthen your training motivation.

Lifestyle alternatives

Some players/athletes feel they are missing out on other life opportunities because of their sport commitments, and that there are alternatives to sport that compete for their time. However, 'good' trainers typically indicate that these alternatives do not weaken their commitment to their training and playing, and that they simply have to take a 'back seat' to their sporting commitments. Make sure you view these alternatives in this way.

Social expectations/obligations

Some players/athletes let external influences such as supporters, fans, the media and the public influence them or put pressure on them to perform. However, 'good' trainers typically harness these expectations to strengthen their commitment to training hard and playing well. On the other hand, some players/athletes are not influenced by others' expectations and instead focus on their own performance expectations rather than living up to those of others. Make sure you harness these expectations to strengthen your commitment to training hard and playing well.

Summary

There are a number of factors that influence your training motivation. In this age of higher standards and professionalism in elite sport, there are increased demands and pressures on players to be fitter, stronger, faster, and to perform better. 'Better' performance requires 'better' training! Factors that affect your training motivation include your life skills, training ethic, social support, social environment, external factors and commitment. As a serious, committed athlete/player it is important that you take the time to understand the variety of issues that influence your training motivation.

The more you can do to develop your training motivation the better you will train and the more your game/race performances will improve.

LANCE ARMSTRONG

'Overcoming injury and adversity'

American road cyclist and 5-time winner of the Tour de France (1999–2003)

Forced to confront his imminent mortality in 1997 after a diagnosis of testicular cancer, American cyclist Lance Armstrong dug into unsuspected mental reserves during his fight with cancer and subsequent recovery from ill-health.

'The illness was a good thing,' Armstrong reflected en route to an emotional triumph in the 1999 Tour de France. 'Of course I wouldn't want to go back there but in a way I would not want to change a thing. The illness made me come back with a new perspective.' [1]

Tougher mentally, more determined and carrying a strong resolution to make the best of his ability, Armstrong returned to cycling after a long, painful, but ultimately successful treatment. He rode in triumph down the Champs-Elysée with the American flag draped on his back after beating the world's finest riders and overcoming a string of malicious allegations, following wins in the first time trial and a testing mountain stage. After the drugs scandals of the 1998 Tour de France, suspicions now fall on any successful rider. [1]

'Do you really see me thoughtless enough to use substances which could damage my health after the ordeal I went through?' he responded. [1] Armstrong demonstrated how the mental characteristics of commitment, mental toughness, and motivation are vital for elite athletes, and not just during competition!

'What I didn't and couldn't address at the time [of my cancer recovery] was the prospect of life. Once you figure out you're going to live, you have to decide how to, and that's not an uncomplicated matter. You ask yourself; now that I know I'm not going to die, what will I do? What's the highest and best use of myself? These things aren't linear, they're a mysterious calculus. For me, the best use of myself has been to race in the Tour de France, the most gruelling sporting event in the world'. [3]

'Every time I win another Tour, I prove that I'm alive – and therefore that others can survive, too. I've survived cancer again, and again, and again, and again. I've won four Tour titles, and I wouldn't mind a record-tying five [achieved in 2003]. That would be some good living.' [3]

'But the fact is that I wouldn't have won even a single Tour de France without the lesson of illness. What it teaches is this: Pain is temporary. Quitting lasts forever.' [3]

PSYCHOLOGICAL REHABILITATION FROM INJURY

17

Injury or illness is one of the biggest mental toughness challenges you will face in your sporting career. Any injury or illness serious enough to stop you playing for more than two or three weeks will present you with a mental challenge along with the physical challenge of rehabilitation and recovery. Sean Fitzpatrick had an amazing rugby career without serious injury until 1997; however, when he suffered a severe knee injury he demonstrated the need for discipline and mental toughness in dealing with the frustration of being out of action.

Your first discipline is to get a clear diagnosis from the doctor and then a specific rehabilitation programme from the physio. You must then approach your rehabilitation programme with the same discipline and commitment that you put into your fitness and skill training. Your recovery is as much a mental process as it is a physical one.

Rehabilitation and recovery is your responsibility

You, and only you, are responsible for your rehabilitation (rehab) programme. The doctor and physio will set the programme, but you are the one who must be disciplined enough to follow it completely.[2] Often athletes/players are tempted to rush their rehab and try to do more exercise or physical activity than prescribed in the rehab programme. It is also common for an athlete to lose heart when the rehab is not progressing as quickly as expected.[2] In both cases you must be disciplined and stick to the programme prescribed by the doctor and physio. You have to take a determined attitude to the 'challenge' of your injury rehab.

Mental toughness and discipline are part of playing sport, and they apply equally to succeeding in other aspects of sport such as injury rehabilitation. Take the view that your rehab and recovery is an opportunity to develop other skills and areas of your performance.[2] Perhaps you have some technical limitations that you can work on improving while you wait for the injury to heal; alternatively, you can use the time to work with your coaches and watch match/race videos to enhance your tactical appreciation of your sport in general and your position in particular. Of course, you can also use the time to increase your psych skills.

Above all else, regard your rehab and recovery as a challenge – just like achieving a fitness goal, playing a tough opponent, or trying to break into the provincial rep team – mentally tough players relish the opportunity to meet any challenge. Use your PST methods, such as goal setting, centring, self-talk, parking and imagery, to help with the psychological aspects of recovery.[2] Set yourself some clear, specific and realistic goals for recovery, identify the target dates and goal achievement strategies, and take immense satisfaction in achieving rehab goals during the recovery process. Use centring and relaxation procedures to help relax the muscles around the injury. Use self-talk to stay focused for quality training in the rehab process (e.g. during a rehab weights programme), to 'park' negative thoughts about the injury, and to maintain your confidence. Use imagery to imagine the injured part of your body repairing itself.[3] There is some research that documents the role that imagery and positive thinking can have in helping the body to heal itself from serious illness and injury.[3]

You can also use imagery to rehearse the technical and tactical skills of your sport and/or playing position – when you take the field/court again you need to be mentally ready as well as physically ready to perform.[4] Your confidence may be shaky if you haven't kept your 'head in the game' during your time off the field/court. Watching videos and using imagery to rehearse and practise your technical and tactical skills can make a huge difference to your confidence when you return to play.

You also need to use your psych skills during the physical activity prescribed for your rehab programme. You need to be disciplined enough to stick to the prescribed amount of exercise – more is not better! You need to focus on quality, not quantity, so that you don't re-injure yourself or stall your rehab process.

Take a 'team' approach to your recovery

Make sure you use a 'team' approach to your injury rehabilitation. The rehab team will include your doctor and physio, probably your coach and your teammates, and maybe your family and friends. You don't have to 'tough it out alone' to be mentally tough – seeking support and help from others is not a sign of weakness, rather it is a sign of strength. We rely on our teammates at training and on the field or court, and they rely on us – so it is in injury rehab; you should seek help from others then look to repay their support in the future. Something as simple as a teammate going to the gym with you for company and to provide encouragement during your weights programme can make an enormous difference to your

motivation and commitment during recovery. Teammates and the coach can also help with 'keeping your head in the game' by talking tactics and reviewing videos with you.

> 'It's the biggest mental test of my career. I haven't had a bad injury before. It's difficult, but I've got to get on with it... The World Cup [2002] is the one thing that's motivating me – it's the light at the end of the tunnel.'
>
> David Beckham

Ready to return = psychologically and physically ready to play

If you have been out of action for a month or more, or you have recovered from a severe injury, you will likely have to face up to some fears when you return to play.[4] There are two common types of fear: the injury – 'Will it stand up to a game/race?' 'Will it still hurt?' 'Will I re-injure myself?' – and your confidence – 'Will I be able to play as well as I used to?' 'Am I fit enough after the layoff?' 'Will I be good enough to get back into the starting team?' Once again your mental toughness takes on a different form – are you tough enough to face down these fears and play to your potential? In order to utilise your mental toughness for return to play, you should make good use of the same psych skills that you have developed for performance.

As Michael Jones observes, you need to be mentally fit as well as physically fit to play again when you return from injury.

The successful achievement of the goals you set yourself during rehab will provide you with some confidence. In addition, you should use imagery to practise and rehearse your successful return to play.[2] If you mentally practise your technical and tactical skills during rehab, when you return to training you will be able to slot back into your performance pattern and be 'up to speed' with your team's game plan.

The bottom line is that you should take a proactive approach to your injury rehabilitation and recovery, instead of sitting around feeling sorry for yourself. Your mental toughness will be severely tested when you get injured[5] – regard it as a challenge!

An example — Gordon Slater's injury comeback[6]

In 1995 Gordon Slater broke his leg playing rugby for Taranaki. Not just bone was shattered, but also the hopes of a young player already earmarked as an All Black in the making.[6] After 18 months of painful and trying convalescence and rehabilitation he emerged in 1997 to display confirmation that the investment in him as a member of the New Zealand Colts, divisional and development teams had not been ill-founded.

Slater's convalescence was tough, physically and mentally. Although he was never told his career was under threat, he was not exactly filled with optimism either. 'They did say it was one of the worst breaks you could get. I had no idea how long it would take.' The doubts crept in, especially at the start of the next year when he attended some training camps with the Hurricanes Super 12 team and came away in some pain. But as Slater commented later, 'It's certainly been worth it. It's everyone's dream to play for the All Blacks and to finally be here, let alone so soon, is just great.'[6]

Gordon Slater demonstrated the need for mental toughness when faced with severe injury. If you suffer a similar fate you will need to use your mental toughness to achieve your goals and realise your dreams. Injury is an opportunity to test yourself and develop new skills, it is an opportunity to 'grow as a player', and it is an opportunity to 'grow as a person'. If you view your injury as a stepping stone rather than a stumbling block anything is possible – be a believer!

RETIREMENT AND LIFESTYLE MANAGEMENT

18

'I think I've found a life
to suit my style.'

Jimmy Buffett, 'Spider John'

Lifestyle management is a very broad area within sport psychology; however, for the purposes of PST skill development the focus is on one of the major life skills that has a significant impact on peak performance. That is, planning for retirement from competitive sport.

'I had no private life – at least not the sort I wanted. In order to play tennis and win, I had to put the private Boris Becker – my spiritual self – into a freezer. But I knew the sacrifices needed to stay at No. I were far too great to carry on indefinitely... Until then I was a very one-dimensional person. All my life had been tennis, and I knew that was starting to jeopardise the things that could happen for me in the rest of my life. It was time to take care of my soul rather than my backhand, time to work on myself as a person, rather than tennis.'

Boris Becker (German tennis player: former World No. I; 3-time Wimbledon Champion)

One of my key recommendations as team psychologist to the New Zealand Olympic and Commonwealth Games Association after the 1992 Olympics was that planning for retirement from elite sport be added to the PST programme for future Games teams. Some of this planning was already taking place on an ad hoc and fragmented basis, but I believed (and still believe) that we need to have systematic education in this area. I was struck by the number of athletes at the Olympics who were quite unsure of their sporting futures, vocational career and lifestyle after the Games.[1]

In recent years the New Zealand Academy of Sport has recognised the need for career and retirement planning for elite athletes/players. The academy now offers an 'Athlete Career Education' programme as a service to all athletes registered with it (see www.nzas.org.nz for website information). While aware of the need to give specialised coaching to a group of elite 'developing' athletes/players, the academy also felt a strong responsibility to ensure they were equipped for life after the game.[2] Consequently, along with the expected sports skill coaching, the academy provides a personal development programme that includes career planning, tertiary study, communication skills, financial planning skills, interpersonal relations, and time management.[2,3] In addition, the New Zealand Rugby Union now employs professional development managers to work with all their professional players on the development of their non-rugby skills (e.g. career planning, vocational training, financial planning).[4]

Despite the work of the New Zealand Academy of Sport and others, many athletes and coaches still deliberately avoid thinking about retirement and 'life after sport', falsely believing that such planning detracts from the athlete's motivation for their current sporting career. However, my experience in talking to athletes is that when they are uncertain about the future that uncertainty can be a major distraction in itself. Indeed, research has shown that athletes who plan for life after sport perform as well, if not better, than those who don't plan – the knowledge that their future is secure gives them the peace of mind to totally dedicate themselves to their current sporting careers.[3]

I firmly believe that systematic education about planning for retirement will help you to train and perform better because of this peace of mind. While some athletes may be doing some of this planning at the moment, it needs to be more systematic and it needs to be provided for all athletes who aspire to perform at the elite level. This chapter also provides you with some practical advice on how to make the career planning and retirement planning process more effective for your personal needs.

Retirement: is it a serious psychological problem?

Retirement or rebirth?

The major issue in this regard is the cause of retirement; that is, whether it is self-chosen (voluntary) or forced retirement (involuntary, as a result of age, injury, selection). Forced retirement can be quite traumatic, and even voluntary retirement can require some signif-icant adjustments of lifestyle for the committed athlete. Either way, retirement involves some 'desocialisation' and relearning of social roles.

Severe, mild or negligible psychological problems? ('When the dream ends!')

Research has found that most athletes successfully adjust to retirement with only mild to negligible problems; however, a number of players take longer to adjust than they would like. For example, 17 per cent of college athletes in the US indicated extreme dissatisfaction with 'self' on retirement.[5] In another study of players in Czechoslovakia, 83 per cent of national team members reported a variety of psychological, social and vocational conflicts on retirement, while only 38 per cent were able to confront and deal with termination immediately (18 per cent were still not coping at the time of the study), and 41 per cent had paid no attention to a career after sport.[6]

Most athletes find forced retirement difficult, but most are able to deal with the issues and problems and get on with their lives. Nevertheless, there is a significant minority who experience mild to severe psychological problems on retirement. These problems are preventable, but you need to learn how to cope with the likely hassles if you are unable to prevent them.

Sports-only 'identity'

This applies when your only source of self-esteem is gained through sport. Athletes who become over-identified with their sport often sacrifice education, work skills, jobs and family. For an athlete with this 'identity' the sense of loss and confusion on retirement can be profound. Consequently, you need to spend some time identifying the role sport plays in your life. It will no doubt be important, but it should not be all-important. Your self-image needs to be based on a balanced combination of different sources of self-esteem, not just your physical ability at sport (see the section on positive self-esteem in Chapter 2).

'It's the one regret I might have. Going to school is part of growing up, developing. Going to parties, getting into a little trouble, all that helps make you a broader person. Also, I might have a good friend. You know, I don't have a really good friend.'

Pete Sampras (US tennis player) describing his regret at leaving school to go into a Tennis Academy and then onto the pro tour

Lifestyle changes

Significant changes to the former athlete's daily schedule or routine, as well as family and social commitments, can be quite disconcerting. In addition, the realisation for the elite athlete/player that she/he is no longer 'famous' can be difficult to deal with. You need to plan ahead and be prepared for changes in your lifestyle.

Keeping sport in perspective – a 'balanced' life

Playing sport 'seriously', with a dedicated focus on trying to perform to your potential, requires you to commit a significant amount of your time and energy to your sport. However, if you are not careful sport can start to take over your life.[7] You must be able to manage your time effectively to fit sport in with other parts of your life and to keep it in perspective (see Chapter 16, 'Training motivation').

The main message here is that you need to be careful to avoid letting your sport take over your life completely. To succeed in sport and lead a happy life you need to live a balanced lifestyle that includes time for your job (or education/ training for your future job if you currently make a living from playing sport), your family and for yourself, in terms of relaxation and recreation.[8] Leading a balanced life is important in helping you be successful as an athlete/player, as well as leading a happy life.

Practical recommendations for successful retirement

Since top-level athletes/players commit a lot of time, effort, emotion and energy to their sport, it is perhaps not surprising that a number of them find it difficult to retire. Fortunately, there are many ways in which you can help yourself to prepare for and cope with the retirement transition. The following practical recommendations have been developed from considerable work in the US, Canada, Australia and New Zealand.[9]

> 'It is very, very dangerous to have your self-worth riding on your results as an athlete.'
>
> Jim Courier (US tennis player; former World No.1)

1. Pre-retirement counselling should be available to help top athletes/players prepare for retirement.[3] Such counselling should help you to find new interests (e.g. polytechnic or university study, a new career, working part-time, or seeking new physical and recreational activities), to understand why you are retiring, and to understand the effects it could have on you. This counselling might consist of team seminars and individual sessions, and should include specific career planning. Ideally this would involve the coach and a sportpsych consultant working with you.

   In the special and important case of 'career planning' there are several recommendations.[3] These are taken from career planning programmes in New Zealand, Australia, the US and Canada.

Recommendations:

- You need to understand the process of developing a 'career', rather than just getting a 'job'.
- You need to develop job-relevant skills for your chosen 'career'.
- You need to spend considerable time to identify your personal career needs.
- You need to identify job-related opportunities while you are still playing sport seriously.
- You need to use your sport motivation skills to help you set career goals.

- You need to remind yourself to 'transfer' the many psychological and physical skills you have developed for sport into career skills.
- You should seek out from coaches and administrators the opportunity for individual counselling that focuses on expansion of self-identity; emotional and social support; enhancement of coping skills; and developing a sense of personal control.

2. It is important that you understand why you are retiring, and it will be easier if it is a voluntary decision on your part.

3. Less pressure from coaches and the athlete/player's family to retire would help – you need to feel that it is solely your decision to retire. As with the suggestions above, this recommendation focuses on prevention rather than cure.

4. Support and understanding from coaches and teammates is needed to help you during the retirement decision and the subsequent transition to retirement. You should also develop a social support network inside and outside of the sporting context to use for help and emotional support.

5. Coaches need to be aware of the resources available to them to help an athlete/player if they do not feel they can help the player themselves. This includes people such as other retired players, sportpsych consultants, financial planners, and career counsellors.

6. Support and on-going contact from your team, club, regional and national sporting organisations is important to counter any feelings of abandonment on retirement.[3,8]

7. On-going consultations by sport administrators with both current and former athletes/players and coaches regarding continual upgrading of 'planning for retirement' programmes would be useful and desirable.[2,3]

8. You should phase out your physical training over a few months if possible. A gradual 'wind down' is better than a sudden change in physical exercise and lifestyle.

9. There is a need for nutrition and weight control advice for many retired athletes/players. Since you will be used to consuming a large number of calories and using large amounts of energy, you may need to learn new dietary habits as your physical training decreases.[10]

10. While still playing, you should ensure that you are keeping open other social networks apart from your sporting friends. You should not allow your sport to restrict your social life and other interests.

11. If possible, try to continue your involvement in your sport in some capacity. For example, you might choose to coach or participate in Masters sport.

12. It is vital that you regard the Psychological Skills Training you have developed for sport as 'life skills' training as well.[11] For example, the PST skills of self-confidence, assertiveness, motivation, commitment, concentration, coping with pressure, and communication that you have developed through sport can be used as coping skills in other life situations (e.g. school/education, work/career, relationships with others).[11]

If you learn specific skills in sport then you can change the 'picture' and use these skills elsewhere in your life.

PUTTING TOGETHER YOUR PST 'GAME PLAN'

19

The PST programme outlined in this book has three major objectives:

- To help you consistently perform to the best of your ability – performance enhancement.
- To help you enjoy sports participation more by reducing stress and improving performance.
- To help you develop psychological skills for use in other life situations (for example, motivation, commitment, confidence, anxiety/ stress management).

Overall, the PST programme is designed to help you reach your Ideal Performance State on a regular basis. Remember, the Ideal Performance State is that mood, feeling or state in which you feel totally focused, mentally and physically, on your sporting performance and are confident that you will perform to your best. It's like being on 'automatic pilot'. Unfortunately the Ideal Performance State usually proves to be quite an elusive state for most athletes – it doesn't happen often enough!

Designing your own PST 'game plan'

Now that you have gained an understanding of the principles of PST it is time to design your own PST programme, or 'game plan'. So how do you put together your PST game plan? As well as following the five-step process below, you should go back to Chapters 5 and 6.

Step 1. Identify your PST skill needs (PST assessment).

Step 2. Prioritise your PST skill needs.

Step 3. Match PST methods to your PST skill needs.

Step 4. Learn and practise the PST methods.

Step 5. Evaluate and review PST skill development.

Step 1. Identify your PST skill needs

Follow the process outlined in Chapter 6 to complete your own peak performance profile. Once you have completed this profile you will have identified your PST skill needs. Follow the example of the 'profiling' process outlined for Jack (our golfer) and Kayla (our netball centre) in Chapter 6 and consider the PST skills and methods that Jack and Kayla used – the PST 'game plans' used by Jack and Kayla are outlined in the appropriate parts of the book and are also summarised below.

Jack's profile indicated that he had a number of technical, tactical, physical and psychological skills that needed improvement (see his peak performance profile on page 46). Jack's coach and fitness trainer helped him with his technical, tactical and physical skill needs. From a psych skills perspective Jack needed to commit himself fully to his golf and his training, take control of his own pre-shot 'psych-up' (i.e. calm down!), sharpen up his concentration, and learn to cope with pressure. Kayla, on the other hand, needed to gain some self-confidence, get back her concentration, improve her decision-making, be a better team player, and pick up her on-court communication (see Kayla's peak performance profile on page 47).

Step 2. Prioritise your PST skill needs

You need to sort your skill needs into different types of training, and decide which of your psych skills are most in need of improvement (you should talk this over with your coach if possible). You will also need to categorise your psych skill needs into the categories outlined in Chapter 5: that is, foundation, performance and facilitative PST skills. For example, in Chapter 6 Jack's first step was to categorise his psych skill needs; these were: (i) commitment (foundation skill); (ii) pre-shot psych-up = peak activation (performance skill); (iii) concentration (performance skill); and (iv) coping with pressure (performance skill). Then, based on this skill categorisation, Jack concluded that he first needed to identify some PST methods that would help him improve his foundation skill need for greater commitment – for this he chose to use the PST methods of goal setting and self-talk.

Kayla needed some help to design her PST programme based on her peak performance profile (page 47). Before she made any definitive decisions it was important for Kayla to discuss her assessments with her coach and compare her assessments with the profile that her coach completed on her. Once Kayla and her coach were in agreement, her next step was to categorise her psych skill needs: (i) self-confidence (foundation skill); (ii) concentration and decision-making (performance skill); (iii) teamwork (facilitative skill); and (iv) communication (facilitative skill).

Step 3. Match PST methods to your PST skill needs

In order to design your own PST game plan you need to select the appropriate PST methods to develop or improve the PST skills prioritised in Step 2 above (see Chapter 5 for suggestions about useful PST methods to match with specific PST skills). For example, once Jack saw some gains in his commitment he was in a position to work on some PST methods to enhance his performance skills of pre-shot psych-up and concentration – he chose to combine the use of mental preparation, imagery and self-talk to work on both these PST performance skills together. Finally, he decided to use self-talk and a CARS plan to help him cope with pressure and be smarter with his on-course decision-making. Based on her classification of psych skill needs, Kayla selected some PST methods to match each PST skill. Following the logic of the PST programme (see Chapter 5) she sorted out her foundation needs first, and used a blend of goal setting, imagery and self-talk to enhance her self-confidence (foundation skill). She discussed this decision with her coach before she started to learn and practise each of the PST methods she decided to work on.

Step 4. Learn and practise the PST methods

Once you have selected the relevant PST methods you will likely find it helpful to reread the relevant PST method chapters (i.e. Chapters 10–15), and to complete the various worksheets provided for each of the PST methods.

Step 5. Evaluate and review PST skill development

Many athletes/players and their coaches use the peak performance profile (or a modified version) as a means for on-going, regular feedback/evaluation of the success of their PST game plan.

Advice to coaches

Coaches are often expected to develop and then teach a PST programme for an athlete/player or team. Consequently, they are often asked to 'coach' a set of skills that they have limited knowledge about. In an ideal situation the coach would be able to call on a sportpsych consultant to help, just as they might call on a fitness trainer for advice on the fitness and strength needs of their players. However, if a sportpsych consultant is not available then the coach will need to educate her/himself about PST (just like fitness and strength needs) and learn to teach the 'basics' of PST to her/his players. Indeed, many coaching courses now have specific modules on PST or mental skills training. My advice to coaches in this situation is to follow the basic process outlined below:

Coach step 1. Educate yourself

Take the time to work through the basic PST skills most commonly needed in your sport (see Chapters 7–9), and the PST methods most commonly used in your sport (Chapters 10–15). See Recommended Reading page 179.

Coach step 2. Educate and inspire your athletes about PST

You need to be prepared to explain the relevance and use of PST to your athletes. It often helps if you have a quote or example about PST or mental toughness from an elite athlete in your sport or an elite athlete that your athletes/players will recognise and respect. Feel free to use any of the quotes you have read in this book. Examples such as these lend credibility to the worth of PST and help defuse any misconceptions your athletes might have about PST.

Coach step 3. Help your athletes identify their PST skill needs

Explain the principles of PST needs assessment and help your athletes/players learn how to complete a peak performance profile. You may wish to offer to complete a peak performance profile assessment of each player as well – as another source of information and as a means to start a discussion with the athlete/player about her/his PST needs.

Coach step 4. Help your athletes 'prioritise' their PST skill needs

Often you will need to be the voice of reason and 'direct' your athletes to the most important PST skills that they should work on. Make sure you understand the three categories of PST skills (i.e. foundation, performance, facilitative) and help your players make decisions about which PST skills they should prioritise. Make sure you value and use your own experience and knowledge of your sport in this decision-making process. For example, logically any 'foundation' skills should typically take precedence over 'performance' skills. Remember that not all of the skills will be necessary to enhance your athlete's performance and enjoyment of their sport; make sure they make the tough decisions about prioritising their needs instead of trying to train all their skills at once!

Coach step 5. Help your athletes match PST methods to their PST skill needs

This selection process should be fairly straight-forward if you have helped your athletes make some tough decisions in Step 4 regarding the prioritisation of their PST skill needs. On pages 34–5 (Chapter 5) I have outlined some suggestions of likely PST methods to use for particular

PST skill needs. Please ensure that your athletes don't try to do too much too soon (e.g. work on all the PST methods at once!), otherwise they will struggle with the time and commitment necessary for effective PST practice.

Coach step 6. Teach the PST methods to each athlete and help them practise

You will need to be prepared to explain and teach the PST method(s) to your players, but then you should give them the responsibility of doing the 'hard yards' of practice. Just like fitness work and technical skills practice, this task is the athlete's responsibility, not yours – they need to take ownership!

Coach step 7. Help your athletes to evaluate and review the success of their PST game plan

In this role you need to ensure that your athletes/players engage in an honest and accurate evaluation of their PST game plan and its successes and failures. No one improves unless they acknowledge their areas of weakness and take responsibility for any failures – the objective then is to learn from any mistakes and to do better next time.

Summary

If you work hard on the PST skills and methods outlined in this book you will be developing the mental toughness that so many players and coaches regard as the basis of consistently successful peak performance. Mental toughness is a product of PST skill development and the development of the 'tough stuff' building blocks of positive self-esteem, assertiveness, and commitment. You need a positive level of self-esteem to successfully create the Ideal Performance State ('To be an achiever you have to be a believer'). In turn, self-esteem requires self-awareness and self-acceptance, being realistic and rational, and the development of the skills of self-responsibility, self-discipline and self-management.

Assertiveness is also a vital building block of the 'tough stuff' ('If it's to be, it's up to me'). You need clear goals, positive self-talk and affirmations, and positive imagery in order to develop and maintain assertiveness. Finally, well-developed self-esteem and assertiveness lead to a strong commitment to achieving your goal of peak performance. Commitment is a product of sport enjoyment, the opportunities provided by your participation in sport, and your personal investment in enjoyment and performance. If you are committed you will be more determined, will work harder, and will set more challenging goals. However, being fully committed to peak performance does not mean over-identifying with sport as your only source of self-esteem – it is important that you keep sport in perspective (i.e. live a balanced lifestyle; see Chapter 18).

The development of mental toughness also requires high levels of motivation and the ability to regulate activation and control anxiety. Motivation is a process of identifying your multiple goals for participation in sport and using goal setting to primarily focus on task and performance goals. Regulation of activation and control of anxiety is a matter of getting the 'butterflies to fly in formation' via the identification of your optimal or peak level of activation and the subsequent use of appropriate PST methods.

To be able to effectively develop a PST programme for yourself it is vital that you assess your PST skill levels via a peak performance profile, then your skill needs should be developed through a well-planned programme of specific PST methods. Too often athletes focus totally on learning particular methods (e.g. imagery, centring) and lose sight of the specific PST skill that the method is designed to improve (e.g. activation control). It is easy to be seduced into thinking of the method as the 'end' itself, rather than as a 'means' to an end (i.e. PST skill development). The methods you choose must have a planned purpose or the desired skill development is unlikely to occur.

The PST programme is not intended to overcomplicate your sporting performance. Indeed, not all of the skills and methods will be necessary for you to enhance your performance and enjoyment. Your task is to identify the PST skills that you believe are needed to improve your performance and then choose the PST methods that you believe are the most appropriate for your PST needs. Don't try to do too much too soon, otherwise you will struggle with the time and commitment necessary for effective PST practice. Remember, psychological skills are like physical skills – they take practice and hard work to improve and to maintain.

In this book you have learned the basics of a number of psychological methods designed to improve your level of psychological skills. These methods, if learned correctly and practised diligently, will help you with your psychological skill needs. I wish you good training – you don't need luck, just hard work and practice!

If you are interested in learning more about these PST skills and methods and about other PST programmes, there is a list of recommended reading at the end of this chapter. Each of the books I have recommended is very practical. If you are also interested in the principles and theories underlying the PST programme you will find a number of theoretical books and articles of interest in the reference section.

While I encourage any coach reading this book to be confident enough to teach these PST skills to their athletes/players, you should not attempt to work as a sportpsych consultant unless you have qualifications in both sport psychology and psychology. Although this book has not prepared you to be a sportpsych consultant, it has provided you with valuable information that you can use for yourself as a player, athlete or coach.

RECOMMENDED PRACTICAL READING

Sport psychology books

Bull, S., Albinson, J., & Chambrook, C. (1996). *The Mental Game Plan: Getting Psyched for Sport.* Eastbourne, UK: Sports Dynamics.

Dugdale, J., & Hodge, K. (1997). *Psychological Skills Training: Practical Guidelines for Athletes, Coaches, & Officials.* Wellington, NZ: Sport Science NZ.

Hodge, K.P. (2000). *Sports Thoughts: Inspiration and Motivation for Sport.* Auckland: Reed.

Hodge, K., Sleivert, G., & McKenzie, A. (1996). *Smart Training for Peak Performance: The Complete Sports Training Guide.* Auckland: Reed.

Jackson, S., & Czikszentmihalyi, M. (1999). *Flow in Sports.* Champaign, IL: Human Kinetics.

Martens, R. (1987). *Coaches' Guide to Sport Psychology.* Champaign, IL: Human Kinetics.

Orlick, T. (2000). *In Pursuit of Excellence: How to Win in Sport & Life through Mental Training* (3rd ed.). Champaign, IL: Human Kinetics.

Orlick, T. (1986). *Psyching for Sport: Mental Training for Athletes.* Champaign, IL: Leisure Press.

Sport-specific sport psychology books

Hanson, T., & Ravizza, K. (1995). *Heads-Up Baseball: Playing the Game One Pitch at a Time.* Indianapolis, IN: Masters Press.

Hodge, K., & McKenzie, A. (1999). *Thinking Rugby: Training Your Mind for Peak Performance.* Auckland: Reed.

McKenzie, A., Hodge, K., & Sleivert, G., (2000). *Smart Training for Rugby: The Complete Rugby Training Guide.* Auckland: Reed.

Rotella, R., & Cullen, R. (1995). *Golf Is Not a Game of Perfect.* New York: Simon & Schuster.

Winter, G. (1992). *The Psychology of Cricket: How to Play the Inner Game of Cricket.* Sydney: Pan Macmillan.

REFERENCES

Introduction to Psychological Skills Training (PST)

1. Bull, S., Albinson, J., & Shambrook, C. (1996). *The Mental Game Plan: Getting Psyched for Sport*. Eastbourne, UK: Sports Dynamics.
   Hodge, K.P., & McKenzie, A. (1999). *Thinking Rugby: Training Your Mind for Peak Performance*. Auckland: Reed.
   Orlick, T. (2000). *In Pursuit of Excellence: How to Win in Sport and Life through Mental Training*. (3rd Edition). Champaign, Ill: Human Kinetics.
   Williams, J.M. (Ed.) (2001). *Applied Sport Psychology: Personal Growth to Peak Performance* (4th edition). Mountain View, CA: Mayfield.
2. Colling, Belinda (2000). Cloud had silver lining. *Sunday Star-Times*, 13/2/00, p. D2.
   Richardson, Mark (2001). In M Butcher, 'The Opener: Mark Richardson'. *North & South*, March 2001, 53–60.
   Fitzpatrick, S. & Johnstone, D. (1998). *Turning point: The Making of a Captain*. Auckland: Penguin Books.
   Rutherford, Ken (1994). Endorsement quote for *Sport Motivation*. In K. Hodge. *Sport Motivation: Training Your Mind for Peak Performance*. Auckland, NZ: Reed.
   Woods, Tiger (2001). Chapter 10: How to Master the Mind: Winning Psychology. *How I Play Golf*. (pp. 255–271). London: Little Brown.
3. Gould, D., Eklund,, R., & Jackson, S. (1992). 1988 U.S. Olympic Wrestling Excellence: II. Thoughts and Affect Occuring During Competition. *The Sport Psychologist*, 6, 383–402.
   Hardy, L., Jones, G., & Gould, D. (1996). *Understanding Psychological Preparation for Sport: Theory and Practice of Elite Performers*. New York: John Wiley & Sons.
   Mahoney, M., Gabriel, T., & Perkins, T. (1987). Psychological skills and exceptional performance. *The Sport Psychologist*, 1 (3), 181–199.
   Orlick, T. & Partington, J. (1988). Mental links to excellence. *The Sport Psychologist*, 2 (2), 105–130.
   Williams, J.M. (Ed.) (2001). *Applied Sport Psychology: Personal Growth to Peak Performance* (4th edition). Mountain View, CA: Mayfield.
4. Howitt, B., & McConnell, R. (1996). *Laurie Mains*. Auckland, NZ: Rugby Publishing.
5. Anderson, A., Hodge, K., Lavallee, D., & Martins, S. (2003). *Athletes' attitudes towards seeking sport psychology consultation*. Unpublished manuscript.
   Sullivan, J. & Hodge, K. (1991). A Survey of Coaches and Athletes about Sport Psychology in New Zealand. *The Sport Psychologist*, 5 (2), 140–151.
6. Jackson, S. (1992). Athletes in Flow: A Qualitative Investigation of Flow States in Elite Figure Skaters. *Journal of Applied Sport Psychology*, 4 (2), 161–180.

Chapter 1: The Ideal Performance State

1. Hardy, L., Jones, G., & Gould, D. (1996). *Understanding Psychological Preparation for Sport: Theory and Practice of Elite Performers*. New York: John Wiley & Sons.
   Mahoney, M., Gabriel, T., & Perkins, T.

(1987). Psychological skills and exceptional performance. *The Sport Psychologist,* 1 (3), 181–199.

Orlick, T. and Partington, J. (1988). Mental links to excellence. *The Sport Psychologist,* 2 (2), 105–130.

Thomas, P., Murphy, S. & Hardy, L. (1999). Test of Performance Strategies (TOPS): Development and preliminary validation of a comprehensive measure of athlete's psychological skills. *Journal of Sports Sciences,* 17, 697–711.

Williams, J.M. & Krane, V. (2001). Psychological characteristics of peak performance. In J.M. Williams (Ed.). *Applied Sport Psychology: Personal Growth to Peak Performance* (pp. 162–178). Mountain View, CA: Mayfield.

2. Jackson, S. & Csikszentmihalyi, M. (1999). *Flow in Sports.* Champaign, Ill: Human Kinetics.

Jackson, S. & Roberts, G. (1992). Positive performance states of athletes: Toward a conceptual understanding of peak performance. *The Sport Psychologist,* 6, 156–171.

McInman, A. & Grove, J. R., (1991). Peak Moments in Sport: A Literature Review. *Quest,* 43, 333–351.

3. Jackson, S. (1992). Athletes in Flow: A Qualitative Investigation of Flow States in Elite Figure Skaters. *Journal of Applied Sport Psychology,* 4 (2), 161–180.

Jackson, S. & Roberts, G. (1992). Positive performance states of athletes: Toward a conceptual understanding of peak performance. *The Sport Psychologist,* 6, 156–171.

4. Jackson, S. & Roberts, G. (1992). Positive performance states of athletes: Toward a conceptual understanding of peak performance. *The Sport Psychologist,* 6, 156–171.

Chapter 2: 'Tough Stuff'

1. Llewellyn, J. (2000). *Coming in First: Twelve Steps to being a Winner Every Day.* Marietta, GA: Longstreet Press.

2. Fox, K. (1997). *The Physical Self: From Motivation to Well-Being.* Champaign, Ill: Human Kinetics.

Shavelson, R., Hubner, J., & Stanton, G. (1976). Self-concept: Validation of construct interpretations. *Review of Educational Research,* 46, 407–441.

3. Brewer, B., Van Raalte, J., & Linder, D. (1993). Athletic identity: Hercules' muscles or Achilles heel? *International Journal of Sport Psychology,* 24, 237–254.

4. Dunn, J., Causgrove-Dunn, J., & Syrotuik, D. (2002). Relationship between multidimensional perfectionism and goal orientations in sport. *Journal of Sport and Exercise Psychology,* 24, 376–395.

Wolff, R. (1993). Perfect Pitch Syndrome. *Contemporary Thought on Performance Enhancement,* 2, (1), 123–130.

5. Connelly, D. (1988). Increasing intensity of play of non-assertive athletes. *The Sport Psychologist,* 2, 255–265.

Horsley, C. (1991). Developing assertiveness skills in sport. *Excel,* 7, 15–19.

Chapter 3: Motivation for Peak Performance

1. Allen, J. B. (2003). Social motivation in youth sport. *Journal of Sport and Exercise Psychology,* 25, 551–567.

Duda, J. L. (2001). Achievement goal research in sport: Pushing the boundaries and clarifying some misunderstandings. In G. Roberts (Ed.), *Advances in motivation in sport and exercise* (pp. 129–182). Champaign, IL: Human Kinetics.

Hodge, K., & Petlichkoff, L. M. (2000). Goal

profiles in sport motivation: A cluster analysis. *Journal of Sport and Exercise Psychology,* 22, 256–272.

2. Hodge, K. & Zaharopoulos, E. (1992). Participation Motivation and Dropouts in Netball. *New Zealand Coach,* 1, 6–7 (1992).
   Hodge, K. & Zaharopoulos, E. (1993). Dropouts in Rugby. *New Zealand Coach,* 2, 7–8.
   Tantrum, M. & Hodge, K. (1993). Motives for Participating in Masters Swimming. *New Zealand Journal of Health, Physical Education, and Recreation,* 26, 3–7.

3. Maehr, M. & Nicholls, J. (1980). Culture and Achievement Motivation: A Second Look. In N. Warren (Ed.) *Studies in Cross-Cultural Psychology.* New York: Academic.
   Roberts, G. (1984). Toward a new theory of motivation in sport: The role of perceived ability. In J. Silva & R. Weinberg (Eds.), *Psychological Foundations of Sport,* (pp. 214–240). Champaign, IL: Human Kinetics.

4. Hodge, K., & Petlichkoff, L. M. (2000). Goal profiles in sport motivation: A cluster analysis. *Journal of Sport and Exercise Psychology,* 22, 256–272.
   Wilson, K. & Hodge, K. (1997). Rugby Union and Professionalism: The effect of extrinsic rewards on player's intrinsic motivation. Presented at the *4th World Congress of Science and Football,* Sydney, Australia. (1999).

5. Riley, P. (1993). *The Winner Within: A Life Plan for Team Players.* New York, NY: G.P. Putnam's Sons.

Chapter 4: Anxiety, Activation and Peak Performance

1. Hardy, L., Jones, G., & Gould, D. (1996). *Understanding Psychological Preparation for Sport: Theory and Practice of Elite Performers.* New York: John Wiley & Sons.
   Martens, R., Vealey, R., & Burton, D. (1990). *Competitive Anxiety in Sport.* Champaign, Ill.: Human Kinetics.

2. Hardy, L. (1990). A catastrophe model of performance in sport. In G. Jones & L. Hardy (Eds.), *Stress and Performance in Sport* (pp. 81–106). Chichester, UK: Wiley.
   Hardy, L., Jones, G., & Gould, D. (1996). *Understanding Psychological Preparation for Sport: Theory and Practice of Elite Performers.* Chichester, UK: John Wiley & Sons.
   Landers, D., & Arent, S. (2001). Arousal–Performance Relationships. In J. Williams (Ed.), *Applied Sport Psychology: Personal Growth to Peak Performance* (206–228). Palo Alto, CA: Mayfield.

Chapter 5: The PST Programme

1. Hardy, L., Jones, G., & Gould, D. (1996). *Understanding Psychological Preparation for Sport: Theory and Practice of Elite Performers.* New York: John Wiley & Sons.
   Thomas, P., Murphy, S. & Hardy, L. (1999). Test of Performance Strategies (TOPS): Development and preliminary validation of a comprehensive measure of athlete's psychological skills. *Journal of Sports Sciences,* 17, 697–711.
   Mahoney, M., Gabriel, T., and Perkins, T. (1987). Psychological skills and exceptional performance. *The Sport Psychologist,* 1 (3), 181–199.
   Orlick, T. & Partington, J. (1988). Mental links to excellence. *The Sport Psychologist,* 2 (2), 105–130.
   Williams, J.M. & Krane, V. (2001). Psychological characteristics of peak performance. In J.M. Williams (Ed.). *Applied Sport Psychology: Personal Growth to Peak Performance* (pp. 162–178). Mountain View, CA: Mayfield.

2. Vealey, R. (1988). Future Directions in Psychological Skills Training. *The Sport Psychologist,* 2 (4), 318–336.

Vealey, R. (1994). Current status and prominent issues in sport psychology interventions. *Medicine & Science in Sport & Exercise*, 495–502.

3. Weinberg, R.S. & Williams, J.M. (2001). Integrating and implementing a psychological skills training program. In J.M. Williams (Ed.). *Applied Sport Psychology: Personal Growth to Peak Performance* (pp. 347–377). Mountain View, CA: Mayfield.

4. Hodge, K., Sleivert, G., & McKenzie, A. (1996). *Smart Training for Peak Performance: A Complete Sports Training Guide for Athletes*. Auckland, NZ: Reed.

Chapter 6: Peak Performance Profile: Self-Assessment

1. Butler, R. & Hardy, L. (1992). The performance profile: Theory and application. *The Sport Psychologist*, 6, 253–264.
Butler, R. (1997). Performance profiling: Assessing the way forward. In R.J. Butler (Ed.). *Sports Psychology in Performance* (pp. 33–48). Oxford: Butterworth-Heinemann.
Hodge, K.P., & McKenzie, A. (1999). *Thinking Rugby: Training Your Mind for Peak Performance*. Auckland: Reed.

Chapter 7: Foundation PST Skills

1. Bandura, A. (1977). Self-efficacy: Toward a unifying theory of behaviour change. *Psychological Review*, 8, 191–215.
Bandura, A. (1986). *Social Foundations of Thought and Actions: A Social Cognitive Theory*. Englewood Cliffs, NJ: Prentice Hall.
Hardy, L., Jones, G., & Gould, D. (1996). *Understanding Psychological Preparation for Sport: Theory and Practice of Elite Performers*. New York: John Wiley & Sons
Horsley, C. (1991). Developing assertiveness skills in sport. *Excel*, 7, 15–19.

2. Hardy, L., Jones, G., & Gould, D. (1996). *Understanding Psychological Preparation for Sport: Theory and Practice of Elite Performers*. New York: John Wiley & Sons.
Horsley, C. (1991). Developing assertiveness skills in sport. *Excel*, 7, 15–19.

3. Llewellyn, J. (2000). *Coming in First: Twelve Steps to being a Winner Every Day*. Marietta, GA: Longstreet Press.

4. Scanlan, T., Carpenter, J., Schmidt, G., Simons, J. & Keeler, B. (1993). An introduction to the sport commitment model. *Journal of Sport and Exercise Psychology*, 15, 1–15.
Scanlan, T., Russell, D., Beals, K., & Scanlan, L. (2003). Project on Elite Athlete Commitment (PEAK): II. A direct test and expansion of the Sport Commitment Model with elite amateur sportsmen. *Journal of Sport and Exercise Psychology*, 25, 377–401.

5. Scanlan, T., Russell, D., Beals, K., & Scanlan, L. (2003). Project on Elite Athlete Commitment (PEAK): II. A direct test and expansion of the Sport Commitment Model with elite amateur sportsmen. *Journal of Sport and Exercise Psychology*, 25, 377–401.

6. Scanlan, T. & Lewthwaite, R. (1986). Social Psychological Aspects of the Competitive Sport Experience for Male Youth Sport Participants: IV. Predictors of Enjoyment. *Journal of Sport Psychology*, 8, 25–35.

7. Pinel, B. (1997). Enjoyment and Fun: Implications for Youth Sport Coaches. *New Zealand Coach*, 6, 10–11.
Pinel, B. (1998). *Enjoyment-Profiling: A Practical Look at Enjoyment*. Proceedings of the Children's Issues Centre Child and Family Conference, July, 1997 (pp. 231–236). Dunedin, NZ: University of Otago.

8. Scanlan, T., Stein, G., & Ravizza, K. (1989). An In-depth Study of Former Elite Figure Skaters: 2. Sources of Enjoyment. *Journal of Sport and Exercise Psychology*, 11, 65–83.

9. Howitt, B., & McConnell, R. (1996). *Laurie Mains*. Auckland, NZ: Rugby Publishing.
10. Mazany, P. (1995). *TeamThink – Team New Zealand: The "Black Magic" of Management Behind the 1995 America's Cup Success*. Auckland, NZ: VisionPlus Developments.
11. Jordan, M. In R. Green (1993). *Hang Time: Days and Dreams with Michael Jordan*. New York: St Martins Press.

Chapter 8: Performance PST Skills

1. Hanson, T., & Gould, D. (1988). Factors affecting the ability of coaches to estimate their athletes' trait and state anxiety levels. *The Sport Psychologist*, 2 (4), 298–313.
2. Hardy, L., Jones, G., & Gould, D. (1996). *Understanding Psychological Preparation for Sport: Theory and Practice of Elite Performers*. New York: John Wiley & Sons.
   Williams, J.M. (Ed.) (2001). *Applied Sport Psychology: Personal Growth to Peak Performance* (4th edition). Mountain View, CA: Mayfield.
3. Orlick, T. (1986). *Psyching for Sport: Mental Training for Athletes*. Champaign, Ill: Leisure Press.
4. Hodge, K.P., & McKenzie, A. (1999). *Thinking Rugby: Training Your Mind for Peak Performance*. Auckland: Reed.
5. Anshel, M., Williams, L., & Hodge, K. (1997). Cross-cultural and gender differences in coping style in sport. *International Journal of Sport Psychology*, 28, 141–156.
   Cresswell, S., & Hodge, K.P. (2001). Coping with stress in elite sport: A Qualitative analysis of elite surf life saving athletes. *NZ Journal of Sports Medicine*, 29 (4), 8–83.
   Gould, D., Eklund, R., & Jackson, S. (1993). Coping strategies used by U.S. Olympic wrestlers. *Research Quarterly for Exercise and Sport*, 64, 83–93.
6. Gould, D. (1996). Personal Motivation Gone Awry: Burnout in Competitive Athletes. *Quest*, 48, 275–289.
   Raedeke, T. (1997). Is athlete burnout more than just stress? A sport commitment perspective. *Journal of Sport & Exercise Psychology*, 19, 396–417.
7. Anshel, M., Williams, L., & Hodge, K. (1997). Cross-cultural and gender differences in coping style in sport. *International Journal of Sport Psychology*, 28, 141–156.
8. Jones, G., & Swain, A. (1992). Intensity and direction as dimensions of competitive anxiety and relationships with competitiveness. *Perceptual and Motor Skills*, 74, 467–472.
9. Lane, A., Rodger, J., & Karageorghis, C. (1997). Antecedents of state anxiety in Rugby. *Perceptual and Motor Skills*, 84, 427–433.
10. Nideffer, R. & Sagal, M. (2001). Concentration and attention control training. In J.M. Williams (Ed.). *Applied Sport Psychology: Personal Growth to Peak Performance* (pp. 312–332). Mountain View, CA: Mayfield.
    Moran, A. (1996). *The Psychology of Concentration in Sport Performance: A Cognitive Approach*. East Sussex, UK: Psychology Press.
11. Schmid, A., Peper, E., & Wilson, V. (2001). Strategies for training concentration. In J.M. Williams (Ed.). *Applied Sport Psychology: Personal Growth to Peak Performance* (pp. 333–346). Mountain View, CA: Mayfield.

Chapter 9: Facilitative PST Skills

1. Martens, R. (1987). *Coaches Guide to Sport Psychology*. Champaign, Ill.: Human Kinetics.
   Martens, R. (1990). *Successful Coaching*. Champaign, IL: Human Kinetics.
2. Martens, R. (1990). *Successful Coaching*. Champaign, IL: Human Kinetics.
   Yukelson, D. (2001). Communicating effectively. In J.M. Williams (Ed.). *Applied Sport Psychology: Personal Growth to Peak Performance* (pp. 135–149). Mountain View, CA: Mayfield.

3. Orlick, T. (1986). *Psyching for Sport: Mental Training for Athletes.* Champaign, Ill: Leisure Press.

4. Carron, A. (1988). *Group Dynamics in Sport.* London, Ontario: Spodym.

   Hardy, C.J. & Crace, R.K. (1997). Foundations of team building: Introduction to the team building primer. *Journal of Applied Sport Psychology,* 9, 1–10.

   McLean, N. (1995). Building and maintaining an effective team. In T. Morris & J. Summers (Eds.) *Sport Psychology: Theory, Applications, and Current Issues* (pp. 420–434). Sydney: J. Wiley.

5. McGrath, J. (1984). *Groups: Interaction and Performance.* Englewood Cliffs, NJ: Prentice-Hall.

   Zander, A. (1982). *Making Groups Effective.* San Francisco, CA: Jossey-Bass.

6. Hodge, K. P. (2004, in press). Team Dynamics. In T. Morris & J. Summers (Eds.) *Sport Psychology: Theory, Applications, and Current Issues* (2nd Edition). Sydney: J. Wiley.

   Steiner, I. (1972). *Group Processes and Group Productivity.* New York: Academic.

7. Hardy, C. J. (1990). Social Loafing: Motivational Losses in Collective Performance. *International Journal of Sport Psychology,* 21, 305–327.

   Swain, A. (1996). Social loafing and identifiability: The mediating role of achievement goal orientations. *Research Quarterly for Exercise & Sport,* 67, 337–344.

8. Latene, B., Williams, K., & Harkins, S. (1979). Many hands make light work: The cause and consequences of social loafing. *Journal of Experimental Social Psychology,* 37, 822–832.

9. Carron, A. (1988). *Group Dynamics in Sport.* London, Ontario: Spodym.

   Westre, K. R., & Weiss, M. R. (1991). The Relationship Between Perceived Coaching Behaviours and Group Cohesion in a High School Football Team. *The Sport Psychologist,* 5, 41–54.

10. Brawley, L. R.; Carron, A. V., & Widmeyer, W. N. (1988). Exploring the Relationship Between Cohesion and Group Resistance to Disruption. *Journal of Sport & Exercise Psychology,* 10, 199–213.

    Widmeyer, N. & Ducharme, K. (1997). Team building through team goal setting. *Journal of Applied Sport Psychology,* 9, 97–113.

11. Brown, N. (1997). *The Cohesion-Performance Relationship in Professional Rugby.* Unpublished Honours Dissertation. University of Otago.

Chapter 10: PST Method – Goal Setting

1. Weinberg, R.S. (1996). Goal setting in sport and exercise: Research to practice. In J.L. Van Raalte & B.W. Brewer (Eds). *Exploring Sport and Exercise Psychology* (pp. 3–24). Washington: American Psychological Association.

2. Weinberg, R.S. (1996). Goal setting in sport and exercise: Research to practice. In J.L. Van Raalte & B.W. Brewer (Eds). *Exploring Sport and Exercise Psychology* (pp. 3–24). Washington: American Psychological Association.

   Kingston, K., & Hardy, L. (1997). Effects of different types of goals on processes that support performance. *The Sport Psychologist,* 11, 277–293.

3. Hardy, L. (1986). How can we help performers? *Coaching Focus,* 4, Autumn: 2–3.

4. Bull, S., Albinson, J., & Shambrook, C. (1996). *The Mental Game Plan: Getting Psyched for Sport.* Eastbourne, UK: Sports Dynamics.

   Hodge, K.P., & McKenzie, A. (1999). *Thinking Rugby: Training Your Mind for Peak Performance.* Auckland: Reed.

5. Hodge, K., Sleivert, G., & McKenzie, A. (1996). *Smart Training for Peak Performance: A Complete Sports Training Guide for Athletes.* Auckland, NZ: Reed.

Chapter 11: PST Method: Relaxation and Centering

1. Gould, D. & Udry, E. (1994). Psychological skills for enhancing performance: Arousal regulation strategies. *Medicine and Science in Sports and Exercise*, 26, 478–485.
   Williams, J.M. & Harris, D.V. (2001). Relaxation and energizing techniques for regulation of arousal. In J.M. Williams (Ed.). *Applied Sport Psychology: Personal Growth to Peak Performance* (pp. 229–246). Mountain View, CA: Mayfield.
2. Weinberg, R. & Gould, D. (2003). Chapter 12: Arousal Regulation. *Foundations of Sport and Exercise Psychology* (3rd Edition) (pp. 263–281) Champaign, IL: Human Kinetics.

Chapter 12: PST Method: Imagery

1. Vealey, R.S., & Greenleaf, C.A. (2001). Seeing is believing: Understanding and using imagery in sport. In J.M. Williams (Ed.), *Applied sport psychology: Personal growth to peak performance* (4th edition) (pp. 247–283). Mountain View, CA: Mayfield.
2. Kendall, G., Hrycaiko, D., Martin, G.L., & Kendall, T. (1990). The effects of an imagery rehearsal, relaxation and self-talk package on basketball game performance. *Journal of Sport and Exercise Psychology*, 12, 157–166.
3. Gordon, S., Weinberg, R., & Jackson, A. (1994). Effect of internal and external imagery on cricket performance. *Journal of Sport Behavior*, 17, 60–74.
4. Beauchamp, P.H., Halliwell, W.R., Fournier, J.F., & Koestner, R. (1996). Effects of cognitive-behavioral psychological skills training on the motivation, preparation, and putting performance of novice golfers. *The Sport Psychologist*, 10, 157–170
5. McKenzie, A.D., & Howe, B.L. (1997). The effect of imagery on self-efficacy for a motor skill. *International Journal of Sport Psychology*, 28, 196–210.
   McKenzie, A.D., & Howe, B.L. (1991). The effect of imagery on tackling performance in rugby. *Journal of Human Movement Studies*, 20, 163–176.
   Pickford, S. (1994). *The effect of mental imagery on rugby goal-kicking performance.* Unpublished honours dissertation, University of Otago.
6. Orlick, T. & Partington, J. (1988). Mental links to excellence. *The Sport Psychologist*, 2 (2), 105–130.
7. Roberts, G., Spink, K., & Pemberton, C. (1986). *Learning Experiences in Sport Psychology.* Champaign, Ill.: Human Kinetics.
8. Iveleva, L., & Orlick, T. (1991). Mental links to enhanced healing: An exploratory study. *The Sport Psychologist*, 5, 25–40.

Chapter 13: PST Method: Self-Talk

1. Zinsser, N., Bunker, L., & Williams, J. (2001). Cognitive Techniques for Building Confidence and Enhancing Performance. In J. Williams (Ed.), *Applied Sport Psychology: Personal Growth to Peak Performance* (4th Edition) (284–311). Palo Alto, CA: Mayfield.
   Hodge, K.P., & McKenzie, A. (1999). *Thinking Rugby: Training Your Mind for Peak Performance.* Auckland: Reed.
2. Orlick, T. (1986). *Psyching for Sport: Mental Training for Athletes.* Champaign, IL: Leisure Press.

Chapter 14: PST Method: Mental Preparation

1. Orlick, T. & Partington, J. (1988). Mental links to excellence. *The Sport Psychologist*, 2 (2), 105–130.
2. Jackson, S. & Csikszentmihalyi, M. (1999). *Flow in Sports.* Champaign, Ill: Human

Kinetics.

3. Orlick, T. (1986). *Psyching for Sport: Mental Training for Athletes*. Champaign, Ill: Leisure Press.

Chapter 15: PST Method: CARS Plan

1. Hodge, K.P., & McKenzie, A. (1999). *Thinking Rugby: Training Your Mind for Peak Performance*. Auckland: Reed.

2. Gould, D., Finch, L., & Jackson, (1993). Coping strategies used by National Champion Figure Skaters. *Research Quarterly for Exercise and Sport*, 64, 453–468.

   Gould, D., Eklund, R., & Jackson, S. (1993). Coping strategies used by U.S. Olympic wrestlers. *Research Quarterly for Exercise and Sport*, 64, 83–93.

   Hardy, L., Jones, G., & Gould, D. (1996). *Understanding Psychological Preparation for Sport: Theory and Practice of Elite Performers*. New York: John Wiley & Sons.

3. Ravizza, K., & Hanson, T. (1995). *Heads-Up Baseball: Playing the Game One Pitch at a Time*. Indianapolis, IN: Masters Press.

Chapter 16: Training Motivation

1. Hodge, K., Sleivert, G., & McKenzie, A. (1996). *Smart Training for Peak Performance: The Complete Sports Training Guide*. Auckland, Reed Books.

   Hodge, K.P., & McKenzie, A. (1999). *Thinking Rugby: Training Your Mind for Peak Performance*. Auckland, Reed Books.

2. Matheson, J. (August 1999). A life less Ordinary. *NZ Rugby Monthly*; p.28–34.

3. McMurran, A. (June 14, 1996). WRC hailed for loosening of purse strings. *Otago Daily Times*, p. 27.

4. Burwitz, L., Moore, P.M., & Wilkinson, D.M. (1994). Future directions for performance-related sports science research: An inter-disciplinary approach. *Journal of Sports Sciences*, 12, 93–109.

   Marlow, C. & Bull, S.J. (1999). Attitudinal factors influencing adherence to fitness training in international women cricketers. *Journal of Sport Sciences*, 17, 64–65.

5. McCarroll, N. & Hodge K. (2004). Training Motivation in Elite Sport: Principles and Practice. *NZ Coach*, Summer, 19–21.

   Mummery, W.K., & Wankel, L.M. (1999). Training Adherence in Adolescent Competitive Swimmers: An Application of the Theory of Planned Behaviour. *Journal of Sport and Exercise Psychology*, 21, 313–328.

   Palmer, C.L., Burwitz, L., Smith, N.C., & Collins, D. (1999). Adherence to Fitness Training of Elite Netball Players: A Naturalistic Inquiry. *The Sport Psychologist*, 13, 313–333.

6. McCarroll, N. & Hodge K. (2004). Training Motivation in Elite Sport: Principles and Practice. *NZ Coach*, Summer, 19–21.

7. McCarroll, N. (2000). *Training Motivation in Elite Rugby: The Fitness Trainers' Perspective*. Unpublished manuscript. School of Physical Education, University of Otago, Dunedin.

Chapter 17: Psych Rehabilitation from Injury

1. Fitzpatrick, S. & Johnstone, D. (1998). *Turning point: The Making of a Captain*. Auckland: Penguin Books.

   Fitzpatrick, S. *Sunday Star Times*, 16/11/97, p. B1.

2. Hodge, K., & McNair, P. (1990). Psychological Rehabilitation of Sports Injuries. *New Zealand Journal of Sports Medicine* 18, 64–67.

   Sullivan, J. (2003). *Psychological Rehabilitation of Injured Athletes: A Prospective Study*. Unpublished Masters Thesis, University of Otago.

3. Iveleva, L., & Orlick, T. (1991). Mental links

to enhanced healing: An exploratory study. *The Sport Psychologist*, 5, 25–40.

4. Ravizza, K., & Hanson, T. (1995). *Heads-Up Baseball: Playing the Game One Pitch at a Time.* Indianapolis, IN: Masters Press.

5. Gould, D., Udry, E., Bridges, D., & Beck, L. (1997). Coping with Season-Ending Injuries. *The Sport Psychologist*, 11, 379–399.

6. —— (1997). Gordon Slater's Injury Comeback. *Sunday Star Times*, 30/11/97, p. B4.

Chapter 18: Retirement and Lifestyle Management

1. Hodge, K. P. (1993). 1992 Olympic report: Sport psychology at the Barcelona Olympics. *New Zealand Journal of Health, Physical Education, and Recreation*, 26, 8–11.

2. Australian Institute of Sport (1999). *Athlete Career Education (ACE) Programme.* Canberra: Australian Institute of Sport.

3. Baillie, P. (1993). Understanding retirement from sports: Therapeutic ideas for helping athletes in transition. *The Counselling Psychologist*, 21, 399–410.
   Murphy, S. (1995). Transitions in competitive sport: Maximizing individual potential. In S. M. Murphy (Ed.), *Sport psychology interventions* (pp. 331–346). Champaign, IL: Human Kinetics.
   Ogilvie, B. C. (1987). Counselling for sports career termination. In J. R. May, & M. J. Asken (Eds.), *Sport psychology: The psychological health of the athlete* (pp. 365–382), New York: PMA.
   Petitpas, A., Champagne, D., Chartrand, J., Danish, S., & Murphy, S. (1997). *Athlete's Guide to Career Planning: Keys to Success from the Playing Field to Professional Life.* Champaign, IL: Human Kinetics.

4. McKenzie, A., Hodge, K., & Carnachan, G. (2003). The Professional Development Programme: A Life of Balance off the Field enables Focus on the Field. *GamePlan Rugby*, 6, 4–5.

5. Greendorfer, S., & Blinde, E. (1985). Retirement from intercollegiate sports: Theoretical and empirical considerations. *Sociology of Sport Journal*, 2, 101–110.

6. Svoboda, B. & Vanek, M. (1981). Retirement from high level competition. *Proceedings, Fifth World Congress of Sport Psychology* (pp. 26–31). Ottawa, Canada.

7. Brewer, B., Van Raalte, J., & Linder, D. (1993). Athletic identity: Hercules' muscles or Achilles heel? *International Journal of Sport Psychology*, 24, 237–254.

8. Gordon, S. (1995). Career transitions in competitive sport. In T. Morris & J. Summers (Eds.), *Sport Psychology: Theory, Applications, and Current Issues* (pp. 474–501). Sydney: J. Wiley.
   Hodge, K.P. (1997). Retirement from competitive sport: Psychological issues and practical recommendations. *New Zealand Coach*, 5, 5–8.
   Sinclair, D., & Orlick, T. (1993). Positive transitions from high-performance sport. *The Sport Psychologist*, 7, 138–150.
   Werthner, P., & Orlick, T. (1986). Retirement experiences of successful Olympic athletes. *International Journal of Sport Psychology*, 17, 337–363.

9. Ogilvie, B. C. (1987). Counselling for sports career termination. In J. R. May, & M. J. Asken (Eds.), *Sport psychology: The psychological health of the athlete* (pp. 365–382), New York: PMA.
   Petitpas, A., Champagne, D., Chartrand, J., Danish, S., & Murphy, S. (1997). *Athlete's Guide to Career Planning: Keys to Success from the Playing Field to Professional Life.* Champaign, IL: Human Kinetics.

10. Pearce, J. (1990). *Eat to Compete: Sports Excellence though Good Nutrition.* Auckland, NZ: Reed.

11. Danish, S., Petitpas, A., & Hale, B. (1993).

Life development intervention for athletes: Life skills through sports. *The Counselling Psychologist,* 21, 352–385.

Hodge, K., & Danish, S. (1999). Promoting life skills for adolescent males through sport. In A. Horne & M. Kiselica. (Eds.). *Handbook of counselling boys and adolescent males* (pp. 55–71). Thousand Oaks, CA: Sage.

Roger Bannister

1. Landon, C. (1982). *Classic Moments of Athletics.* Ashbourne: Moorland.
   Palenski, R. (1997). *Key Moments in the 20th Century: Sport.* Auckland, NZ: Wilson & Horton.

2. Palenski, R. (1997). *Key Moments in the 20th Century: Sport.* Auckland, NZ: Wilson &

PROFILE REFERENCES

Horton.

3. Landon, C. (1982). *Classic Moments of Athletics.* Ashbourne: Moorland.
4. Romanos, J. (1992). *A Sporting Life: The Best of Broadcaster Peter Sellers.* Auckland: Moa.
5. Quercetani, R. (1990). *Athletics: A History of Modern Track & Field (1860–1990).* Milan: Vallardi.
6. Agnew, I. (1976). *Kiwis Can Fly.* Auckland: Marketforce.
7. IAAF (2003, 23 December). http://www.iaaf.org/statistics/records
   Bannister, R. (19??). First Four Minutes.

Sir Edmund Hillary

1. Booth, P. (1993) *Edmund Hillary: The Life of a Legend.* Auckland: Moa Beckett.
   Hillary, E. (2000) Foreword. In C. Gilson, M. Pratt, K. Roberts, & E. Weymes (Eds.) *Peak Performance.* London: Harper Collins.
   Palenski, R. (1997) *Key Moments in the 20th Century: Sport.* Auckland, NZ: Wilson & Horton.
2. Booth, P. (1993) *Edmund Hillary: The Life of a Legend.* Auckland: Moa Beckett.
   Palenski, R. (1997) *Key Moments in the 20th Century: Sport.* Auckland, NZ: Wilson & Horton.
3. Hillary, E. (1975). *Nothing Venture, Nothing Win.* London: Hodder & Stoughton.
4. Booth, P. (1993) *Edmund Hillary: The Life of a Legend.* Auckland: Moa Beckett.
5. Hillary, E. (1955) *High Adventure.* London: Hodder & Stoughton.
6. *Otago Daily Times,* 24/7/99; p. 18.

Dame Susan Devoy

1. Devoy, S. & Scott-Vincent, R. (1993) *Susan Devoy: Out on Top.* Auckland: Moa Beckett.
   Stratford, T. (1988) *Guts, Tears & Glory: Champion New Zealand Sportswomen Talk to Trish Stratford.* Auckland, NZ: New Women's Press.
2. Stratford, T. (1988). *Guts, Tears & Glory: Champion New Zealand Sportswomen Talk to Trish Stratford.* Auckland, NZ: New Women's Press.
3. Devoy, S. & Scott-Vincent, R. (1993). *Susan Devoy: Out on Top.* Auckland: Moa Beckett.

Michael Campbell

1. Duncan Johnstone, *Sunday Star-Times,* 6/2/00; p. B2.
2. *Sunday News,* 6/2/00; p. 40.
3. *Otago Daily Times,* 15/2/00, p. 23.

Sir Murray Halberg

1. Walsh, D. (2000). *Sunday Star-Times,* 2/1/00; p. B2.
2. Roger, W. (2000). The man who wouldn't accept defeat. *North & South,* February 2000; pp. 48–59.
3. McLean, T.P. (1990). *Silver Fern: 150 Years of New Zealand Sport.* Auckland: Moa.
4. Halberg, M. (1963). *A Clean Pair of Heels: The Murray Halberg Story.* ???
5. McMurran, A. 'Old resolve helps Halberg through crisis. *Otago Daily Times,* 8/3/00; p. 31.

Bob Blair

1. Brittenden, R. T. (1958) *Great Days in New*

Zealand Cricket. Wellington: A.H. & A.W. Reed.

McLean, T.P. (1990) *Silver Fern: 150 Years of New Zealand Sport*. Auckland: Moa.

2. Brittenden, R. T. (1958) *Great Days in New Zealand Cricket*. Wellington: A.H. & A.W. Reed.

    Brittenden, R. T. (1983) *Big Names in New Zealand Cricket*. Auckland: Moa.

    Reid, J. (1962) *Sword of Willow*. Wellington: A.H. & A.W. Reed.

3. Brittenden, R. T. (1958) *Great Days in New Zealand Cricket*. Wellington: A.H. & A.W. Reed.

    Brittenden, R. T. (1983) *Big Names in New Zealand Cricket*. Auckland: Moa.

4. Brittenden, R. T. (1958) *Great Days in New Zealand Cricket*. Wellington: A.H. & A.W. Reed.

5. Reid, J. (1962) *Sword of Willow*. Wellington: A.H. & A.W. Reed.

6. Brittenden, R. T. (1983) *Big Names in New Zealand Cricket*. Auckland: Moa.

7. Brittenden, R. T. (1958) *Great Days in New Zealand Cricket*. Wellington: A.H. & A.W. Reed.

    Brittenden, R. T. (1983) *Big Names in New Zealand Cricket*. Auckland: Moa.

    Reid, J. (1962) *Sword of Willow*. Wellington: A.H. & A.W. Reed.

8. Brittenden, R.T. (1983) *Big Names in New Zealand Cricket*. Auckland: Moa.

    Reid, J. (1962) *Sword of Willow*. Wellington:

A.H. & A.W. Reed.

9. Reid, J. (1962) *Sword of Willow*. Wellington: A.H. & A.W. Reed. (pp. 73–74)

10. Brittenden, R.T. (1958) *Great Days in New Zealand Cricket*. Wellington: A.H. & A.W. Reed.

    Brittenden, R.T. (1983) *Big Names in New Zealand Cricket*. Auckland: Moa.

    McLean, T.P. (1990) *Silver Fern: 150 Years of New Zealand Sport*. Auckland: Moa.

    Reid, J. (1962) *Sword of Willow*. Wellington: A.H. & A.W. Reed.

Lance Armstrong

1. *Sunday Star-Times*, 26/12/99; p. B9.
2. Armstrong, L. (2000). *It's not about the bike*. New York: Putnam.
3. Armstrong, L. & Jenkins, S. (2003). *Every second Counts*. New York: Broadway. www.lancearmstrong.com

QUOTE REFERENCES

The author gratefully acknowledges the following authors and publishers, from whom the text quotes in *Sport Motivation* have been sourced (numbers in brackets refer to page numbers of this edition):

Bertrand, J. & Robinson, R. 1986. *Born to Win: A Lifelong Struggle to Capture the America's Cup.* Sydney: Bantam (1); Charlesworth, R. 2001. *The Coach: Managing for Success.* Sydney: Macmillan (145); *North and South* March 2001 pp.52–60 (M. Richardson 116, 211, 219, 227); *Otago Daily Times* (M. Richardson 1; M. Hingis 1; C. McMillan 25; C. Perks 35, 57; A. Agassi 43; L. van Welie 44, 94, 161; J. Oram 45; V. Adams 58; J. Capriati 104; A. Lawrence 115; I. Khan 119; S. Ulmer 121; P. Tataurangi 226; M. Campbell 252); *Player* April 2003 p. 30 (M. Richardson 207); *Sunday Star Times* (J. Ackland 1; C. Watson 12; N. Astle 27; K. Biggar 34; R. Dixon 38; G. Tallis 51; S. Bond 118; D. Kirk 127, 261; L. Muir 142; V. Adams 190; J. Wilkinson 219; P. Tataurangi 249; B. Becker 254; J. Seuseu 255; P. Sampras 256; P. McDonald 260); *Sunday News* (R. Waddell 218; M. Campbell 242; D. Beckham 251; C. Hutchings 267); Woods, T. 2001. *How to Master the Mind: Winning Psychology* London: Little Brown pp.255–71 (12, 26, 33, 50, 92, 125, 129, 191, 229, 239).

INDEX